And So...

And So...

THOUGHTS AND STORIES OF A LIFE

John Strauss

Epigraph Books
Rhinebeck, New York

And So . . .: Thoughts and Stories of a Life © Copyright 2025 by John Strauss

All rights reserved. No part of this book may be used or reproduced in any manner without the consent of the author, except in critical articles or reviews. Contact the publisher for information.

Hardcover ISBN 9781966293224
Paperback ISBN 9781966293217
eBook ISBN 9781966293231

Library of Congress Control Number 2025921527

Book and cover design by Colin Rolfe

Epigraph Books
22 East Market Street, Suite 304
Rhinebeck, New York 12572
(845) 876-4861
epigraphpublishing.com

Contents

Acknowledgments	xi
Introduction	xiii
Mosaic	1
The Person and the Taj Mahal	3
If/Then	5
So, What Have You Learned?	8
Susan Died	16
Hi, This Is Don	21
Stories and Science	23
Bill Called Yesterday	30
Bernice	34
Dear Sirs	38
Walter Clark	40
Mrs. Joyce	43
My Mother	48
My Mother II	52
Me and My Mother	57
Dear Professor Shippey	60
Vera Lynn	67
Other Reflections Prompted by Vera Lynn	72
"Angor Animi"	74
The Kids	77
Ann Mott	83
Corinne	84
Who Was Right?	86

A High School Acquaintance	91
Little Things	96
Trees	98
The Airport at Atlanta	102
A Drop of Water	105
Birds Darting	108
Collage	111
Dry Cleaning	113
The Box	115
The Great Waltz	122
Stones on the Beach	125
So I Walk into This Café	127
It is a Quiet, Gentle, Pensive Rain	130
Indian Dance	132
Solutions?	135
You Want Peer Support, I'll Show You Peer Support!	137
Biopsychosocial Fondue	142
Why Do People Get Mentally Ill?	144
A Little Bit of Schizophrenia	147
Methodology II: Putting Yourself in Someone Else's Place	150
Doing Readings	156
The Normal and the Pathological	159
Impasto: Understanding Human Development	162
Biopsychosocial? We Have Barely Begun to Try	165
What Music Can Teach Us about Mental Illness	169
Psychosocial Construction	174
Implications of Complexity Theory for a Biopsychosocial Psychiatry	173
The Story: Its Role in Medicine and Other Human Science	176
Doing a Reading as Human Science	187
Everything is a Story	191

Eighty-eight Years Old	197
Getting Old	199
Becoming an Old Man	202
What Can You Do When Someone Is Dying?	205
Death and Stuff	207
Death	211
Nothing to Write About	217
Il me manque	219
D Day	224
X14-598	227
Gute Nacht	229
"It's Not the 1940's, After All"	233
Im Spital ist im Spital	236
Humanity	238
Scenario One	243
Scenario Two	247
Taking Someone Seriously	250
Nurses	253
Human Nature	257
Ich Weisz Nicht	261
My Self	265
Still a Brahms Fan	267
N Dimensional World (N=Indeterminate)	269
N Dimensional World: Alice and Jerry for Mental Health Types	272
A Strange Thing Happened	275
Another Strange Thing Has Happened	278
Doing the Humanities	282
Loos Geerlings	285
Stories, People, Science, and the Mental Health Field	287
Tempus Fugit: Nobody Says "Ain't" Any More	292
Behind the Wooden Door	294

Comfort	297
But What If It's Not Like That?	300
He Has a Problem with Communicating	302
New Mexico Experience 2009	306
Science and Art, Technique and Feeling	310
How Can a Story Have Such Power	315
Hannah Would Understand	317
More Stories	320
It's a Long Long While from May to December	326
Writing Assignment One	329
Writing Assignment Two	331
A Formulation	333
A Story	335
Congratulations	337
Doing Autobiography	340
Feelings	343
Kindness	346
Magic Moments	349
Stories and Psychiatry	351
Subjectivity	367
The Delivery	369
The Island	373
The Past Isn't Even the Past	377
The Plague	383
The Project	387
Twenty-two	391
Understanding a Life	396
Is John Still Alive?	398
To Build a Fire	399
Being Human and the Mental Health Field	401
Points of View	404
Poisoned Sauce	407

The Dance	408
Too Much	410
Knowledge	413
And Now for Something Completely Different	416
The Ghost of Christmas Past	424
Scrap Trailer in Driveway	429
Taps	431
But My Favorite is . . .	433

Acknowledgments

With profound thanks to my wonderful editor and friend, Anne Ranson, who has contributed so much in so many ways to this project.

Thanks also to Lexi Davidson, who has regularly contributed her expertise. And to Cecelia Montgomery who has been a kind of magical spirit for the project.

And thanks to my wonderful children, Jeff and Sarah, for being so helpful through all this.

Cover photograph of author and his great grandson Jasper by Jasper's mother, Sophie Strauss.

Introduction

The picture on the cover of this book is of me and my great grandson, Jasper. It was taken by Sophie, Jasper's mother and my granddaughter (to whom, thank you). I think Jasper and I are both loving the experience of reading together, which is why I find this picture so appropriate here. I originally had another candidate for the cover, which tells another but still relevant story of continuity. It shows Jasper, at the age of almost three, next to the pond of the Luxembourg Gardens in Paris, a place that is very dear to me and so much a part of my story. He is with his father, my son Jeff. I have a picture taken of Jeff himself when he was much the same age next to the same *bassin*. Unfortunately, I didn't have the chance to see the Luxembourg Gardens until I was twenty. By that age I was too sedate to play with a little rented sailboat in the same way, but I certainly felt totally at home in the same place. My father first visited Paris in his late twenties, and I would like to think of him as having very similar experiences and feelings as he visited that same place. My thoughts turn to the string of human beings who have been there in the sixth arrondissement of Paris. The many writers—Dos Passos and Hemingway, for example—who were there between the first and second world wars. And earlier, American diplomats such as Benjamin Franklin with his fur cap and John Adams among the many others who perhaps were in the same place. One can range much further afield in time and place, to the people who lived their lives in ancient Greece, for example. It is not hard to imagine that there were, with specific details changed, people over the years who had similar experiences and feelings. So the stories in this book (I hate the word *memoires*—it seems so dead) may reflect in some ways experiences common many other humans over time. At least, I hope it is not too grandiose to think so.

But what is the purpose of such a writing? As I finished my autobiography a couple of years ago, I was delighted and relieved. At last! It was something I really wanted to do, and to complete, "before it was too late," as Nancy Ryan, my wonderful secretary for twenty-five years, might have said. Why? That sounds like a question sung with great force in an opera, maybe *La Bohème* or something like that (I know, it's not really in it). And the response (again, a bit like Mimi asking why they call her "Mimi" when her real name is Lucia): "I don't know." Me too, mostly just "because." Which makes it, however, no less of a felt imperative. Sophie, my granddaughter, said it gave her an idea of the background of her family. That's as close as I can come to a response, for her, for any generations beyond mine who care. But it was also for me. I should really try to figure that out.

Whatever the reason, I learned so much from writing the autobiography, new understanding, new connections among events and situations, new ways of thinking about my life and about human life in general. But one thing that surprised me was that even after "finishing" it, I kept thinking about all the things I had left out. Was it because even without meaning to, I was writing a story, with a clean line of evolution, and leaving out things that didn't fit that story? Whatever it was, I didn't realize it until after I finished and I kept thinking of new pieces of my life, or even just new things. So, what the hell, a couple of months after finishing the autobiography I woke up in the morning and thought: "That's it, I'll put together another thing and call it Volume Two. It won't be the development of a counter-story to the autobiography. Nor will it be a redo. It'll just be a collection of some of the things that I have been writing over the years that I think might be relevant." So that's it, here we are.

Mosaic
[*6/23/23*]

Why "mosaic"? In reading over these pieces I could see that they did not together construct a story, at least not in the usual ways. Still, they somehow revealed a story, if not in any linear fashion. Looking for a parallel in the arts, I could only think of Marc Chagall as a painter who more or less did that nonlinear thing. In one of his works there is a house with a horse or donkey upside down in the air above it as well as many other objects and beings scattered, as it seemed, around. I believe it was just such a painting that gave rise to the musical *Fiddler on the Roof.*

So, what could reflect this agglomeration that seemed to me to represent better the reality of life, of a life, than the usual structures? It was my son, Jeff, who suggested one could actually call it a mosaic. (My daughter, Sarah, is also a major contributor to my work but in other ways.) So yes, of course, why hadn't I thought of that? These stories provide a kind of mosaic of my life.

Originally, as a first try, I had grouped the pieces into categories: "early life," "thoughts about psychiatry," "later years," and so on. But I hated that organization. It seemed to me lifeless and stupid, a surrender to my tendency to use obsessive solutions to problems that did not fit that kind of understanding.

Ah, but mosaic, what exactly did you have in mind? Well, when Jeff was two years old, his mother and I bought a low-standing teak coffee table. In the middle of the table was a partly carved out rectangle, meant, I guess, for an inlay of some kind. So I bought a bunch of small square ceramic tiles of various colors that we could put there to form a design. The problem was that Jeff, as soon as he was able to walk, would pass that table, look at the tiles we had put in that rectangle, and begin to put them in different patterns. Occasionally, when he passed, he would look at it again and put the tiles in yet other patterns. Enjoying this idea and his creativity, one day I took the square tiles and cracked them into smaller and more varied shapes to increase the possible range of his efforts. He loved that, and so for several years we had this ever-changing table, each of the designs giving a different view of its elements.

Having also been influenced by works like *Choses Vues* (Things Seen) by Victor Hugo and the compendium of writings that is Eugène Delacroix's *Journal,* I found that "mosaic" is exactly the idea I would like to communicate with these many pieces of writing. See them and choose them as you like, in any order that you like, noticing any relationships or non-relationships that you like. It is both my mosaic and yours, and each way of seeing the various parts and their relationships or non-relationships may be of interest, may even have its own validity.

So here they are.

Oh yes, one other thing. In reading over the last draft, I decided that there was too much stuff related to mental health and I should delete all but two pieces about that. But reflecting further, I concluded that most of the "psychiatry" pieces were primarily about who we are as people generally and that I should leave most of them in. So I have, and if you find them annoying for whatever reason I suggest that you just skip over those pieces.

The Person and the Taj Mahal
[*4/11/21*]

Have you ever been to India? Several years ago, when I was doing some research for the World Health Organization (WHO), I went to Agra, India, for our meeting there. I arrived a couple of days early to have some time to see the city and, of course, the Taj Mahal. I knew something about the building, how it had been built by Shah Jahan to celebrate his beautiful wife Mumtaz Mahal, that it was considered one of the wonders of the world. But you know how that is, "Oh sure."

But it really was one of the most beautiful, magnificent structures built by humans that I had ever seen. I mean really! It is beyond language to describe. There it stood, at the far end of its long reflecting pool, very big, a beautiful dome, incredible symmetry. There in the morning, gleaming white, the sun reflecting off it, and the colors of its inlaid stones sparkling. I mean you really have to see it.

At noon I went back to see it again and found, just as people say, a different building, The colors were brighter now, shimmering in the sun. Then, totally captivated, I went back in the late afternoon. Yes, of course, a different building again. With shadows falling across it, even the shape seemed to have changed. It was still incredibly beautiful but in a new way. I had never seen anything like that. I have never seen anything like that.

I have two little boxes of the white marble with the beautiful multicolored stone inlays to remind me. One I bought at the time of the visit. The other was given to me many years later by Ani, my wonderful Indian friend.

What did Henri Poincaré say, a house is not a pile of stones? The Taj Mahal is certainly not merely a pile of marble. People are like that too. Wondrous, variegated. I have a friend whom I like very much. She is bright, fun, thoughtful, creative. A friend of mine who works with her says she complains a lot. I never see that aspect of her. I know a lot of people, psychiatrists, biologists, who study mental illness. They study people's chemicals and nerve pathways but not the whole person. It seems to me that this is like studying the stones that make up the Taj. Interesting, important, but it doesn't give them much information about the whole thing, the whole package. It often seems that they, and the whole mental health field, rarely notice what they're not seeing, the person. Julien La Mettrie in the eighteenth century insisted that the physical part of a person and the mental part, which he called the soul, were intimately connected with each other. I believe that is one of the early statements of what we now call the biopsychosocial perspective on the human being. Oliver Sacks more recently noted that even in people with major brain damage, there is a human side that is reachable. In the mental health field we have traced some possible connections between certain chemical and brain findings and mental symptoms, experiences, and behaviors. But essentially, very little attention is paid to the Taj Mahal as a whole, to how all these things fit or don't fit, interact or don't interact with the functioning, even the structure of the whole building. What is the connection or non-connection of the woman's complaining connected to her being bright, fun, thoughtful, and creative? How do these relate to her feelings of uncertainty and doubt, her experiences of a difficult marriage, her headaches and episodes of depression. A pile of stones is not a building, a pile of neurons and chemicals is not a person. We need a conceptualization of the whole being.

If/Then
[*1/18/18*]

The first complete draft of my autobiography has been rejected. Two critics said the first part feels like I was in a hurry, that there needs to be more reflection and context; a third critic, an editor with Yale University Press, said that I should write about working with patients. My first reaction was: I have written what I wanted; I'm not going to write some coherent story just to fit what people expect. Then, yesterday morning, in fact, I decided that I should try to put myself in the place of a reader and fill out areas she/he would need to know to understand better what I was saying and being.

There are two questions actually: Can I make it more understandable without losing me; and is there a theme and if so, what is it? Regarding that second question, I offer these thoughts. A patient once told me she shouldn't have married her husband. She did so because she was getting older and wanted to have kids, but she shouldn't have settled. Last night, during the intermission at a folk concert, my friend Richard recounted something about his life and said he had made the wrong decision. He added that many people regret certain decisions they have made. (I don't!) The woman next to me hearing our conversation said there was a musical on Broadway a couple of years ago called *If/Then* in which the plot follows the life of a character in one direction that results from a single decision and simultaneously tells the parallel story of the life that would have followed the opposite decision. The woman then said people would end up the same way no matter which decisions were taken. I disagreed, saying one decision or an event leads to another and then to another and another, and thus to an entirely different evolution. But now I'm not quite so sure. There are certain ways of being I have, for example, that keep me pretty much on the same course no matter what happens. I'm stubborn and have an idea of what's important to me that seems pretty unalterable. Or do I? What if I had never met Frank Fox, who almost by chance became my Sunday School teacher? Would I have ever learned about Spinoza and Buddhism? Or what if I had not gone to study in Geneva? What if I had had a less troubled, warmer, and more available mother or, for that matter, had a mean, destructive father? What if, many things? Is there a "theme" to our lives? Is it unalterable? Do specific events or conditions matter in the evolution of one's life?

An autobiography, how do you write it? How do you write it without shutting off those questions which are really complex and not definitively answerable? To think about microhistory, what is the connection between the individual's life and the contexts in which he lives? What would have happened to Napoleon if he had been born in 1715, to Nelson or Wellington if Napoleon had been born in 1715? Can we speculate on how life A prime would have been different from life A? Should an autobiography be a microhistory, as my friend Annie, an anthropologist working especially with people who have major psychiatric problems, says, taking both the individual and the context "seriously?" How would that look?

If/Then. Maybe it's an issue of constraints and probabilities (uncertainty theory?). If Piaget had sent me a telegram saying, "No, you can't come to study with me in Geneva," then I probably would have gone into the air force after my residency, never have gone into research and meaningful academia, and maybe ended up depressed and running a hardware store. If my mother had been able to stay in New York and work at the United Nations, would she have had a happy and healthy life? Better, at least, than the one she had, with breakdowns but, in between, meaningful work? So much uncertainty!

There are two issues, and, of course, they relate. The first is form. One possibility is to think of a life from a stochastic predictability point of view. The chances of my being on time to meet someone are about ninety-five percent. What were the odds of that woman running the red light and totaling my car; or of Piaget saying it was OK to come, or not to come, or just not answering; or of my deciding to hitchhike around the country as a teenager or to choose Swarthmore over Harvard. An alternative is to choose a story form. As Barbara Turner, a wonderful storyteller and teacher, said to me when I was telling a story, "Stay there," meaning stay at that point in the story and expand on it, describe it more, expand the narrative. I'm not clear at the moment about the implications of the difference between the story approach, which is more interesting and idiosyncratic, and the stochastic approach, which is more general, not applicable to a single person, and more solid.

The second issue is content. The examples above concern a human life, but let's think about mental illness. What is relevant or most or more relevant for mental "illness," thinking in a statistically predictive form about its causes, course, and treatment? Or should we be thinking about a more coherent but less statistical form. Are we dealing more with statistical probabilities or more with closely knit specific interacting sequences, "stories"?

So, What Have You Learned?

I was sitting at my kitchen table, looking out the window to the back yard on a quiet rainy day and resting for a moment between tasks. In a mood of rebellion, my mind posed the question to me, "So you've been in this mental health thing for quite a while now, at least sixty years. What have you learned?" "Whoa, that's not fair," I thought, "I was just resting for a minute." But the question was too good to be ignored. What had I learned after spending thousands of hours, a lot of my life really, trying to figure this stuff out?

Well, my first response was "not much." I mean I haven't learned, for example, what the cause of schizophrenia was or how to have a consultation with a person with schizophrenia and say, "You need to do [such and such]. Then come back in a week, when it will have been cured, for a follow-up visit to make sure everything is fine." I mean that's what happened two months ago when I heard a horrible tearing sound and felt a sharp pain in the back of my left leg as I was pulling off a tight boot. "A torn hamstring," I thought. During the appointment with the orthopedist the next day, he took a two-minute history, palpated my left thigh, and came up with diagnosis, treatment, and prognosis, "You have a torn hamstring. Fortunately, it wasn't the muscle pulling off the bone, just a tear in the muscle. Don't use it too much, and in a week to ten days it will be fine." "There's no way a medical consultation can be that easy, clear, and definitive," I said to myself. But a week later it turned out that he had been totally correct. "Wow, if psychiatry could only be like that," I thought.

But it isn't. When I started to consider what I have learned over these years, what came to my mind first were the faces and voices of some of the patients I have known over all that time. These were people, most often with the diagnosis of schizophrenia or other severe mental disorders. But first and foremost, they were people, not just "schizophrenics" or "bipolars" or "depressives." And I don't say that out of some effort at being politically correct. I don't consider myself to be a "torn hamstring," but that diagnosis pretty much captured the problem for which I saw the orthopedist. No, these people were really people. The schizophrenia, or bipolar disorder, or depression wove itself into their personalities, but it was not who they were. Far from being mere political correctness, that observation is, I believe, a crucial basis for what I think I have learned. It has allowed me, among other things, not to limit observations to the things that are more superficial and easy to measure but to inquire more deeply into the nature of those variables we can measure, to explore variables more difficult to measure, to consider the interactions of all of these, and even to posit more complex variables in the goal of trying to make sense of what we see, constructions such as phases of improvement or the role of the person with the disorder.

Early on in my career, first as a medical student and then as a first-year psychiatric resident, when I was on the wards and working with a patient, I would ask a supervisor, "How come Mr. (or Mrs.) X is diagnosed as schizophrenic?" It was not that I was particularly interested in diagnosis at that time, just trying to learn how the term applied to the patient. In those days in American psychiatry, I realized later, the efforts at diagnosis were deplorable. One supervisor told me that my patient was considered schizophrenic because he was "on this ward." (Really!) In another rotation with another supervisor, I was told that a woman was considered to have schizophrenia because she had been sick for so long. (Really!) In still another rotation with yet another supervisor, I was told that a woman was considered schizophrenic because she had such a hard time relating to people.

A few years later for several reasons, including an invitation to become an investigator in an international study and because I thought it would be great to have that chance to travel, I became seriously interested in the focus of the study on psychiatric diagnosis. As many classification systems were to be viewed, I thought it might be a way of "cutting nature at the joints," a way of defining types of illness to provide better understanding and more effective treatment. But, as I became involved in research with my colleagues, especially Will Carpenter and John Bartko, in the International Pilot Study of Schizophrenia (IPSS), I learned (one of the main things I have learned over the years) that in the field of psychiatry things are not so simple. The problem of classification, of "nature's joints," in our field is incredibly complex. Far from being able to consider people as "a hamstring tear," for example, we are dealing with multiple interacting phenomena and cannot separate our concept of mental disorders from the people who have them.

In the traditional model of the disorder first called "dementia praecox" and later "schizophrenia," its prognosis was a defining characteristic, almost pathognomonic. And the universally grave prognosis at the time was that patients with schizophrenia could not recover or even improve. We found this not to be true. Further, we were taught that the key symptoms of the disorder could be identified reliably and discretely. That also was not always true. Delusions and hallucinations, for example, actually form a continuum of experience from more or less pure ideas (delusions) through a mix of "well, it's like a voice, but it's also like a thought," to a more or less pure perception (hallucinations). And then, most powerful of all for me, there was the young woman with schizophrenia who, during a series of follow-along research interviews where we were asking about the harmful or helpful impacts of symptoms, treatments, living setting, work, and friends, asked me one time, "Why don't you ever ask me what I do to help myself?"

She opened up for me the whole field of subjectivity. Not just the subjectivity we had been dealing with before, the subjectivity of symptoms and the problem of putting people into discrete symptom-cluster groups, but now, too, the subjectivity of the person with psychiatric disorder as an active being, with issues of meaning, willing, desiring, acting, and responding.

It should have been obvious all along, of course, but it wasn't. This was partly because the traditional medical model usually views diseases as separate, in some ways autonomous, problems that it is up to the professional to diagnose, treat, and cure. That model is beautiful and powerful, but for some conditions it is just not sufficient, and sometimes it is just not accurate. So that is another thing I learned.

Proof for such a hypothesis as the importance of the patient's subjectivity that extends beyond symptom concerns and includes a patient's active role is very difficult to come by. Nevertheless, there are so many patients with schizophrenia and other severe disorders who will tell you things like

"The most important thing in my getting better was someone who cared" or "someone who took me seriously." Others, in response to the question, "How have your psychiatric problems affected your life?" (thank you, Susan Gottschalx for suggesting this question), will look at you wide eyed and say, "You know, you are the first psychiatrist who has realized I have a life?" As you learn to listen for and open up the possibility of asking the right questions, you will also hear things like, "One day I decided I could do better than this and set myself to pulling myself together." Or "I followed your suggestion and rather than shouting at my voices I listened to them respectfully, and now they are not nearly so much of a problem." I can think of many similar instances.

So, subjectivity. Complicated! Not exactly a torn hamstring (although I suppose that can be complicated as well). I've learned that severe mental disorder is probably not "an illness like any other" but is really complex, such that you probably can't treat a person with severe mental illness without understanding the person. (This is not trivial. It is made almost impossible in many treatment systems these days where the psychiatrist is supposed to see a patient for perhaps ten to fifteen minutes once every six months, perhaps to "bring the patient to baseline.")

From the point of view of understanding, of conceptualizing, of helping the person get better, a major question is how to deal with such complexity. Interestingly, in such a problem, we are not alone. Other fields such as economics and physics have various ways, not of reducing complexity to something as relatively non-complex as a torn hamstring, but at least ways to consider how to deal with multivariable systems that also have nonlinear interacting processes. Complexity theory, systems theory, uncertainty theory, even chaos theory are various ways of making the best of complex phenomena. And for us, another tool is the use of narrative, of stories, as a way of putting the complexities together in order to frame hypotheses, to help us provide ways of thinking about complex causality, and also to help us consider subjectivity, the role of meaning, desire, decision-making, and action in working with people struggling with severe psychiatric disorder.

Narratives, stories we construct to help us frame hypotheses, could, of course, be something like *King Lear* or *The Heart of Darkness* or even *Anna Karenina,* but our efforts don't need to be so long or so beautifully written. Even a narrative paragraph or two is helpful and much better, along with a traditional medical history, than the medical history alone. It is important in such considerations to take a moment to inquire into what such a story-generated hypothesis might entail. Take *King Lear,* for example. A hypothesis drawn from that play might be, "psychosis can be caused by a rigid elderly man being severely disappointed by his daughters." I suggest such a hypothesis almost tongue in cheek since it is such a flagrant example of how a magnificent, powerful story can be reduced to rubble by an inadequate objectification. It reflects, among other things, how much objectification dedicated to more measurable variables considered as generating a linear process can leave out and thus risks not being very good science. Leaving out the power and beauty of a story loses an important part of the story, its feeling, and leaving out large amounts of data because they are difficult to measure generates bad science. The problem for the field is how to have relative objectivity and still represent nuanced and complex interactions. Perhaps this can be best obtained by describing a patient with both an objective summary and a more free and open brief narrative.

What would a brief narrative suggesting the possibility

of a relevant hypothesis be? For *King Lear*, recognizing that any brief narrative is just a pale shadow of such a magnificent story (or any human life), how about this: An elderly, powerful king decides it is time to hand over his throne to his three daughters if they will state how great their love is for him. The two oldest confirm their devotion, but the youngest, his favorite, Cordelia, says she will not take part in such a bargain. The king divides the kingdom between the two "loving" daughters and disowns the third. After his turning over his kingdom to the two daughters, their progressive cruelty removes from Lear all his worldly goods and his sense of self and poisons his view of the world. The shock of these losses drives him mad. Lear recovers briefly from his psychosis and is reunited with Cordelia, who has remained loyal to him. But she is then killed, and he, too, dies, but not before seeing himself as a "foolish fond old man." Did a kind of "urhomelessness" (total loss of his sense of the world and of his own identity) contribute to King Lear's becoming psychotic, and/or could it have been his shear fury at having been totally wrong and mistreated?

Clearly, Shakespeare would have nothing to fear from my meager effort at summarizing his play—perhaps you would like to try your own hand at doing better—but even this limited effort suggests more than "rigid elderly man severely disappointed by his daughters." The wonderful teacher of an acting class I took several years ago often said, "The life is in the details. There is nothing general about life." In acting a role you immediately perceive how much that is true. Can we understand psychiatric disorders without some understanding of the life of the person who lives it?

Attention to the individual and his or her story has other benefits as well as those of delving more deeply into the data of human experience. Finding unexpected phenomena is one important benefit. In my own work, I have found that patients when given the opportunity begin telling you about all kinds of things you never thought about. For example, the continua of symptoms ("Well it's a voice, but it's also like a thought"), which suggests factors about the psychology and biology of symptoms, and the active role of the person in the improvement process ("Why don't you ever ask me what I do to help myself?"). These are just two examples.

There is a growing interest in fields such as history regarding the power of the intensive narrative of a single person to provide a basis for a broader understanding of the major issues of the field itself while still adhering to scientific principles. Such approaches also suggest how alternative stories can be generated by narratives to provide alternative hypotheses for evaluation. We can learn from these efforts and perhaps have something to teach them as well.

So I guess I have learned something in all these years. Not the things I was expecting, certainly not solving the problems in the definitive way in which I would have hoped, but something important, nevertheless.

Susan Died
[*12/16/21*]

Klop klop klop
Vier kann oft gallop
Uber something uber steiner

Da da da da
Da da da da
Klop klop klop
Vier kann oft gallop

Now where did that come from? I didn't even know that I knew that. It's a song from my childhood, my early childhood. Maybe when I was four or five years old. I haven't thought of it since then. If you had asked me if I knew it, I might even have said no. But I can actually sing it for you. Here I'll do it....

So it's maybe eighty-four years since I've thought of that song. I looked it up on the internet and found it, except they say it starts with "Hop hop hop." Later, I looked again and found the version "Klop klop klop." Damn! I've forgotten some of the words, of course, but what I do recall is right.

I know what's going on, at least in general.

Susan, my sister, died two weeks ago. She was the last of my original family, other than me, to go. Susan, my sister, four years older than I. She taught me to ride a bike. On her bike! "OK, now you get on the bike and put your feet on the pedals and start to pedal and I'll run alongside you and hold you up." And I did, and she did, and then she let go, and there I was, riding a two-wheeler! I could go anywhere I wanted! When I was about five, I broke her favorite record, Beethoven's Minuet in G. I don't know how I did it—not on purpose, I think—and she never even got mad at me.

Especially when my mother was gone—physically or psychologically—during a lot of my childhood, Susan was always kind. She was always present in the early years.

After Susan went off to college, when I was about thirteen, we somehow lost that close contact, but at the core, the deep feeling of closeness remained. Once, the first year she was at college, at Christmas she came home with a friend, Mary Peterson. I pretty much fell in love with Mary. She was kind, smart, interested, thoughtful, and before she left, she gave me the record set she had brought with her. Jazz, Stan Kenton or Duke Ellington, I think. Funny thing, I never forgot her.

Anyway, Susan, my sister, didn't even finish that year at college. She was at Antioch, which had a work-study program, and Susan went off to work in New York and never went back to school. Antioch was pretty wild, my parents said, unstructured. They said Susan needed more structure and was having psychiatric problems. But after she moved to New York, we didn't have much contact. She had a lot of problems I guess, then married Mike.

I sometimes stayed overnight with Susan and Mike in their New York apartment. Later, they'd come up to New Haven for Thanksgiving dinner. I'd fix the meal—turkey, chestnut stuffing, cranberry sauce, candied sweet potatoes, salad, chopped liver for hors d'oeuvres, and wine and cognac. They'd bring a pie for dessert. But my friends who joined us—very tolerant friends—really couldn't stand Mike, who always had to dominate the conversation. So we stopped doing that. Finally, I got a little tired of Mike too. Once I called Susan and said it would be nice to have lunch with her and I could come down to New York. She said "good," but when I called to set a date said she wanted Mike to come too. I never brought it up again, and we never had lunch together.

Then Mike died. He went pretty fast, in a couple of months, glioblastoma. I tried to help out with their contacts with doctors and stuff, explaining things to them, and then afterwards, helping her deal with the people who were trying to straighten out their finances. They'd never paid much attention to money. Mike had no life insurance. His brother had given them half a million dollars most of which they'd gone through. They seemed to think he had so much money he should have given them more.

After a while, the money situation became more chronic than acute, and things seemed to stabilize more or less at an okay level. Susan also moved beyond the acute shock of his loss (they'd been together over sixty years), and she and I began to talk on the telephone.

At first, Susan was a little like a robot on the phone. I hated that. But then she became more relaxed. She would even call me sometimes, and we would have great exchanges about life, about politics, about when we were kids, about our parents. We reminisced about people like Dot and Pal Felheim, friends of my parents. Only Susan and I remembered them. I remembered what Dot looked like—short, with curly hair and an almost triangular face. Susan remembered that she was bright and knew a lot about books. Pal was a quiet man, a colonel in the air force during the war. After Dot died, he moved to New

York and married Adele, who was a sophisticated New Yorker and sort of distant. Susan and I talked about Ethel, our aunt, my mother's youngest sister, who died in her thirties of breast cancer. I remembered her at the Island a few months before she died with a big bandage around her chest. Years earlier she had a car with a rumble seat and took Susan and me for a ride in it. Susan remembered that Ethel studied at Julliard in New York and was a wonderful pianist.

Susan and I talked on and on, knowing things and bringing them back to life, things that no one else in the world remembered. I had a sister again, a real sister, for the first time in sixty-five years!

After a couple of months of being wonderfully together, over the phone, with my sister, I began to lose her again. She started to fade and then was no longer there. While it was clear that we still cared for each other somewhere way down deep, our calls became hollow, sad, and awful. Only a shell of her could be touched. When I went down to see her, it was much the same, although our fondness for each other persisted down deep. (Seeing her again after Mike's death, I realized that she was becoming fatter and fatter. When I asked her how come, she said it actually started when our parents died several years earlier, and somehow she just didn't care.) She withdrew more and more except on the surface. Then some on the surface too. She got worse and worse. She had some strokes. Then she died.

I saw her buried on Zoom. I didn't go to New York because I was having some dental procedures, and they were having trouble stopping the intermittent, unpredictable severe bleeding. So I watched on Zoom, with David, Mike's nephew, doing the camerawork. Arlene was there. Susan was in a long box. They put it in a long hole in the ground and shoveled dirt over it. The weather was cold, and I felt terrible that Susan would be so cold that night, there in the ground, without a coat, and with all that dirt over her.

    Klop klop klop
    Vier kann oft gallop.

Hi, This Is Don
[*10/3/17*]

I was awakened from my nap by the ringing of my telephone. When I take a nap I put the phone next to the couch, so I leaned over, picked it up, and turned it on. An enthusiastic male voice, "Hi, this is Don, from the Fulfillment Division. Your fulfillment packet is ready to ship." I receive so many sales calls: "Hello, I'm from credit card holders company," "This is a call to update your home security system," "I'm calling to help you update your Windows computer programs," "I'm from the disintegrating toilet paper company," things like that, so I turned the phone off and put it back on the floor.

"Just a minute," I thought, fulfillment division, that could be perfect! Then a second thought, "No, that's stupid. No one would call from a place with a name like that. I must have been dreaming." I turned over but then turned again and picked up the phone, pressed the button to show the last call, and there, sure enough, "Fulfillment Division." "Oh, how could I have not done that?" I thought, "but now it's too late. I've missed my chance." But then I thought, "No, along with the name there will be a phone number. You can call them back."

So I did. "Hello, Fulfillment Division," a woman with a lovely voice answered. I explained to her how I had just received a call from them and not thinking because I get so many sales calls, had hung up. Would it be too late to ask them to send me my Fulfillment Packet? "No," she said, "which one would you like?" "Well, I would love a job sending people fulfillment packets. Could I have a packet that would get me that job?"

"Of course," she replied, "but I need to tell you that naturally, a person can only get one packet." "I understand," I said, "but it would be so neat to call someone to let them know I had just found the woman perfect to be the wife they had been looking for, or the cure for their inoperable lung cancer, or even the publisher for their many times rejected autobiography."

"All right," she said, "but don't forget, just one such packet." I hung up the phone all excited. "Just think" I mused, "after all these years, I can send people their fulfillment packets. In a world of Donald Trump and Mike Pence, and Mitch McConnell, and Paul Ryan and Steve Minuchin, I can at least send people their fulfillment packets."

(The first paragraph is totally true.)

Stories and Science
[*4/29/17*]

I find our discussions these last weeks both fascinating and frustrating. I do not assume that either of us is necessarily "wrong" but realize how hard it is to "get" the point of view of the other. Let me try to explain how I see this. I see you as taking the view of the best of traditional science. And where applicable, I see that view as both powerful and beautiful. I, on the other hand, have been impressed these last few years with the degree to which our field essentially ignores three things: (1) feelings, not just "affects" or even "emotions" but complex feelings that have so many nuances and roots in various meanings; (2) the almost infinite diversity of human experiences and approaches to coping with life; and (3) the active role of the person. For me the value of stories is that they provide a way of taking that diversity of experience, feelings, and meaning, and active role to create a kind of gestalt, a source for combining bio, psycho, and social in a coherent way. I do not think that stories prove anything, but they are unequalled for generating hypotheses that include not just the usual readily measurable variables scientifically considered under the rubric of biopsychosocial but also the phenomena that we encounter every day but do not include for adequate attention in our efforts at mental health science. A rule of good science must certainly be that it's not acceptable to ignore huge masses of data simply because they do not fit your paradigm. This does not mean that we have to go back to accepting some highly speculative structuralist theory like psychoanalysis for example, only that we have to think more seriously about the data that are around us all the time and appear to many clinicians to be of major importance in processes that concern us. I think in the mental health field we are dealing with a human science that has the need for both traditional scientific thinking and also a way of incorporating diversity, feeling, meaning, and the active role of the person, a pluralist approach to understanding our field. The traditional scientific paradigm alone is adequate for dealing with many medical problems, such as cholera or a fractured tibia. However, I think another and broader paradigm is essential for our field, where factors that are not a fundamental concern regarding illnesses like cholera need to have a major role in our understanding. I believe this is probably as true for disorders like schizophrenia as it is for problems like anxiety or depression. Which of the various kinds of mental disorders are more "unitary," like cholera, or more colored by human diversity— "feelings," meaning, and "active role," remains to be determined, but this cannot be adequately accomplished if we continue to view these "human" factors as essentially peripheral or even noise. In brief, I think it is folly in most instances to consider mental disorders without considering the person who has one. We can't consider that person fully without some kind of story. Thus, stories in my view need to be part of thinking about mental disorders.

Let me try to write in a bit more detail what I am trying to explain. Two months ago I was taking off a particularly stubborn boot and heard a horrible ripping sound in my thigh accompanied by a severe pain. "Damn, hamstring tear," I thought. I called an orthopedist and made an appointment for the next day. He took a ten-second history, little more than I have just recounted, did a ten-second physical exam, and said I had a hamstring tear. He told me that, fortunately, it did not involve the attachment of the muscle to the bone and to rest the leg, and in one week to ten days it would be much better or even entirely resolved. He added that I might want to follow up with some physical therapy.

I thought there was no way this thing was going to resolve by itself in such a brief period, but he seemed knowledgeable, attentive, and kind, so I followed his instructions. Within eight days the pain in my left thigh was entirely gone and the leg was entirely functional. He had taken the briefest of histories, done the briefest of examinations, made a diagnosis, prognosis, and indicated what treatment was necessary—and he had been right! Oh, that the field of psychiatry could more often be like that!

But what if psychiatric disorders are not like a hamstring tear, or cholera, or even a parathyroid adenoma, conditions to which can be applied the magnificent power of the traditional medical model of premorbid course, signs and symptoms, medical history, physical and laboratory examinations, diagnosis, prognosis, and treatment? What if there are such intricate interweavings of bio, psycho, and social, that these factors including the feelings, decisions, and actions of the person and perhaps even the developmental history of the person are so important that major modifications in the traditional disease paradigm are essential? How should we deal with that possibility?

I heard Steve Suomi yesterday talk about his work on "subhuman" primate development. I've known him and his work for over forty years and always have the same reaction. He's contributed hugely to learning about the interactions of biology, psychology, and social issues in understanding normal and abnormal development, far beyond what we who work with humans can untangle. Although child development studies and even research on PTSD have made important inroads in understanding certain psycho, bio, social interactions in mental illness, in studying these disorders in adults we have often assumed they are disorders like Huntington's disease, pneumococcal pneumonia, or multiple sclerosis, essentially "ideal types" (Weber), "regular" illnesses, perhaps with premorbid components, but we have not looked at them as understandable also from a developmental perspective. I believe that a developmental perspective is the most likely to integrate the biological, psychological, and social aspects that appear to be involved.

A major problem arises: If the reality of severe mental illness is, in fact, a biological, psychological and social interaction process, how do we proceed to untangle these complexly woven threads? It is possible, of course—at least theoretically—to conduct the infinite number of controlled bivariate studies that would be necessary following traditional scientific protocol. But, given the number of potential variables and interactions involved along with the probable existence of nonlinear properties as critical stages, emergents, and feedback loops, such a strategy appears to require alternatives that could also be used. Hypothesis generation and testing approaches would provide valuable assists in making such efforts more feasible. Of course, as noted above, assuming that the disorders are genetic, and/or "illnesses like any others," would appear to avoid the problems of multivariate interaction altogether. Although it may be useful to pursue such simpler strategies, it is far from certain that they would be adequate.

I am proposing that an additional approach be added to the armamentarium. That is, the use of stories based on human experience that can include a large number of variables, interactions, and even critical periods and feedback loops. These features, after all, are the foundation of stories. By taking stories of real people with psychiatric disorders, or even of those who have avoided such disorders, it may be possible to suggest the most likely variables and interactions that play major roles. Although there is an important tradition in medicine of crucial "case histories," I suggest that the tradition be enlarged to include factors that may be crucial in psychiatric disorders not commonly included in traditional case histories. These expanded case histories could involve the actions and efforts of the individual, his or her feelings and reactions, and the demands and traditions of the social setting, and so on.

Even more radically, fictional accounts might also be of potential value. There may be aspects of experience in the plays of Shakespeare. For example, consider *King Lear*, which communicates more than "don't be a stupid old man" or even "be careful what you say to your daughters" and can perhaps help to elucidate experiential sequences important in understanding mental illness. Fictional accounts may even highlight crucial processes that can be more hidden in accounts of actual experience.

From the point of view of the mental health field, stories should be viewed as having methodologies as much as do traditional scientific methods, statistical methods, and so on. Just as even an apparently simple traditional scientific question, is person "A" like person "B," is incredibly complex methodologically as well as conceptually, getting into all the problems of diagnostic typologies and dimensions and their possible combinations, so stories too have their methodologic complexities. Not only are there different approaches to constructing and understanding stories (consider, for example, Jane Austen, Shakespeare, Franz Kafka, and James Joyce) so there are different ways of interpreting them. Approaches to stories are perhaps more like Clausewitz's view of conducting war (*On War*), involving a combination of rationality, feeling, knowledge, and creativity. Although the comparison is perhaps an odious one, still both types of endeavor attempt to deal optimally with extremely complex phenomena. That complexity may inhibit their easy translation to traditional scientific methods and criteria.

Stories are not, of course, meant to substitute for traditional research methods any more than those methods can substitute for stories. Stories are meant to provide hypothesis generation for the complex interactive realities of the human world that pose such a serious problem for knowledge that does not limit itself to assumptions of simple limited variables and limited interactions.

We cannot carry out the kind of studies possible in primate research to untangle the possible threads in severe mental illness, but there are other possible strategies, not to replace controlled research paradigms but to complement them, that can be crucial to studying the kind of complex biopsychosocial phenomena with which we may be dealing.

To accomplish this bringing together we are best served by following the principles of pluralism in science, as expounded. For us I think such pluralism involves using the approaches of traditional science as well as attending to narratives to deal with the interactions of objective and subjective data. Although there are problems with the potential diversity of narratives used and the establishment of a definitive "truth," not including a narrative leaves out an element essential to our understanding. Yes, I can tell you the plot of *Anna Karenina* limiting the data to one sentence: A woman who gets married, is unhappy, has an affair that doesn't work out, and kills herself by throwing herself under a train. Thus, I can spare you from reading the seven hundred or so pages of the novel, but you will have little understanding of the true nature of the situation. I do not think our narratives need to be seven hundred pages long, but to restrict them to traditional medical summaries is almost certainly inadequate. For example, concepts such as a patient's "baseline," which can ignore the desires and goals of the patient, are almost always unacceptable. As the pluralism model states, it is not a question of using the narrative instead of the more traditional concepts and methods but using narrative along with these approaches.

Bill Called Yesterday
[6/14/23]

Bill called yesterday. It is part of a gigantic plot to get me to look at my life, as people in college used to say "qua life," as a life. Ok, I might as well, since I mostly don't seem to do much to help myself avoid it. Who is Bill ? Bill is a friend from high school, ninth grade to be exact. Bill and Bob and I were friends. Bill, though, was a bit too cool for me so while the three of us were friends, he and Bob were friends in one way and Bob and I were very close too. So we were a funny kind of trio. Bill was the person who suggested we join the debating team, saying, "You'll be fine, the people in the audience will always know less than you anyhow." That was Bill. Anyway, Bill went off to the University of Chicago in tenth grade. I think they had a special program to accelerate smart kids into college. I saw very little of him after that time, but he and Bob remained friends.

So, seventy-six or so years later, I think it was just after Bob died, Bill called me, and he has continued to do that about every eight months or so since. And it has been very nice. I have called him a few times too. He is now living in another city having retired from his publishing position

He is less cool now and, in my opinion, much more real. And it's nice having each other like this. So we talk, about our lives, about Erie, Bob, things. In this call, Bill has some cognitive issues, but still seems very much together. That's kind of scary, of course, but since I often can't recall people's names right off, we all have things we have to get used to. But they are ominous.

Now, how can I communicate to you this sense that we're talking together about entire lives? Entire lives, ours, not this event or that event, not this experience or that, not even about this marital condition or that. Even when we do mention one or another thing or person, we, or at least I, have the distinct impression that it's from the perspective of viewing a whole life, our whole life experiences, which we both now know are not going to go on forever. We are looking across a vast expanse. It's really weird.

OK, this is really important so let's see if I can be more helpful in explaining it. When I was hitchhiking across the country one summer as a student, on the second day I got to Kansas. I walked through the little town of Belleville, through a park where you could hear the kids playing in the municipal outdoor swimming pool, and I got to the western end of the town, where I went into the small drugstore and bought a chocolate ice cream cone. IT COST A NICKEL! (When months later I was back in Erie, I wrote a little story about "The last nickel ice cream cone in the world.") As I ate the cone, I continued walking to the edge of the town. Looking west over the cornfields I experienced a sight wildly different from anything I had ever seen in my life. I could see forever! There was a grain silo, maybe ten, fifteen miles away. It looked very small, although I knew it was at least four stories high. The view was so immense that it was like being able to see the whole world. It just went on and on and on, and I could see it all. When you're out at sea, as I was later when I took various ocean liners across the Atlantic, you can see long distances too, but it's different. Maybe seeing miles of cornfields is just different from seeing the ocean. Maybe it's seeing a single object like the grain elevator that makes the difference. Maybe it's different because it was my first view of such an expanse. Whatever the case, although I have looked out from mountain tops and airplanes and other high places, I have never had the experience of seeing the sheer physical vastness of the world as I did that day on the west edge of Belleville, Kansas.

That's what being ninety has felt like. When I was in Moscow and first saw Red Square, it seemed in that setting of huge space surrounded by the walls of the Kremlin and other buildings that we people were like ants. It was really creepy. But the view from Belleville was completely different. The world seen from the western edge of Belleville was magnificent, breathtaking. I have been told that some people find open spaces such as the prairies of rural Kansas frightening, but I found it wonderful.

So time itself has been reshaped. That's apparently one aspect of being ninety. Maybe you have other experiences of space that can help you understand what I'm trying to explain.

Bill for example, talks about Bob at one point wanting to borrow money from Bill. Even though Bob and I had a much closer ongoing relationship than that between Bob and Bill, Bob had never asked to borrow money from me. That tells you something about the difference in relationships. Maybe Bob did not want to present to me as someone who needed money. But Bill had never met Bob's wives or kids whereas I had spent a fair amount of time with them and had gotten a feel for them.

But Bob is dead now, and Bill and I are talking on the phone. He has read my autobiography and makes appreciative comments about it. We talk about Bob's dentist father (Bill's father was a dentist too), or Bob's mother, or the girl I wrote about in the book and how after seventy years she and I are still awkwardly in contact. At each call, after about twenty or thirty minutes, Bill makes noises about wanting to finish, he has to go for dinner with his wife or something, and we stop. And there we are. There's this vast landscape of which we have parts in common, and we share that now, and there is nobody else, or almost nobody, who would really know what we're talking about, not in the same way, Bill from his house in another state, and me from my house in New Haven, CT. Bill and I, who haven't seen each other in over seventy years and who have no idea of how the other even looks now, talk like we're in Mrs. Ryder's classroom at Academy and she's just left the room for a couple of minutes. We each have this amazing view of the whole world, at least of our whole worlds.

Bernice
[7/26/08]

I met her on the train today. She got on at 125th Street and since the train was quite full, sat down next to me. She had a big white bag of fried chicken from Popeye's and started pulling out pieces and dipping them in a white sauce before she ate them. After a couple of minutes, having never seen a white sauce for fried chicken, I asked her what it was. She turned to me and smiled, a little embarrassed, and said "ranch dressing, I just love ranch dressing." I asked her if she bought it separately and she said no, they will just give it to you, and then added, "Would you like to try some?" I said, no, that I'd just had a huge lunch. The lunch was unusually good, slices of turkey, ham, corned beef, lox, cream cheese, tomatoes, onions, Swiss cheese, onions, potato salad, great rye bread, and mayonnaise, my favorite things, and cheese cake for desert, all very fresh and of very high quality—as I suppose befits the Barclay Intercontinental and all those wealthy people on the board of NARSAD (National Alliance for Research on Schizophrenia & Depression) and maybe even us (more or less) distinguished scientists from all over the country. Anyway, Bernice, she told me her name about halfway to Bridgeport where she would be changing trains en route to visiting her mother. She was Bernice Jones. I told her my name too. Bernice and I talked all the way from 125th Street to Bridgeport.

She told me she worked as a security guard and was going to take an eight-hour course so she could become an armed guard, trained in how to shoot a pistol and do many other things. I said I had never shot a pistol but had always wanted to and maybe I'd see about going to a place in New Haven where I could do that. "Yes, I would," said Bernice. She also said that in the past she'd done a lot of things, been in the fashion field, been a dancer, and her first job out of school was as a librarian. I told her that I had always loved libraries and that when I was a little kid growing up in Erie, Pennsylvania, my mother would take me to the public library, so I got to know all the librarians and where all the books were. I felt so comfortable there that over the years it became like a second home to me. Bernice had always lived in New York, I think, but had a sister who lived in New Jersey—Atlantic City, if I recall—and another, in Alabama? They both had kids. Bernice didn't much like New Jersey but thought Connecticut was really nice. Her mother, whom she was going to visit—but just for the day since she had to be back at work tomorrow, Sunday night, the 4-to-midnight shift—lived in Taunton Massachusetts, and since she, Bernice, wasn't married any more, her mother wanted her to come and live with her, but she wasn't about to do that. "No way, my mother is always after me to pick things up, to have things just so. I know that when she sees me today she's going to say, 'Why you showing so much?'" In fact, her rather copious breasts bulged agreeably over her low-cut dress. I said, "Your mother's in Taunton and you're in New York. After what I've seen in midtown Manhattan, compared to a lot of people there, you're not showing so much." I added that I know adult kids often live with their parents these days but that would drive me nuts, either as a parent or as a kid, I need my independence. Well, she liked her independence too. Her husband of twelve years had just taken off and left her three years ago and moved to Reno. She didn't have any kids, He took her Pekingese with him, and she really missed the dog. But since the husband had a Pomeranian and the two dogs grew up together, she thought it better that they stay together. I told her I really understood her feelings about the Pekingese, that we had had a Springer Spaniel, Barney, and I really loved that dog. Barney died when he was about twelve, and I really missed him.

We talked about loss, about divorce, about whether we would ever marry again, about travel. She had taken some cruises, a great one from New York to the Caribbean. I mentioned that I had visited Martinique once, and she said the ship had stopped there but she really preferred Antigua. I had never been there. I said I had traveled quite a bit, though, and she asked me what places I liked best. I told her Paris, India, and Bora Bora, and I described how incredibly beautiful Bora Bora was and how fascinating I found India and some of the people I met there. She said she would love to go to India and Bora Bora some day.

Around Stamford, she asked what kind of work I did. That's always a problem, and after I told her I was a psychiatrist, I quickly added that when I told people on airplanes that they often said, "Oh, you can read my mind" and then I'd tell them I can't even read my own mind. She liked that. She said actually she was a security guard at a homeless shelter and how bad she felt about the people there. Some of the staff treat them like dirt, but she and some others sit and talk with them. They're people after all. She likes to give and get massages and would give them massages if that was allowed but, of course, it isn't. "You know," she told me, "Some of those people are really troubled, and helping with the body is important. You know, the body can affect the mind." I said I totally agreed with her and added, "Unfortunately the field of psychiatry hasn't figured that out yet." I also said I also loved to give and get massages.

One of her sisters had some mental problems and was taking medications. If they were too much, she didn't think very well and got very heavy. I said that really was a problem. We both agreed that although medications could be important, people needed other things, like someone who cared about them.

I told her I thought she was pretty smart and said things so well and with so much feeling that she should be a teacher. She smiled very broadly and said, "How did you know that is exactly what I would want to do?"

We continued on like that. Shortly before we got to Fairfield, Bernice (she said someone told her her name was French) said that what she would really like is to be a missionary, to teach the Bible. There was a pause, and I said I had tried religion but, as with so many things you're supposed to do or believe, I found myself arguing with it. Ladies in fancy fur coats who go to temple, I mean how religious is that? She said yes, they don't care at all about the animals, and she smiled warmly, totally accepting my apostasy.

Well, we got near Bridgeport, we exchanged e-mails and phone numbers. (She only gave me her phone number since she was always changing her e-mail address.) I said I'd send her a card from Paris. We gave each other a big hug, she stood up with her white bag from Popeye's with the chicken that was left, the train pulled into the station, and she got off.

Dear Sirs
[*12/15/18*]

I am a (very) longtime listener to NPR and particularly love your series, "Missed Connections." It makes me think of a connection that has had a tremendous impact on me, but I have never been able to thank the person to whom I owe this wonderful experience.

In 1955, following my sophomore year at Swarthmore College, I decided to spend the summer hitchhiking around the country. I set out from my home in Erie, Pennsylvania, never in my life having been west of Cleveland, Ohio. My three-month, nine-thousand-mile trip took me to San Francisco and back by way of Hannibal, Missouri, Belleville, Kansas, Cheyenne, Wyoming, Grand Junction, Colorado, Gallup, New Mexico, the Grand Canyon, Salt Lake City, Utah, Glacier Park, Sand Point, Idaho, Spokane, Washington, the Oregon coast, and Santa Rosa, California, among other places. One night it brought me to Provo, Utah. I arrived there after sunset, ordinarily a bad time to arrive anywhere when hitchhiking since when you come to a new town in the dark you have no idea of where to find a place to sleep. On the other hand, a ride is a ride and it is wise to take it as far as it's going. When my ride left me off, I appeared to be in a residential area and all was dark, not a light on anywhere. In *Les Misérables* there is an episode where the hero arrives by foot at a town with which he is totally unfamiliar and where he is a complete stranger. I felt a little like that, totally alone and disconnected. After walking about trying to find a place to put down my sleeping bag for the night, finally I saw a light coming from a distant building. Approaching it, I saw that it was a bus garage. Closer still, I saw that there was a man working on one of the buses. Before entering the premises, I coughed loudly so as not to startle him and then called out to ask if he knew of a park nearby where I might spend the night. He got up and came toward me, and I explained my situation. He was very kind and told me about a nearby park. When I went to leave, he said, "Wait a minute." As I turned back, he handed me a five-dollar bill. I was very grateful but explained that I didn't need it since I had recently been lucky enough to earn $50 selling hot dogs at the Frontier Days Rodeo in Cheyenne (that's another story). But he insisted. He told me that when he had been doing what I was doing someone had given him five bucks, and he was just passing it on. As suddenly as that, no longer was I a lonely isolated human being. I belonged now to a whole line of connected people struggling to find themselves and their way in the world, a whole lineage of people who in a sense formed a network of experiences, assistance, and compassion. I took the money with much thanks.

As you can see, now almost sixty years later, I have not forgotten him. I have never forgotten that experience and have tried to carry its message. That wonderful man at the bus garage in Provo, Utah, revealed to me a beautiful truth.

Of course, I never saw him again. We didn't even exchange names. I would so have loved to have told him what an impact he had. I think it is possible that he is no longer living, but is there someone in Provo, Utah, perhaps related to a man who was a mechanic for the municipal bus company who may have heard of such an incident?

Thank you so much for your series.
Sincerely,
John Strauss

Walter Clark
[*11/11/08*]

How do you write about Walter Clark? I mean, he was not a person who stood out, which is one reason why he was so special. He was not flamboyant or aggressive, he was a lovely, kind person. He was not loud and obtrusive, he was quiet with a quiet sense of humor.

Walter and I were roommates in our senior year at Swarthmore. Or did I have a single then? Maybe it was our junior year. Anyway, we were never in each other's way even though the room, in true Quaker style, was small. Walter loved Gerard Manley Hopkins. Walter was an English major. Although, as I mentioned, he was generally a rather quiet person, occasionally he would come out with a line or two from Gerard Manley Hopkins or read a piece of one of his poems to me.

Walter was from New Hampshire. The way he talked and the things he loved and how he dressed, you would think he was from the woods. He did love the woods and hiking, but not like today with all the fancy, high-tech equipment and competitiveness. I think he just liked walking in the woods. He always wore old low leather boots, like a New Englander might wear. He loved Lake Winnepesaukee and his family place in Wolfboro. He would walk around Swarthmore in those boots, wearing simple worn pants and a simple shirt, and talk with his slightly country New Hampshire accent.

Walter was a Catholic, I can't remember whether he went to church or not. Sometimes he did, I think.

Walter went to Peru, over a summer maybe. He told me when he came back that he had learned some Quechua and that they had poems that were beautiful. I had never heard of Quechua before or since, for that matter, until about four years ago when daughters of friends of mine, Sophie and Susan, went separately to spend extended times in Peru. Then I heard the word Quechua again, which reminded me of Walter.

Walter and I had keys to the Cutting Record Collection. It consisted of tons of classical music recordings housed in a rather small room in a second-floor towellike extension of the building called the Lodges, the rest of which was only one story tall. The architecture was more or less Tudor and the windows of the Cutting Collection cranked open sideways. We had gotten the keys from Shel Weeks, a tall thin quiet guy from a wealthy socially famous New York family who was a communist and who had gotten meningitis when he had traveled to Yugoslavia where U.S. citizens were forbidden to go. Shel was always doing stuff like that, going to Yugoslavia, or to debutante balls in New York, and somehow getting keys to Cutting and, later, pass keys to all the Swarthmore buildings, which he gave to us.

So, Walter and I had those keys, and we would go up to Cutting fairly often. Sometimes when we were there, individually or together, especially in the spring, which is super beautiful at Swarthmore with a large campus and beautiful green fields filled with all sorts of flowers and trees donated by the Hoyt Scott (Scott paper towel) Foundation, we would open the windows wide and play Scarlatti harpsichord sonatas really loud so people walking over the fields could hear them from far off. And, of course, we loved listening to them too, and feeling them too because the sound system in Cutting was quite powerful.

We graduated, and my next memory of Walter was three years later when I was spending the year in Geneva. I had taken the time off from medical school to study with Jean Piaget. Walter, who had been drafted into the army, had just finished his service and arranged to be discharged in Europe. He came by where I was living, a very small room in the huge heavy stone mansion of the Reverdin family, whose great-great-great uncle sat on a horse in the park in front of the University. The house stood on the rue des Granges in the very center of the old city of Geneva. You entered it through a large stone archway and then a courtyard, on one discrete side of which was a stone stairway up to a narrow hall off which was my tiny room. Walter said he wanted to spend some months in Europe, maybe in Germany studying with the frauleins. But a month or so later he sent me a card from Spain saying he'd had enough and was going back home. I knew that feeling sometimes myself.

We had no contact after that until our fiftieth reunion. I don't know why we didn't. It was that kind of friendship, I guess. At the reunion I joined him and his wife for lunch, but he seemed distant, and I felt sad. My feelings about him hadn't changed at all. His wife seemed lovely, like a New Hampshire girl. I think she was probably just right for him.

Two days ago, I got the Swarthmore Alumni Bulletin and read the class notes from our class. Walter was dead. How could he be?

He had been walking in the New Hampshire woods and just died. A heart attack, I imagine. He was retired but had taught English and creative writing at the University of Michigan. He was beloved as a teacher, had gotten many awards for teaching, and written some books of poetry.

I tried calling his wife, Francilia, but she wasn't home.

Mrs. Joyce
[*4/14/14*]

I drove up to the massive red brick building, parked, and took out my set of heavy steel keys. Building 6, in this thing they called a campus, was like the rest, distinguished only by the sign indicating its number. I walked up to the huge front door, opened it with one of the large steel keys, and went in. Inside, the plaster was a dull dirty yellow, no pictures. A few heavy wooden benches, empty, lined the walls on both sides.

Today, I was dressed in my grey flannel pants, jacket, and tie, trying to look at least respectable, maybe even dignified. A sign said "6C," with an arrow pointing down a long corridor to the right. I followed it and after about forty yards came to a massive solid varnished wooden door on my left marked "C." I selected another key from the ring still in my hand, put it in the keyhole, turned it, opened the door, and entered the ward. Before me was another long corridor, but this one had door openings on both sides, openings that led into small rooms, each furnished with one or two plain beds, a plain heavy wooden table, and one or two heavy wooden chairs. This part of the psychiatric ward for chronic patients was empty of human occupants at this time of day, but the other end of the long hallway opened into a large room where I could see patients sitting in chairs. They sat facing ahead, not talking with anybody or doing anything. A brief scream came from one of the rooms at the far end of the hall, but it stopped quickly, and no one seemed to notice it.

Also at the end of the hall, off to one side, was the nurses' station. Unlocking its door with yet another key on my steel ring, I went in and asked the aide who was doing some paperwork, "Can I see Mrs. Joyce? I'm Dr. Strauss and I'm doing some interviews for the clozapine study."

"I'll show you where she is. You can use one of the patients' rooms that's empty for the interview." Locking the door to nurses' station behind us—with a key from his own large ring of keys—he led me into the "Day Room." "This is Mrs. Joyce," he said, pointing to a woman sitting in one of the chairs. Dumpy, pretty old, grey stringy hair, even her face was grey, and wearing a formless, colorless Mother Hubbard dress.

"Hello Mrs. Joyce. I'm Dr. Strauss. I've come to interview you as part of the clozapine study you're in." She looked up at me, expressionless, and without saying a word, began to struggle to get up out of the chair. "Can I help you?" I said. She neither replied nor looked at me but managed to stand up by herself. The aide led us to one of the empty rooms. I arranged a chair on each side of a wooden table and invited her to sit down, which she did.

I explained, "As you know, you're having interviews as part of the clozapine study you're in, so that is what I would like to do today. Would you read this paper that says you are agreeing to be interviewed, and if it's all right, would you sign it?" Mrs. Joyce looked briefly at the page, took the pen that I offered her, and slowly and with some difficulty signed the paper. We went through the same thing with another page saying it was all right for me to record the interview.

I set up the tape recorder on the table, took the interview forms out of my briefcase, and started. "Can you tell me how it was you came to this hospital?" Mrs. Joyce didn't answer. She didn't seem to mind being questioned, and I guess she understood, but she just looked at me. I decided to try something else, direct questions to which she could just answer yes or no. "I want to ask you about some of the problems you might have. Can you just tell me yes or no about these? Have you felt sad or depressed?"

"No." Her voice lacked feeling, and I couldn't tell if she meant it or not.

"Have you been feeling anxious at all?"

"No." I still couldn't tell if she meant it or not. I felt stupid. Somehow there was absolutely no connection between us. Was I exploiting her? Was she just in a state where she wasn't relating, not paying any attention, just going through the motions?

I had never had this kind of situation before, although I had done literally hundreds of these interviews, Not knowing what else to do, I continued asking my questions and making my little check marks. After a few minutes I stopped making my check marks since this was the most non-interview of any interview I had ever performed.

Soon after I decided this was the dumbest interview I had ever done. This woman was almost totally "negative symptoms," and I wasn't getting any meaningful information. "Negative symptoms" are supposedly one of the signs of schizophrenia. They include things like social withdrawal, no expression of feeling, minimal activity of any kind. Boy, Mrs. Joyce sure had them all! My colleagues and I had brought this concept back from its 19th century origins because we had found that negative symptoms predicted bad outcomes in people with schizophrenia. It was often thought that they were more or less permanent and biologically based, perhaps part of a "deficit syndrome." As I said, I had done hundreds of these interviews, often with very sick patients, but Mrs. Joyce was more pure negative symptoms than anyone I had ever seen.

I gave up on the interview form and decided just to try to talk with her. "What kind of food do you have here, is it good?"

"Okay."

"Can you sleep all right at night?" More questions like that. But Mrs. Joyce's answers were no different from before, totally dead in tone of voice, in lack of attention to the question, in attention to anything. But I kept trying, "Do you get outside much?" things like that. Same total lack of everything. "How do you like being on the clozapine study?"

All of a sudden Mrs. Joyce's eyes lit up. She smiled brightly. Her voice sparkled with feeling and pleasure. "People like me better."

I saw Mrs. Joyce six months later as planned by the study for a follow-up interview. She looked better, more engaged, happier. Was it the clozapine? I didn't even know in my role as interviewer if she was one of the people who had received it or if she was in the placebo group. Or was it that "people like me better," that in the depersonalized dehumanized environment of the hospital ward she now stood out and was interviewed by people like me and others? I had no idea.

I got out my recording equipment, we sat down, and I started to go through the questions. Now she paid attention and answered in a meaningful fashion. As I generally do when I carry out these interviews, I engaged in some small talk with her, about comments she made in answering the questions, about the food, about the weather. At the end of the interview I thanked her and wished her luck. She said she was hoping to contact her family again, something she hadn't tried for over fifteen years when she first came into the hospital. I thought: "Oh, my god! They may not want to see her. She is probably totally gone from their lives. The poor thing, she'll reach out after all these years, and they won't reach back, or at the very least, they'll be shocked. Oh,

I hope it works. The poor thing." But, of course, I didn't say any of that. Not knowing what to do or say, I offered something inane like "That's nice." I worried for her. All these years lost from them in this hospital.

I was busy packing up my recording stuff, standing at the table. Mrs. Joyce walked over to me and suddenly reached out and hugged me. "Thank you," she said, "for being so nice." I almost cried. As I said, I'd done hundreds of these research interviews before. None of the people I'd interviewed had ever hugged me. This woman, with the flattest affect, the worst negative symptoms, the most non-contact, the most "not even there" feeling, who had this chronic, theoretically biological, withdrawal, this woman came up to me and hugged me, for interviewing her, for being so nice.

I can guess what you might be thinking. "Maybe she was bipolar." "It was the clozapine." (If that's what you're thinking I need to tell you about the film *A Sister's Call* that I saw last year at the APA, and Resperdal [see below, in the essay "The Project."]) Or maybe you're thinking, "She was being bizarre." And I would say, yes, those thoughts fit best in our way of thinking. But you really can't know any of that. Maybe it was because people liked her better. But for some reason, for many of us, it would be difficult to consider that.

My Mother
(as she might have described herself,
around age sixty-five)

Life has been a real struggle for me. I love beautiful things, the arts. I have worked in politics to help try to improve the state of the world. I love being with people and am very good at that and most other things. Yet, in every endeavor I run up against things that block me. It's very discouraging.

I come from a wonderful family. Dad worked his way up from poverty to become very wealthy. He was very domineering at times but loved us all. He was an excellent musician. In fact, my mother was a good singer, one of my sisters, too, had a lovely voice, and my youngest sister was a fine pianist and particularly kind. But that sister died of breast cancer when she was only thirty-five. My mother died of cancer too. She was older, but all her life she was plagued by episodes of anxiety that made it very difficult for her. She was probably too submissive to Dad, but those were Victorian times. I don't think she was very happy. She was, however, a wonderful cook.

I went to high school in Cleveland, where I was brought up. I had a lot of good friends who came from important socially active families, and I was very popular. At a time when it wasn't all that common for girls to go to college, I did—I started at Smith College. But just before exams the first year I became very anxious and called home. When I talked with Dad he said just come home, girls don't need to go to college anyway, and so I did. Oh, I wish I hadn't done that.

Back in Cleveland I went to what was called a teachers

training school and became a teacher. But I got married before I started teaching, and then I couldn't get a job because they wouldn't hire married teachers. They were afraid married women would get pregnant and that it would be bad for the students to see that.

I married Walton. He was funny and bright and played the piano beautifully. But he tended to dominate me with his talking even though sometimes I would stand up for myself. He didn't like fish. I did, though, and would serve it occasionally for dinner. Then he made so many jokes about the food that pretty soon I didn't like fish anymore.

Then the Depression came, and we had to move to Erie so that Walton could manage a group of apartment buildings he had bought with my father. I hated Erie. It was small and dominated by a stuffy Protestant elite. The people were so petty. The women just talked about their illnesses,

Soon Susan, my daughter, was born, and four years later my son, John. After giving birth to John, I developed a hip abscess that took months to get better. I should never have been a mother. I wasn't very good at it, although I really tried to be. What I really loved was my time teaching foreign policy at the local Catholic college. Yes, I didn't finish even one year of college myself, but I taught a college course and did it well.

As I said, I hated Erie. I started a branch of the United Nations Association of the USA there. Some school groups came but no one else, so it closed down. Later I had a studio where I made hand-woven table sets and scarves with my looms and sold beautiful jewelry from fine shops in New York, but it was Erie, and people didn't care for those things there. For several months I lived in New York City and worked for the just born United Nations. Now that was something! Exciting people doing important things. I worked with Mary Lord, who succeeded Eleanor Roosevelt as the U.S. delegate to the UN Human Rights Commission, and even met Mrs. Roosevelt. I also worked for the Adlai Stevenson's presidential campaign. Of course, he lost, but he sent me a personal letter of thanks, which I framed.

Oh, I didn't tell you, I also had what they said was a mental illness. I was depressed, I guess, at the beginning, which was about 1944. Nobody knew how to handle things like that in those days, certainly nobody in Erie. I had some good friends there, Lenore, a social worker, and Laura, who was developing important community social programs, and they recommended I see a doctor in Cleveland or New York. I went to Cleveland to see Rudolph Reich, a famous diagnostician, and he said I should go to New York. I was first seen at New York Hospital, which was a disaster. They said I had some psychotic things as well as the depression. They gave me electroshock and then insulin coma treatments. Thank heaven, I finally got out of there to the Weiss Cornell Psychiatric Hospital in White Plains, where Dr. Patricia Donovan became my doctor. She was wonderful and remained my psychiatrist even after I returned to Erie. In fact, she treated me until she died about thirty years later. I also had a wonderful occupational therapist at White Plains who taught me to weave.

Yes, Dr. Donovan was my doctor for years. I had many relapses and went back several times to the hospital. It was during one of those times, after I was discharged from the hospital and was staying at a hotel in New York and seeing Dr. Donovan, that I started working for the UN. I really loved that, but when I told Walton that I would love it if we could move to New York, he said that wasn't possible since he needed to make a living by running the apartments in Erie. He probably didn't want to move anyway. He came from a small village about a hundred miles from Cleveland and loved the small town feel of Erie. Also, he could make friends anywhere. So, I had to go back to Erie. Funny, we never bought a house there because I didn't want to. I always hoped we would move back to Cleveland or, better yet, to New York.

We did finally move to Cleveland a couple of years after Walton retired. That's where we are now. But most of my family have died, and I am starting to forget things and not be able to think very clearly. Besides, it's too late to start anything new now. I take medicines for my psychiatric problems. They help some. I have a psychiatrist here who's good. My son, John, who's a psychiatrist himself, found him for me. Susan lives in New York and has a lot of problems. Johnny has been very successful but is so busy that he doesn't have much time for us. We call him and Susan every Sunday morning.

My Mother II
[9/1/08]

When my mother died thirteen years ago—after having been senile, bedridden, and totally "not there" for two years—I was shocked that her death caused me so much anguish. Returning to New Haven after the funeral, I went back to work at the Mental Health Center and stopped in to see my former secretary, Maggie Ferrucci, whose office is just inside the door. I told Maggie, who is of Italian descent, about how shocked I was by my strong reaction. She gave me a hug and said, looking me in the eye, "You only have one mother."

I could have titled this "My Mom," but she doesn't feel like "Mom" to me. Never did. However, when Lucile Bruce and I were talking about subjectivity and mental illness and I mentioned that my mother had a mental illness, Lucile suggested that I should write about my subjectivity and her. I thought that was a brilliant idea and why hadn't I come up with it. Several days later I realized that I had, in fact, written about her subjectivity, or tried to (see above). Friends who read it thought it was good, but I felt my effort had been a complete failure, that I hadn't really accessed how things felt to her at all. Anyway, I'm glad I had forgotten. A great thing about forgetting, a quality I have long shown for certain things, is that those things always feel new, unknown, and unexplored. And, of course, in some ways they really are. Look at all the paintings Monet did of water lilies. Anyway, thanks Lucile, and here goes:

"Augusta wanted to change Erie." That's my mother

all right, although I never realized it until Laura said it. My daughter, Sarah, is making a video documentary of my life. This past week we drove the three hundred and fifty miles to Erie, Pennsylvania where I grew up, and then on to Akron, Ohio, so that Sarah could interview Laura Wallerstein. Laura is the last friend of my mother's who is still alive. She and her husband, Leon, moved from Erie to Akron three years ago to be near their son Larry since Leon has pretty much lost all of his recent memory and Laura, too, is losing hers. Nevertheless, they greeted us with great warmth and seemed pleased to see us. They were quick with repartee, and Leon even remembered some things from the distant past, such as the name of his high school French teacher, though he had to ask me, apologetically, about every two minutes where I lived now. They had known my parents since I was about three, living near us in my Dad's apartments, where we also lived, and remaining good friends forever. They went with us to visit my family's island north of Toronto.

Now, in their Akron home, Sarah set up her camera on a tripod and miked Laura while Leon and I went into an adjoining alcove, where Leon forgot they were filming and kept trying to talk. Still, I could hear a little of the interview and noticed when Laura said, "Augusta wanted to change Erie." Laura's words really struck me. First, I had never thought of my mother as "Augusta." I knew that was her first name, of course, but she was just "my mother," and that word "Augusta" somehow turned her into a real person, a person with a name, this woman "Augusta." Then I wondered—and I don't have an answer—how did a Jewish woman from Cleveland, whose father left school in the "eighth reader" to drive a grocery cart for his mother, come to have a name like Augusta? Her mother, "Nanny," Fannie Englander, sang opera though not professionally, and I know very little about her family. She did have a brother, Uncle Art, a car dealer who had lost a leg under a Cleveland trolley when he was young. He married a rich woman, Julia, and they had one son Arthur, Jr. Nanny was also related to the Newmans, although "cousin Paul" never answered my letter when my daughter at age six was teased by her classmates for saying he was our cousin. But "Augusta," where the hell did that come from? A Roman noble woman? Probably I'll never know. But it fit her. She liked beautiful things, She brought with her to Erie crystal water glasses with silver rims, fine china plates with gold rims, heavy sterling place settings, and a Marie Laurencin watercolor that now hangs on my wall. Like the names that Native American people give their children to match their temperament, Augusta was a perfect name for my mother. And Augusta wanted to change Erie. Laura came from New York and a pretty wealthy family involved in the Ethical Culture Movement. Laura came to Erie, adapted, was very successful in developing social services, and now has a large social services building named after her. Mom has nothing named after her. She started a progressive school, the Erie Day School, with Ross Fink, but that later became fashionable with the city's social elite and not too interested in progressive education. The school exists to this day. Sarah and I visited it and talked to the new headmaster. He knew the family of Zella Selden, one of those that endowed the school, but he had never heard of my mother.

My mother started a chapter of the United Nations Association of the USA in Erie. A few students and school classes came, but it was not much used and closed. Mom attended Smith College but left before the end of her first year because of anxieties around exams. Her father, my grandfather, "Sambo," said when she called home, "Come home if you're anxious, there's no reason for girls to go to college anyway." But my mother, who had never finished even one year of college, taught foreign relations courses at Gannon College, the local Catholic college, for several years. I don't know why she stopped.

My mother had wanted to work at the United Nations in New York shortly after it was founded. She was a volunteer there for a while after convalescing from a stay in a White Plains psychiatric hospital. I think she was offered a job, but Dad said, "We can't move to New York. I can't move the apartments to New York and where would we get money?" So she returned home to Erie.

Mom set up a weaving studio in Erie, where she wove beautiful cashmere things and sold stuff from Georg Jensen and other high-class New York stores, but she never sold much. What I remember most are shared experiences with her: at age eleven, working quietly with her in our "Victory" garden in the field behind the house to raise corn, tomatoes, and other vegetables during World War II and dancing together to records of Strauss waltzes; at eight, driving with her to buy oranges that came up from Florida at the farmers market; at five, her buying a linoleum rug for our cellar playroom that had the map of the United States on it so my sister, Susan, and I could drive our cars across the country. She loved to play her favorite record by the French singer Hildegarde, "Je t'attendrai." She campaigned for Adlai Stevenson, who sent her a letter of thanks that she framed. Every Sunday morning while we were at breakfast, she would call her family in Cleveland from the phone next to the dining room. "Hello, how ARE you?" She always started in this exaggerated fashion, and at the dining room table we would all smile. During the week we would hear her call Meiser's, the fancy grocery store in Erie that delivered. "Hello, may I speak to Kenny? Kenny, how are your lamb chops? Good, I'll take six of those." Then she would complete the rest of her order, all to be delivered. I remember her sitting quietly fuming at the dinner table when Dad took over the conversation. I remember her buying me soft poppy seed rolls from Kuhneman's bakery, my absolute favorites. But when I was a teenager she would always be up in her room when I had breakfast or got back from school, and I only saw her at dinner. A few years before her death, just as she was beginning to lose her memory, I was visiting their apartment when one evening she drifted off slightly and, as though preoccupied, said to no one in particular, "I never should have been a mother. I was not a good mother." My reassurances could not convince her otherwise.

Mother never changed Erie. Mother hated Erie. Dad, who had been raised in Loudonville, Ohio, said she was unrealistic. By the time they moved back to Cleveland she was about sixty-five and it was too late to start a career. They took some cruises and did other stuff, but she still had major psychiatric problems and then became senile. She died in a nursing home, pretty much a vegetable, at the age of ninety-three.

Augusta Rosenthal. Her last name was German, commonly Jewish. Her first name was that of an ancient Roman aristocrat. I wonder if they knew that. She tried to live up to it, almost succeeded. But she was dealing with impossible odds.

Oh yes, Laura Wallerstein said several times during our visit, "And I remember you, Johnnie. Once, when you were outside, about four years old, you were pulling at a weed and saying, "No weed is ever going to get the best of Johnnie Strauss." I don't know if I ever got the weed out or not. But I'm still trying to put the arts and sciences together even though Aristotle said you couldn't do it.

I guess this isn't very subjective. Or is it?

Me and My Mother

I never had much of a mother. I couldn't have told you that as recently as yesterday. But today, at age eighty-two and after one phone call, I feel that I can see her and our relationship better. It's not that she didn't try. As Dad would point out, "Your mother loves you. See, she bought you poppy seed rolls and lamb chops." And she really did try. But mostly it didn't work. She was struggling with her problems. Sometimes she was away in New York, getting treatment, psychotherapy, ECT, sometimes even hospitalized. But even when she was home, she was often up in her room and mostly "wasn't there".

Bob, a very close friend since eighth grade, called last night from Los Angeles. He was upset because a woman in his retirement place whom he had befriended was whisked off to only her daughter who has power of attorney knows where. That brought up for Bob a lot of memories about how almost all his father's family disappeared when Bob was four. There was some family dispute, and he essentially lost all of them, although they all lived in Erie. I never knew that, never knew they lived in Erie, never even knew that they existed, except for an advertising dentist who Bob told me was his dad's brother but alienated from him. In turn, I told Bob about my piece "Uncertainty Theory," in which I wrote about my mother, about the character Carol Milford from *Main Street* by Sinclair Lewis who feels stifled by life in a small Midwestern city, and my finally understanding that Mom's hatred of Erie was not so weird (even though none of the rest of us felt that way about it). (This article, which was originally published in the journal *Psychiatry* in 2017, is reproduced in my autobiography, *To Understand a Person* [2020].)

We kept talking, and the realizations kept coming. Bob said that he was always surprised when he was over at the house (we spent huge amounts of time in each others' houses after school and on weekends) that no one seemed to pay much attention to whether my mother was there or not. She was often in New York, but when she was at home, it was, Bob said, as though no one noticed. Thinking about it now, I can see that that's how it was, she pretty much didn't exist. Of course, she did, enough that it never occurred to me that in large part I didn't have a mother, at least not consciously. If anyone had asked, I would have thought the question stupid. But for me, mostly I didn't. As I told Bob I couldn't even remember her birthday 'til she was in her eighties. I guess, basically, I never forgave her. "OK, if you're not going to be here, I'll just accept that you're not. So there!"

Not there, even when she was. She would be just up in her room, or wherever, or not around at all. When I was about thirteen, I learned how to make gunpowder (I still remember). You could buy the three ingredients in the pharmacy of any decent-sized drug store. One day I did and decided, like Jim somebody from a Masefield story, I think, to make a cannon. I took my kit for making lead soldiers and a lead pipe about one inch in diameter, melted some lead and used it to plug the end of the pipe, made a hole in the still soft plug with a nail, and threaded through it an old firecracker fuse. From the other end I put in the gunpowder I'd made, a plug of cotton, and then some small pieces of lead leftovers from the toy soldier kit. I set it up in the backyard, put a light bulb a foot in front of it, lit the fuse, and ran.

Huge bang!

When I went to look, the end of the pipe where the explosive charge had been was split open, the plug was nowhere to be found, nor the light bulb. Then Mom called out from her bedroom window, "A neighbor called to complain. You shouldn't do that again." "OK," I said.

And that was pretty much that. Even when she was home, she was barely there. It was very sad—for all of us. But each of us, too, did what one could. I was lucky. I had Dad, our wonderful housekeeper Martha, and Bob. And in the early years I had Susan, before she went off to college. We all made it. Sort of. I was luckier than Susan. And probably luckier than Dad, although he was really a survivor, very impressive.

Dear Professor Shippey
[5/20/14]

Thank you so much for your wonderful series "Heroes and Legends"! Your knowledge, creativity, and intelligence combine with the works themselves to make your teaching both beautiful and powerful. I was particularly impressed by your discussion of *Don Quixote* and *The Deerslayer*. Perhaps I can add a small something to your understanding of the latter by describing experiences of my own that suggest that some of your statements about Fenimore Cooper relate not entirely to things of the distant past but to some that have continued to exist at least until the mid-20th century. It may perhaps be difficult for someone raised in Britain to understand fully, but some of my childhood and young adult experiences affected me like some combination of your ideas about Cervantes, the idea of a wannabe versus the realist, and about Cooper and the independent, competent hero of the wilderness.

My grandfather bought some islands on Georgian Bay, Canada, in 1918. "Bought" is not quite the right word. At that time, the Canadian government was giving away islands on Georgian Bay for a dollar each if the purchaser agreed to build a permanent structure on them. Georgian Bay is a "bay" off of Lake Huron and is almost as big as a great lake. On the east side of the bay are about thirty thousand islands, of which my grandfather obtained three. He did build some houses on them, but most of our islands as well as those around us were covered by primitive forest. My grandfather said they constituted the most beautiful place in the world (and after having traveled much of the world, I agree). He saw them as a place where our extended family and their friends could spend time together in the summer. I started going there in 1935 at the age of three and for much of my life went every year after that, often for two months, except for one year when both my grandmother and aunt died of cancer and no one went up.

One reached our islands from Parry Sound, a small town about a hundred and sixty miles north of Toronto. In the early days, until I was about fourteen, from Toronto we got to Parry Sound by a narrow road, of which the last fifty miles or so was gravel. At Parry Sound we went to Scott's boat livery, where our Chris-Craft, the *Scram*, was ready for us. We then drove the boat through fourteen miles of bays and channels between islands on a trip that I will remember to my dying day. We crossed the small bay in front of Parry Sound, through the Two Mile Narrows, past Devil's Elbow, across Five Mile Bay, through the Seven Mile Narrows, along the dips and weaves of the channel, around the island of Bear's Head, and then, turning right a few minutes after passing Bear's Head, we traveled for another five minutes to reach our islands, or as we called them "The Island." Seeing "The Island" again every summer was magical.

In the early days most of the other islands were not owned, and there were very few people nearby. When you heard a motorboat in the distance, you could tell from the sound of its engine whose it was—Hitchy Mitchell's one-lunger, the Riley's Royal Canadian, or the Supply Boat, with its the deep chug-chug. The last would stop at Riley's every Tuesday afternoon, and when we heard its whistle or horn we would row over through the channels and buy Cracker Jack and a Cadbury chocolate bar. Years earlier the Supply Boat had stopped at our islands instead of Riley's. But that was before I was born.

There was no electricity on our islands or any of the others.

Water was pumped by hand. Ice came from the icehouse, which the Indians filled each winter with huge blocks of ice cut from the bay. We heated the buildings with wood stoves and cooked on one in the kitchen. The toilets, of course, were outhouses, into which lye was poured periodically to minimize the smell. We washed ourselves by soaping up before swimming in the lake and washed our clothes in the lake, too, using a tub and a washboard. (The latter, a corrugated metal board on which you scrubbed your clothes, was very hard on the clothes.) We used "coal oil" lamps for light at night, but everyone went to bed pretty early so they were only needed for a couple of hours. Once I was bitten by a dog called Wewim and had to be taken to the doctor in town, Dr. Applebee—by boat, of course. On the way back in the dark, my uncle Herb ran our boat up on a submerged rock. He and my father pushed it off, and we finally made it back to the Island.

When I was older, I bought a canoe for myself, a second-hand wood and canvas canoe, and became very proficient in taking it over a broad area in all kinds of weather. I even learned how to "gunnel," stand at the stern with one foot on each gunwhale and propel the canoe forward by bouncing up and down and steer it by shifting my balance. I also learned to paddle without rubbing the paddle on the side so I could slide almost silently through the water, the only sound coming from the tiny little ripple of our passage.

I could navigate my way through all the small channels and tiny bays in the area. When at the age of sixteen I had a girlfriend at Riley's, Émue, I knew that to get there you headed straight at what looked like a solid rock wall of an island, but when you went over a little to the right there was a tiny slanted opening, only big enough for a canoe to pass and you could get right to Riley's Bay and their dock. Ralph Riley had once landed with a float plane in Riley's Bay. He had been a pilot in the Royal Canadian Air Force during the war. When he landed in the bay, he maneuvered the plane right to the dock where they tied it up. Many, many years later, when I was sixty-seven, my kids, Jeff and Sarah, and I were sitting in our house on the only island left to us. (My parents' generation had sold off the big island, and my cousins had sold off the other smaller one. Our remaining island, the smallest of all, was located in front of the big island. In the old days we'd sit out on the screen porch of the big house on the big island and snicker, "Can you imagine anyone building a thing on that small island?") As the three of us were sitting in the living room of the house on that small island, we heard a float plane. It came closer and closer and then settled down out in the bay before us. I had never seen a plane land there before. I love float planes. They are one of the most beautiful manmade things in the world. Jeff said, "That's for us." The kids had arranged a birthday present for me, a float plane ride over the islands!

Oh my gosh! Was that ever beautiful! I had never seen the islands from above before. The whole area that I had thought was mostly water (since we traveled it always in a boat) was mostly land!

But to get back to the Rileys when I was in my teens: Old Peggy Riley was the matriarch of the family. Sometime she would send out Émue's older sister to look for Émue and me because we'd be sitting until late on one of the massive rocks that form some of the islands. Going home from Riley's at two or three in the morning after being with Émue, on moonless nights I would be in total darkness except for the pinpricks of distant stars. If you didn't know your way by feel, you could never have made it home. At night the islands lost their features and blended together into a mass of blackness, blacker even than the sky above or the water that at that time of night was smooth as glass. And the whippoorwill would long since have stopped calling, leaving me surrounded by silence, except for the little ripply sound of the canoe going through the water.

During those years as a teenager, I got pretty tired of being with the family and spent more and more time with the Indians who worked for us, Joe Pegamagabo and Thelma and Winnie Wheatley, the daughter of Cap Wheatley. Cap was part Ojibway and part white, what we then called a halfbreed. I don't think anyone considered that label pejorative. In fact, I always figured he combined the best of both groups and so was better than anyone. A legendary boat driver and hero to many of us, he worked for Scott's and knew absolutely all the channels and everything about the islands and never made any mistakes. His real first name was Wellington, and he was a big heavy man with a weathered lined face and skin browned by the sun. Sitting next to Cap as he drove his boat, with all the white people in your family sitting behind, was like being next to God's right-hand man.

As I spent more time with the Indians, they began to teach me a little of their language. They said that the name Chicago came from the Ojibway word "shgog," which meant skunk. Chicago, they said, was founded in a swampy area that smelled bad. They gave me an Ojibway name, Kiash Koonz, which meant "little seagull." Sometimes Joe and I would go wandering through the woods. He was magical there. One day, he was at my side and, then, suddenly not. I heard a noise up a tree next to us, then a thud on the ground in front of me. And Joe was back, taking off his belt, forming it into a loop, and passing the loop around the hind leg of the stunned raccoon he had knocked off a branch. It all happened just like that. I hadn't even realized the raccoon was there. Winnie was like that too.

We were canoeing one evening and suddenly she said, "Turn around." I did, then I asked her why. There had been a bear in the water a ways in front of us. Again, I had not even seen it.

Being at the Island, I learned many things, not just canoeing but how to build a dock, how to fix an outboard motor, how to shoot a rifle and skin a rattlesnake, and a bit about how to maintain and repair many of the things that were so basic to our wellbeing. Clearly, I was not the Deerslayer, but the idea that one could learn to be self-sufficient was there, especially with my Indian friends. And as you said, the IDEA of the Deerslayer was a beautiful possibility. Not that I would ever get there, but the idea was out there, and it seemed a reality.

I related similarly to the second half of your lecture where you talked about the West. When you linked that with the Eastern wilderness, you were totally right. The feelings these places evoke are very much connected. When I was twenty, for the first time I didn't go to the Island for the summer. Instead, I hitchhiked for three months and nine thousand miles from Erie, Pennsylvania, to San Francisco and back by way of Glacier Park, New Mexico, Arizona, and Spokane, Washington. Talk about infinite beauty, literally. Looking down into the Grand Canyon brought a new kind of awe. And there at the campgrounds the man who was settled next to me turned out to be an old earth scientist, a miner or something, and when we walked down the canyon the next day he explained the rock layers to me.

So you see, it has been like that for me, a bit of Don Quixote, a bit of the Deerslayer. The next summer I hitchhiked all over Europe. I was in many wonderful, exciting places, stayed at great youth hostels at night, and met fascinating people everywhere. It was great but so different from my experiences in Canada and the United States! No immense spaces, no being completely alone. One time I was given a ride by some English people in France. At four o'clock they stopped the car at the side of the road, set up a card table, and prepared tea. When they learned it was my twenty-first birthday, they all sang, "He's twenty-one today." That was lovely and fun. But Europe is really very different from North America, or at least it was.

Vera Lynn
[*7/22/20*]

Vera Lynn just died. She was a hundred and one years old. "We'll meet again, don't know where don't know when, . . . we'll meet again some sunny day." Can you sing along? "When the lights go on again all over the world." "I'll be seeing you, in all the old familiar places, where this fond heart of mine embraces, all day through. In the small café, the park across the way, . . . the wishing well. I'll be seeing you . . . ." Actually, lots of other people sang this one too, but I associate it with Vera Lynn and World War II.

We learned some of the British songs at school, I was ten. It was 1942, fifth grade. "There'll be blue birds over the White Cliffs of Dover, just you wait and see." It was the time of the Blitz. German Heinkel 111K bombers and Dornier bombers were coming over to bomb London every night accompanied by the two-engine Messerschmidt 110s to harry the British fighters. The latter, the Spitfires and the Hawker Hurricanes, would have taken off from fields around London when news came from the observers by the Channel that the Germans were coming—again. When I first visited London, in 1953, there were still huge holes in the ground where buildings had been destroyed and not yet replaced. "Hello, this is Eric Severeid coming to you from London." When we listened to the nightly news, we could hear the bombs exploding in the distance. Our radio was a big thing, standing on the floor, about four feet high. We'd gather around it to listen. Churchill gave incredible speeches: "This was their finest hour." Roosevelt delivered his fireside chats, telling us what was happening, what America was doing to help Britain, the only European country left after the Germans had swept through continental Europe and were now attacking Russia.

By 1942 we were at war too. Before that we were sending supplies to Britain on a pay-later basis in a program called "Lend/lease." Sometimes our supply ships were sunk by the German submarines, submarines that lurked even outside New York harbor. Tensions with Germany were high. But it was the Japanese attack on the totally unprepared Pearl Harbor in December 1941 that brought us into the war.

We started to have air raid drills. The sirens sounded throughout Erie. We would pull down the blackout curtains we had installed, really shades. And wait. After a time, the "All clear" would sound, and we would raise the shades. There was no real danger, of course. Erie was well inland from the coasts. We were always hearing about the lurking danger of the "fifth column," traitors who might blow up factories and reservoirs, but we didn't really worry too much about that.

We had our songs too, mostly like the British ones, songs of longing. "He wears a pair of silver wings," things like that. And also songs of return, "Kiss me once and kiss me twice, it's been a long long time." And, of course, more militaristic ones: " Praise the Lord and pass the ammunition" and "Over hill, over dale, as we hit the dusty trail. And those caissons keep rolling along." What the hell are caissons? I'm not sure, but I think they're wagons carrying munitions, It's the song of the Field Artillery. And, of course, there was "Off we go into the wide blue yonder" the song of the "Army Air Corps."

There was gas rationing—we had a B card, not as skimpy as the A card—and meat rationing. We were asked to bring animal fat into grocery stores so it could be used for munitions.

"Ladies, please don't bring your fat cans in on Fridays" was one of the jokes. It was said that our neighbor sold black-market meat, and maybe the German refugee from across the street did too. The latter was the father of my sort of friend George and had a beautiful Hungarian-born wife.

The movies, of course, were war movies. Perhaps my favorite was *Waterloo Bridge*. An American soldier in London falls in love with a beautiful English girl. He goes off into combat. She thinks he has been killed and in despair becomes a prostitute. Then she learns he is really alive and has come back. Bereft, she throws herself off Waterloo Bridge in London and drowns in the River Thames. And *Mrs. Miniver*. Greer Garson, in all her optimistic beauty, makes it through the war, tragedy notwithstanding. Very uplifting.

But mostly there was the radio. Our programs? My friend Douggie Young and I listened to *Jack Armstrong, the All-American Boy* at 5:30, *Captain Midnight* at 5:45, *Little Orphan Annie* at 6:00, and *Terry and the Pirates* at 6:15. All of them were fighting the Nazis and the Japs, mostly their spies and fifth-column people, all very sinister.

Early in the war, Dad and a couple of other men brought over three German Jewish refugees, all young men, Walter Strauss, Fritz someone, and a third whose name I don't even remember. Dad and the others had signed an affidavit, whatever that was, to vouch for them. Walter (not a relative) was short and thin, bright and very kind. He became friends with us and our friends the Gottliebs. Walter joined the army, thinking he should repay the country that had rescued him. (The others did not.) Soon he was shipped to England, and he left me his small radio and his sergeant's stripes, both of which I cherished. We sent him letters by V-mail, or Victory Mail, a postal system set up to expedite mail to troops overseas. We had to use special, very thin paper. We started a pretty big Victory garden, growing corn, peas, beans, squash, and tomatoes.

Meanwhile, when I reached sixth grade, I began attending Glenwood School. That's where I met Douggie. He had a paper route and was skilled at folding the papers into a tubelike shape and throwing them up onto people's doorsteps without having to leave the main sidewalk. A lot of houses had what were called Blue Star Banners in their windows, displaying a blue star for each kid in the service. A gold star indicated that a child had been killed. There were a lot of "gold star mothers." Douggie would see these up close when, once a week, he went "collecting." He would ring the bell of each house and when a person came to the door, say "collecting" (Douggie wasn't much for words). The person would pay the fifteen or twenty-five cents owed for the papers. The regular paper cost three cents, but the Sunday paper with its color comics and other features, was more. In those days, a quart of milk was eleven cents, and the milkman delivered to your door whatever number of bottles you took (and picked up the empties). I don't think we had homogenized milk yet so the cream collected at the top. Postage stamps were three cents for letters. Postcards cost a penny, and the Postal Service sold prestamped penny cards that cost only a penny for both card and postage.

On D Day, the day the Allied invasion of France began, Douggie had "Extras" to sell. We stood at the corner of Peach and Cherry (really!) and shouted "Extra, Allied troops invade France," just like in the movies, and people stopped to buy the special papers. I only learned weeks later that our Walter had landed on a Normandy beach on the second day of the invasion and been killed. Sixty years later, some French friends invited me to the apartment they had rented one summer in Normandy. I asked if we could tour the various museums, and we visited the Normandy American Cemetery on a bluff overlooking Omaha Beach. The damn thing is huge, so many people killed. I went to the small cabin near the entrance and asked an old American guy there if he could tell me if Walter was buried in this cemetery. He took out a huge book with names written in it in long hand, found Walter's name, and then gave me a little map showing where his grave was. I and my friend and her two young sons made our way there. It stood among thousands of similar gravestones, row after row, but had the Jewish star and Walter's name on it. I broke down in sobs. I had no idea that the deep feelings I had for Walter still existed *le long de toutes ces années.* Of course, we had given our son the middle name "Walter," and it was the first name of my friend Danny Gottlieb's son. Maybe I should have guessed. The world is very strange.

So the war went on, more movies, Once, Susan and I took the train from Erie to New York to meet our parents there. The cars were filled with soldiers in their khaki uniforms who had their duffle bags up in the baggage racks. They weren't rowdy, I guess they were going to New York to be shipped out. At home I had big maps of Europe and the Pacific pinned to my wall and followed the progress of the war with little pins with national insignias on them.

Vera Lynn. "I'll be seeing you." "There'll always be an England and England shall be free if England means as much to you as England means to me."

These times now—with the coronavirus and all enveloping the whole country, the whole world—feel something like those war years. Of course, then we had a president. Now we only have a con man who hopes to get the U.S. ambassador to Britain to move the British Open to his golf course in Scotland so he can rake in more money for himself.

Other Reflections Prompted by Vera Lynn
[6/20/20]

I just read in the *New York Times* that Vera Lynn has died at the age of a hundred and three. Immediately, without even thinking, I began singing "We'll Meet Again, Don't Know Where Don't Know When."

It's funny how songs, music generally but especially songs, will come to you like that. A few years ago I was in Rome for a conference. Walking along the Tiber, I all of a sudden came to the Castle Gondolfo with its striking huge round turret. Then, too, without thinking, I started singing something from *Tosca*, an opera that I love. Even though you may forget the words, the songs, even just the music, can carry the memories, the feelings of a memory or an event, the feelings especially.

When my friend Eve Gardienne at a conference presented her work on "peertivity"—how people with severe mental illness often understand others with similar problems in a way that is more direct, more powerful than is true for most "caregivers"—it made me think about the multiple ways we have of understanding and communicating. Having a similar experience, language, music, facial expression, and so on are all diverse ways of being able to "get it," really understand and be able to communicate an experience, one's own or that of someone else. A couple of years ago I was reading *Les Misérables* and came to the part where Jean Valjean has been released from the galleys, given a little money on discharge, and is making his way northward in France. At nightfall he arrives in a village and goes to an inn to buy dinner and stay for the night, but when they realize he is a former *forcat* (convict condemned to the galleys), they kick him out. Since that is the only inn, he goes to the jail and asks if he can stay for the night, but the warder says if you want to stay for the night you have to commit a crime first. So Valjean goes to a park and tries to fall asleep on a bench. I have not had exactly that experience, but when I was hitchhiking around the country for three months as a student, I learned how it was to find yourself in a town where you knew no one—and in those days before cell phones, you felt lonely and at a loss, totally alien. For a few moments, it was a grim and unpleasant experience. Well, Jean Valjean is the first person I have "met" who could understand that situation. I know it is not the same, but no one I have known has come even remotely as close.

Different ways of being, different ways of knowing, different ways of communicating, radically different ways. Theater people are those most likely to get these realities. Many of the rest of us don't even notice it. Even if you are only trying to figure out "What it is like to be a bat" (as Thomas Nagel describes so well) these are the various approaches you must consider to approximate that kind of "knowledge."

"Angor Animi"
[*11/16/05*]

The term refers to the sense that one is dying, and it is the title of a piece by the poet-physician John Stone. When I was a resident, I attended a seminar on literature and medicine at which we were asked to read the story. It began: "How long have I known this man, I thought, my head bowed, the crying over, done with, here in the hospital room?" There were eight of us in the class, ranging from a young woman, a third-year medical student, to a very old male shrink. The rest were psychiatry residents and fellows. Paul, our leader, was an associate professor in the psychiatry department. Usually, he started us off by having someone read a piece aloud. This time, though, he had each of us in turn take a paragraph as we went around the table. Later we expressed our thoughts.

The story, only four pages long, was about a boy, a college student, with severe heart trouble and the doctor who had known him and been involved with his care since the boy was five years old. When he was little, the boy had lots of physical problems with his spine and his heart, but after open-heart surgery and the replacement of a heart valve when he was a teenager, he had done better. He went to college, studying computers, and had been able to go camping with a friend. Then, a month earlier, things had started to go wrong. He had trouble breathing, experienced confusion, and returned to the hospital, where there was nothing left to do but give him morphine and oxygen as he slowly died. The doctor, who had known him through all this, talked often to David's mother and to David himself and then watched over David as he died. The mother, who had taken an hour away from her vigil to try and get a little sleep, returned to David's bedside in time to see the EKG monitor still registering a faint heartbeat. After she leaned over to kiss David's head, it stopped. It was raining outside.

As each of us read our paragraph and listened to others read, we thought of our little Tommy Byrd, our Jim, our Connie, our Frank. Tommy was my first pediatric patient, a quiet little black kid, maybe nine years old but looking like seven. He had pneumocystic disease, and in those days, forty-five years ago, there was almost nothing anyone could do for it. As his lungs filled up and became blocked, Tommy was slowly running out of breath. Each week it took more and more effort to breathe, and he got quieter and quieter. He was so nice, smiling, trying to be a good patient. Tommy had a mother, too. I was a third-year medical student and after my six-week pediatric rotation finished, I would drop back to the ward once a week or so to see the nurses and Tommy. One day there was no one in his room. The bed was newly made, the sheets were clean and white. The room had only the standard bed, the little bedside table, and a chair like all the other rooms. Nothing, no one else. I turned to Susan, the nurse, though I really didn't need to. "Where is Tommy?" "He died last night."

In our little seminar, Bill recalled Jim, an alcoholic patient he had had several years earlier with severe cirrhosis and ascites. Ascites refers to a massive fluid accumulation in the abdomen that presses against the lungs and makes it hard to breathe. Bill had put a needle into Jim's abdomen to withdraw some of the fluid to make his breathing easier. Jim moved a little in the middle of the procedure. Angry that he hadn't stayed still, Bill looked up at Jim and then realized he had just then died. A code was called, people came. Bill went to the window and cried and watched it rain.

We thought of our psychiatric patients too, not just the ones who died but people like Peter, an eager college student who had started having delusions during his second year at Princeton. I was his doctor. He asked me if he got better whether he would still be able to write poetry. He got better and left the hospital. But then he came back, more delusional than before. Again, he got somewhat better and left the hospital. Again, he came back. I left that job a few months later to move on to my new position.

Jean and James, as they read and listened, had tears come to their eyes. We all did. Even Paul, who had read the story many times. We had never talked about those things before. Shirley, the medical student sitting next to me, didn't say much.

The seminar finished. When we walked outside to the parking lot and our cars, it was raining.

The Kids
[*4/22/19*]

When I learned we were going to have a second child I worried that I would be supposed to give up some of my loyalty and affection for Jeff, our first. At the moment Sarah was born, however, I learned something that now seems obvious (though I would never have believed it before), that you can love more than one kid. It doesn't even need to be a contest. Sarah was the quiet one. In fact, she was the one who taught me that different people could really be different. Whereas Jeff had come out screaming, Sarah arrived quiet and serene. When you put Jeff to bed he would cry and cry. It was very upsetting to hear him there in his room going on and on. But he just couldn't stay up forever—or could he? But Sarah, never. You'd kiss her good night, she'd turn over and tuck her knees under her stomach in a kind of a ball, and she'd be asleep. In the mornings when I got Jeff up, he'd be all smiles and hugs. I would carry him downstairs in our tiny side-by-side duplex apartment, he'd wiggle, and I'd put him on the floor. He'd crawl over to the television that we had been lent—a big box sitting on the floor, with a tiny screen—and pull off the knobs and then crawl over to the kitchen to have something to eat. Four years later, when we had moved from Boston to Washington, in the mornings, Sarah would look at you from her crib, stretch out her arms to you, hug you as you took her to the kitchen, and sit quietly in her chair as you got out her orange juice. The kids were both lovely, but so different!

You'd think, maybe, that Sarah was always sweet and lovely.

With Jeff, you could reach over at dinner time and take a piece of potato that looked particularly appealing from his plate and taste it. Jeff would look at you and smile. One day when we had gone to Hicks and McCarthy to get ice cream cones and I was carrying Sarah, I reached out my hand to get to her cone, which looked particularly appealing. "Here, let me taste it." She let out a scream, and I jerked my hand back, "OK!" As I said, they were, still are, different. Terrific, but so different!

When she was still little, Sarah didn't pay much attention to her hair. It was very curly and often would start to form small "rats' nests." She would sit on my lap while I carefully pulled them apart, to a chorus of "ows," and then brush her hair 'til it was smooth again. After dinner we often played games like battleship or rollerball. We both liked to win and would find ourselves again and again in a heated argument. From the kitchen, Jane would call out, "OK, you two, cut it out." And we would, just like that, both relieved, I think, that we had gotten unhooked.

Both kids were good athletically, but in very different ways. Jeff became a very good skier, but when he played baseball in grade school, I saw him one time in the outfield watching the birds in the trees that surrounded the playing field. Jeff had been like that since infancy, curious about everything, always looking at new possibilities. When we went camping before he could even walk, we would be fixing dinner and suddenly realize that he'd disappeared. He'd have gone crawling off to the people in the neighboring campsite, where he'd be welcomed with eager hellos and laughter.

Sarah never did that, nor did she ever get distracted as she got older and started to play softball. At one of her games that we attended when she was in high school and playing third base, the batter hit a sharp ball along the third base line and Sarah, with outstretched arm leapt toward the line and grabbed it in the air, falling but holding on to make the out. She was also a fine basketball and soccer player and accumulated many trophies during her high-school career. But baseball—yes, baseball, not softball—was the game she loved the most, a love that has continued to this very day. When Sarah was still in grade school, every afternoon we would get out our gloves, mine a catcher's mitt, and she would pitch to me—hard! Or I would throw the ball high over our poplar trees, and she'd be there to catch it on the other side. She never failed to catch it.

Sarah often seemed shy. When she was little, she was sometimes uncertain. One day during the Poor People's March, when we were living in Washington, we invited some of the people involved over for dinner. Sarah had not seen many black people, and Jane let her know that some of the people coming over had black or brown skins. Sarah forgot the details and, shortly before dinner, went to Jane and asked, "What color are these people going to be, green?"

Unlike her brother, Sarah was not very outgoing or adventurous. Hence, it came as quite a surprise when around the age of eight she announced that she was going to be in a school play. We went, of course, and sure enough, there she was. She was actually the mistress of ceremonies, no problem at all, master of the stage. It was the same when she was pitching for Little League, one of the first girls allowed to do so. She just strode out to the mound as though born to the task and went right to work.

Each kid was uncontrollable in his or her own way. Sarah wouldn't let me taste her ice cream cone, argued fiercely when we played games, and insisted on her quarter cheese sandwich and a Ho Ho for lunch at school. Jeff, perhaps knowing that I had done a lot of hitchhiking years earlier, paid no attention when we forbade him to do the same. We found out when, as a high-school student, he got picked up by a man who just happened to be a member of my group at the hospital. I have recounted elsewhere the occasion on which he woke me up in the middle of the night to tell me that he had taken LSD and was on a bad trip. I stayed with him in his room 'til he finally fell asleep.

Both kids, very smart, a lot of fun, lovely, sometimes each a real pain in his or her own way, each so different from the other.

Now I'm eighty-six. Jeff is fifty-six, and Sarah is fifty-two. Sarah and I can still get into those arguments. She doesn't like to have me drive her, the only person who has trouble with that. It makes me furious, but I stay quiet and go along with it. Jeff has parts of his life that I don't understand at all. He apparently has lots of money. I don't think he's made any for years—oh, a little here and there—but he made tons when he was a successful writer for television and then with investments in the stock market. His wife, Mindy, has worked consistently as a kind of interface between the creative aspect of the programs and their business implications. The couple bought a small vineyard, a beautiful place in Napa Valley, have fancy bikes, and travel a lot with their whole family, often in first class, "based on credit-card awards." But they rent out their Napa place on weekends. Why? Because they need the money? Who knows? And I don't ask. Jeff has always told me what he wants to tell me and not told me about things he doesn't want to tell me. I am OK with that, actually more okay than I am with Sarah not liking my driving.

More important, a wonderful transition has taken place. Whereas in the past I was the giver and, to some extent, the planner and controller, the kids have, especially in the last seven years or so, started looking out for me—of course, each in his or her own very different way. Sarah has worked on making a film about the life of me and my (our) family. We visited Loudonville, Ohio, where my father grew up, and she interviewed on film people who know me or knew my parents. We took a trip to Erie and Ohio a couple of years ago, and, of course, we got into our usual battles. For example, Sarah wanted to carry my suitcase down the stairs in the B&B where we were staying, and I insisted on doing it myself. It's funny. When she was a baby, she insisted "Me do it," and now I'm the one doing that. We've had the same kind of fight for fifty years, less frequently now, but the anger is still bitter and maybe even more lasting.

Sarah calls several times a week, just to talk mostly. We discuss baseball and sports generally, which we each feel deeply but somewhat differently about, or talk about our lives, what we're doing, working on, pissed off about, whatever. Jeff and I talk, too, maybe once a week or every ten days, but it's different. He and Sarah planned a weekend on the Cape for my last birthday. They gave me the best room, a room with a huge picture window looking out over the water. They took care of everything. Several years ago we were up at the Island on the day of my birthday, and a float plane landed there. I love float planes. They land so gently and powerfully on the water and take off so gracefully as the step on their pontoons at last leaves its hold on the water and they become airborne. Jeff had ordered it for my birthday so I could for the first time in my life take a ride on our own float plane, see the islands at last from the air, feel that release from the water amidst the roar of the engine, and feel us settle back onto the water an hour later. It was bliss. When Jeff was little, he and I went to model airplane contests together to watch the gas-powered models fly. Now he and I flew on a float plane together. A couple of years ago Jeff and I were in Paris together. He is so easy to be with, loves restaurants and food stores, made all the reservations, except at my hotel where I made them. Best of all, it was at the time of the Tour de France. We went to see the cyclists arrive on the <u>Champs-Élysées</u> at the foot of the rue Royale. The place was crammed with people of course, but because of my age I think, they let us go to the front of the crowd. We saw the bikes come out of the tunnel, flow around the circle, and head up to the Arc de Triomphe. And do it time after time. What bliss, ohmygod!

So things change and things don't change, but they are both very special kids.

Ann Mott
[*5/1/13*]

Ann Mott had a big mop of curly red hair and a round kind face. She was slender and, I think, played soccer but was not really a jock. I'm sure she was smart but not one of those incredible five or six people each year who graduated with highest honors. She was a year ahead of me at Swarthmore. There were about two hundred students in a class so you knew everybody in your year and most of the people a year ahead and behind you. But I don't think she knew who I was, and we certainly never talked to each other, though we might have said "hi" as we passed each other in the hall at Parish or eating in the dining room. As I said, she had a kind face, often smiling. The sight of her gave me the feeling that there's kindness and warmth and pleasure in the world, it's okay to be here. I'm sure she didn't have a halo around her head, but she might as well have.

    I got my Swarthmore quarterly alumni bulletin two days ago. Ann Mott has died.

Corinne
[1/3/22]

She was beautiful, full of life, kind, interested. I met her over coffee. She was sitting at the small table next to mine. I made a not too nasty crack about the waiter, and she laughed. So there we were. I was thirty and I'd guess Corinne was twenty-six, maybe twenty-eight. It took us about twenty minutes to begin to fall in love. Why so long? Well, you don't want to rush things. She had reddish hair, I guess what's called auburn. She was tall, but not too tall and had a lovely round face, dark sparkling eyes. We talked, about the day, about the people walking by, about what each of us was doing in Paris anyway. I had to leave but asked if we could meet again, maybe for dinner, maybe in two days, Thursday. She was staying in a hotel near mine so I said I'd pick her up. I left the café, my heart singing. The sun had come out. I hummed a lovely melody from *La Bohème*.

I picked her up as planned, and we headed off to the restaurant. On our way, walking through a residential area, Corinne disappeared for a moment. I looked up and saw her in her fur-trimmed coat lying in a long planter box attached to the railing of a house. She looked really fine resting there, but I noticed that in the planter box, at her feet, was a baby lion, also resting or maybe even sleeping. I said that there was a lion cub at her feet, but neither of us seemed too troubled by that. Soon Corinne and I were continuing our walk to the restaurant.

It was a nice, small, not too fancy place. You went down a few stairs into a room where there were some benches around the walls on which you could wait for anyone joining you before you actually entered the restaurant itself. The restaurant reminded me a little of the Old Heidelberg in New Haven and even of The Den, a small informal restaurant in Erie where, as a senior in high school, I had my first restaurant dinner date. It was with a lovely girl in my class, a cheerleader, Marilyn Larson.

Well, Bob, my friend ever since eighth grade (and still!), had not yet arrived, so Corinne and I each lay down on one of the benches in the anteroom. Her head was very near mine, and she reached over to kiss me. It was lovely. Just at that moment, Bob entered, and we felt a little embarrassed, embarrassed because it was all slightly awkward but also because Bob would feel his not having someone like Corinne. There was no serious problem, however. Corinne and I got up, and we all went into the main dining room of the restaurant.

I awoke. I had that very special feeling of how it is to be freshly in love, in a wonderful relationship, that feeling of tremendous affection, pleasure, comfort, and ease. And before the two of you begin to notice all the things "wrong" about the other, too much of this, not enough of that, all the things the other person lacks, and the areas of tension between you. That wonderful early warm beautiful soft feeling of being in love. Like this, the recording, Barbara: *Septembre (quel joli temps):* https://www.youtube.com/watch?v=el5Mm0oRmi0

Who Was Right?
[*1/12/20*]

I will finally find out who was right, my father or I. True, he's been dead for twenty-five years, but some of these things take time. Here's how I'll find out. As I've told you, Dad was raised in a small village in central Ohio, Loudonville. When he was in high school he fell in love with a classmate, Lucille Budd. Lucille was the daughter of Paul Budd, a rough giant of a man who was the school principal. He was tough and sometimes mean, helpful characteristics when you were head of a school where most of the kids were farm kids and pretty rough themselves. Anyway, Lucille became Dad's girlfriend. I learned that in my early teens (Dad always told many stories about life in Loudonville). When my daughter, Sarah, and I went to Loudonville a few years ago for her work on a family history, she found a newspaper clipping that said that Dad and Lucille were engaged.

Dad went away to college at Oberlin, but it was 1918 and World War I was still going on. Dad was drafted and went to basic training, but the war ended before he was sent overseas and he and all the other recent draftees were released. Somehow, rather than go back to Oberlin, he started his sophomore year at Harvard. But his mother died—according to Dad, from a botched operation at the Cleveland Clinic—and his father was hospitalized with major mental health problems, probably syphilitic in origin. A Loudonville friend offered to support Dad in continuing his studies at Harvard, but Dad quit and instead went to Cleveland to work in the steel mills. He married my mother.

They had my sister and me and moved to Erie, Pennsylvania, where Dad ran an apartment complex he co-owned with my mother's father. The latter was the family patriarch, a dominating presence, and Dad was very much the junior partner. Dad had a tiny office, but he managed. In the evenings after a day of taking in the checks of the tenants, settling arguments, making sure that repairs were done on time, and so on, and after dinner, Dad would sit down at the piano in our rather small three-bedroom house and sightread Mozart, Beethoven, Brahms, Chopin, and Gilbert and Sullivan. He played beautifully, having been taught by his mother. Sometimes the conductor of the Erie Philharmonic, Fritz Mahler (nephew of Gustav), came over, and Fritz and Dad would play four hands.

At some point in our Erie life Dad was elected president of the Temple Men's Club, maybe even of the Temple itself. He was also elected as the only Jew to the Erie School Board and had many other civic roles. Since he attended to these jobs in the evenings, I came to liken him to Superman: During the day the mild-mannered Clark Kent and at night Superman, who was capable of all these Herculean tasks.

When Dad was about seventy, he and Mom moved "back" to Cleveland, something she had always wanted. They lived in a retirement center. Dad kept his beloved grand piano and would give concerts to the residents. He said it was easy since the "old folks" would fall asleep and not notice when he made mistakes (he was ninety by that time). Every day he would go to the center's pool and work out and joke with the young lifeguards, who really liked his company. Dad had always loved being with people and got along easily.

One evening when I was visiting, Dad, then in his late eighties, was playing the piano. He suddenly stopped, turned to me, and said, "You know who I saw today?" Weirdly, I did, or at least I thought I did. They knew tons of people in Cleveland, and Dad was fantastic for noticing famous people when we were walking in New York or wherever. But it must have been the tone in his voice, because I answered, "Lucille Budd." I knew the name because when I was a kid he would mention her once in a while among other Loudonville people of his youth, but I'm sure I hadn't heard it in years.

"Yes!" he said. "I was at the museum, and there at the other end of the room were these three women". "Did you go over to find out if it was Lucille?" I asked. "No" he said, "Why start that up all over again?"

I was astonished that feelings I didn't even know he harbored could have lasted all those years. I felt terrible he hadn't gone over to find out—and a little disappointed in him for not having more pzazz.

Later in my own life I took a different approach. I was finishing my autobiography just a year ago when I got news of someone from the Swarthmore quarterly who was connected to Ann. This prompted me to call Swarthmore, get Ann's address, and write to her.

Ann, who's Ann? Ann is my Aristophanes woman. I'm talking about Aristophanes as he appears in Plato's *Symposium*, who explains that primeval people were originally spherical. But the gods got angry—I guess because the people didn't need them enough—and decided that the spherical people should be split in half, so they had to go through life desperately searching for their other half. Ann was my other half.

We met during my junior year in college and fell deeply in love. But something was going on that I still don't understand. Much of the time we were blissfully happy together, but then sometimes we were like fingernails on a blackboard. It was wonderful, then horrible, back and forth. We had many beautiful times together studying on weekends at the Trotter classroom where in the spring on sunny Sunday mornings I would bring my record player and we listened to the Prokofiev concertos, her visit to Erie, watching the nine o'clock dog and its master walk by while we were having breakfast at the Danton in Paris. But awful times too, quietly horrible. Feeling at such odds. I can't explain it. During my second year as a medical student at Yale and in psychotherapy, my therapist, a really good guy, said he just couldn't treat me if Ann and I continued going together. But we did, and he did. After three years mostly together, which included some of those horrible times, and breaking up for a period, we were in Paris together, alternating as ever between the wonderful and the horrible, and finally I decided that when she left to go to school in Oxford for a year, that would be it. I described in my autobiography how, at the end of our summer together in Paris, I watched her going down the quai to her train and thought that was really the end. I felt horrible but also relieved.

But it wasn't quite the end. I hadn't even told her yet. I wrote from Geneva, where I was studying that year, to tell her of my decision. She came once to Geneva and then another time to Paris when I had moved there. In Paris she sat cross-legged on my bed and tried to persuade me that we could get back together. I held my ground with great difficulty, but that was that. We both finally got married—not to each other—and had kids. Then we both got divorced. After twenty years, I called her and we had dinner together in Washington, where she lived and I had gone for a meeting. I don't know how she felt, but I decided separating had been the right decision.

Then, in 2021, thirty-seven years after that last Washington dinner and spurred, I guess, by that communication from Swarthmore, I got her e-mail address from the college and wrote her. One thing led to another. The old force fields are still there. After all these years!

We're meeting in May when I go to Boston for Ely's graduation. Ann will come down from Deer Island, Maine, where she is living now. I often thought Dad should have been stronger about his desires rather than avoiding things. I think he may have admired my just going off and doing stuff like hitchhiking across the country or spending a year in Europe. But was Dad's decision about not finding out if it was Lucille the right one? Or is mine with Ann? I'll let you (and me) know.

Postscript: 4/21/21

But, of course, the pandemic hit, and that put an end to plans of getting together. We could only correspond, perhaps every two months or so. Over subsequent months I mentioned the autobiography. She didn't seem all that interested. And then she was. I sent by e-mail a late draft of it.

I'm still not sure who was right about not trying or trying again with a relationship, my Dad or me.

A High School Acquaintance
[*6/10/11*]

Sonya was a thin girl in my class at Academy High School. (My parents said that "Academy" was a strange name for a public school, but there it was.) Sonya seemed always cold and uninteresting. Smart enough but nobody you would be very friendly with. Was she aristocratic? No, not really, mostly just cold and not particularly interesting. She was friends with Jill Miller and Monica Howard, if she was friends with anybody and they were like semi-aristocrats. It seems funny to use that word for them now, sixty-eight years later, when they don't seem like aristocrats, but they did then. What do I mean by "aristocrat" here? Nice enough but somewhat distant, somehow just a little better than other people, less touched by the Sturm und Drang of everyday life and worries, above it all. Now they are all dead. Monica was a diabetic, which I only learned at the fiftieth high school reunion, when she was already dead. Jill was still alive. So was Sonya.

Sonya went out with Jim Fowles from as early as ninth grade, I think. They got married sometime after graduation. Jim was kind of an aristocrat too. He lived above us in Glenwood. Glenwood was the part of Erie to the south. As you got away from the lake, which was on the north side of town, the land rose and by the time you got to Glenwood it was pretty high. Academy was at the north edge of Glenwood, and from the top of the school I seem to remember you could see the lake.

So we lived on Cherry Street, maybe number 4524. Jim lived about three blocks farther up and a little over. His house was bigger than ours. His father I learned somewhere later was the head of the American Sterilizer Company, one of the big industrial plants on 12th Street along with Bucyrus Erie, which made steam shovels and sold them all over the world. Jim was good looking, nice, bright, and a little distant, like Sonya, but nowhere near as much. His house had an attached garage with a basketball hoop so sometimes we would go there and shoot baskets. I think I met Jim maybe in ninth grade, when we were both starting on the swimming team. In tenth grade, like all the Fowles boys before him, he went off to Exeter, but somehow I still knew him.

Jim had that aristocratic thing too. It wasn't off-putting, it was just a thing, just the sense that he was a little bit more sure of himself, more established in the world, and I suppose a little bit better than other people. I ran into something like that when I was hitchhiking around Europe after my second year in college. I landed at a little town in Italy called Lerici and went to the youth hostel there. It was located on the top floor of a castle, a real castle, overlooking the Mediterranean. The sleeping quarters, of course, were pretty basic, but a real castle! An American girl—was her name Mary? was she from Wagner College?—arrived later that day, and that evening we went up to battlements atop the castle. The crenelated walls were about seven feet thick so we could lie in one of the notches, watch the moon in the black night, listen to the lap of the waves of the Mediterranean way below, and hear music coming up from a café on the beach. Man!! I didn't do anything. I think she would have been fine with it, but I was pretty naïve in those days, and the whole thing was very special anyway.

The next day, we were down in the town with a couple of others from the hostel and met three young English people who had just come to stay at the hostel. These people had the same quality, whatever it is, as Jim Fowles but in spades. They seemed so confident, so knowledgeable, and like they so belonged in charge. There was nothing obnoxious about it, none of the pushy aggressiveness you saw from some Germans, it was all super smooth.

When Sarah and I went back to Erie a few years ago—I think it was a year or two after my sixtieth high school reunion—we went to the Erie Day School, which I attended from nursery school through fifth grade. The principal told us that Harold Fowles, Jim's oldest brother, was on their board and had been very helpful to the school. He mentioned a Mrs. Sloan as a major founder—were the Sloans connected with one of those big factories too?—but he didn't know that my mother and Ross Fink had really set the school up, with its progressive education program.

Anyway, I'm pretty sure Jim and I began on the swimming team at the same time. Another swimmer was John Sims, who had red hair and was called "Red" by people who didn't know him well. His father drove a potato chip delivery truck. Jim and John and I were walking home from practice one day when John started making comments about "Mike, Mike the kike." I figured he was getting at me, so I just walked off ahead of them by myself. Jim didn't say anything one way or another. I saw John Sims at the fiftieth reunion, the first one I had attended. He had married Mona Stevens, who was a cheerleader in the class half a year ahead of us. She was okay in looks, personality, and brains. They invited me over to their house for lunch the next day. They had a nice place, and in the course of the conversation John asked how Henry Stein was doing. Well, Henry had been in our class, but he and I had never particularly been friends, so I figured that John was still in his Jewish thing, all these years later. It's funny because John and I had been together all during high school on the water polo and swimming teams—he was a back stroker and I did free style—and we knew each other well. I became captain of the swimming team but don't remember that he had a problem with that. Other than one guy whom I barely knew on the city swimming team who made a Jewish joke after a practice, I never ran into any of that crap. After lunch with John and Mona, I took some pictures of all of us and then left. About a month later Mona wrote me to say that John had died of a heart attack and since I was the last person to take a picture of him, could she have a copy. I enclosed one with my condolence note but never heard back from her.

I didn't see Jim Fowles much after he went off to Exeter. Then, after so many years, I saw him and Sonya at the fiftieth reunion. He had graduated from Williams, done some stuff with race relations there, and maybe been part of the faculty. Then he had gone to the University of Chicago, perhaps in the divinity school? Had he become a minister? He was working on race relations in Chicago. I don't remember much else. Sonya was pretty much the same, polite, perhaps a little less distant.

For some years in New Haven I studied French with a French woman called Delphine Bouyer. She was recommended to me by the French Department at Yale. She and her husband, Patrice, had just arrived in Connecticut, Patrice having taken a position as researcher in the renal department at the medical school. Delphine hated being in the United States, but we got along beautifully. She had never taught before, but she was a natural teacher. We met regularly at Atticus over coffee and scones. and she was wonderful. True, she was a bit tough. She'd say "Nul!" (a nice form of "stupid") when I made a mistake or grade me "0 sur 20" (zero out of 20) but made it sound more teasing than mean.

Anyway, I became friends with the family. Delphine had her baby, Antoine, and I loved to play with him. When he could run, he would chase me around the house. When he got older, I would take him for hamburger, French fries, and milkshake at Clark's. We got to know the waitress "Mary" there and she us. Then, with things tightening at Yale Medical School, Patrice didn't get his position renewed. Instead, he found a position at the University of Chicago. Three years ago I planned a visit to Jeff in Los Angeles and decided to stop off in Chicago to see the Bouyers and stay overnight with them. While there I arranged to have lunch with Jim and Sonya.

I met them at their home near the university, a small but comfortable house. It was really nice seeing them, and we talked easily. Jim was doing his work with race relations, and Sonya was doing good stuff too. She was still thin. They had worked some with Michelle Obama and apparently become friends. I think it was Jim who said that Sonya had cancer. She looked pretty good, but they said there was no further treatment for it and she probably wouldn't live more than a few months. When I went to leave, I shook hands with Jim but then Sonya hugged me. She said, "You have always been such a warm person." Tears came to my eyes. I knew I would never see her again.

Little Things
[*9/10/12*]

It's funny how little things can make such a big difference. Tomorrow, I'm having a cardiac workup for an arrhythmia. It will probably turn out to be pretty benign, especially compared to the problems of some of my friends who are now dead. However, there seems to be something going on between "my" cardiologist and one of the people in her group whom she had me consult with. She doesn't want him to talk with me about some questions I have thought of since seeing him. I'm pretty pissed off now because (a) I'm not used to having a health problem of this degree and (b) they should just cut it out and let things unroll logically.

So here I am generally upset, and I get this e-mail. Well, I need to back up a bit with my story. I have a storm door on the front of the house that doesn't close automatically, so I put a sign on it a couple of years ago saying: "Postperson, please make sure you close this door after you put the mail in. Thank you." When I first put it up, a young woman in one of my writing groups made a joke about my use of the word "postperson" during the meal before one of our group meetings. She has since left for a job far away, but a few days ago she sent me a photo and a beautiful letter, so I sent her an e-mail to thank her. And now tonight, when I'm in this tizzy about this cardiac shit, I get an e-mail from her, "I'm so happy you liked it! It was a pleasure to put together, just to imagine you getting it from your 'postperson.'" My tizzy disappeared. Just like that. Really.

So what's that about? When I was in college I was very

involved with this woman, also a student. We had never had sex, but at the beginning of summer vacation when we had gone to our respective homes I got this letter from her, "I think I may be pregnant. I don't know what to do." If she was pregnant, it should have been by me, but that was impossible. Nevertheless, I was very worried. So I told my friend-since-eighth-grade Bob (with whom I remain friends even though he lives in California and I live in Connecticut). And Bob says, "Don't worry, if she's pregnant, I'll marry her." (He didn't even know her.) Immediately I stopped worrying. I knew it was crazy, the whole thing was crazy, she couldn't be pregnant, Bob wouldn't marry her. It didn't matter, I stopped worrying.

That makes me wonder: Remember K, the central figure in Kafka's *The Trial*? If someone had said to K, "Don't worry K, I know a good lawyer, we'll get you out of this." Or, if someone said to a person just admitted to a psychiatric hospital, "I've brought you some flowers. Here, take them. I had a problem like yours two years ago, and it's much better now." Or something like that? What if a doctor just asked a psychiatric patient, "How is your problem affecting your life?" Just recognizing that the person had a life and was not merely an illness. Maybe we need to take it more seriously when a person who has improved from a severe mental illness says, "The most important thing to me in getting better was someone who cared about me" or ". . . someone who took me seriously."

I think the "little things" can be really important. Maybe, our theories to the contrary, the little things aren't really so little. Maybe we need a theory about <u>that</u>.

Trees
[*10/15/19*]

It turns out, I just realized I don't know how to write about social class. It is hard to do without sounding academic, phony, bigoted, or all those things. Please try to be as kind as you can to my being caught in all that as you read the following.

In the *New York Times* today there is a description of how a lot of people in Dayton, Ohio, discouraged by factories moving away and unions weakening, felt abandoned by the Democratic party so left it to vote for Trump and now seem pretty much at sea. Somehow, without realizing it, I accepted and understood this completely. I know those people; I was raised among them. What! Until the moment of reading this article, I have been merciless in condemning these red necks who are dedicated to a vicious, lying con artist!

Must have been in how the article was written. Of course, I understand them. These aren't mean people or nasty people. Well, some are, but most are kind, good human beings. When I was hitchhiking these were the guys who picked me up and bought me lunch. We talked about their experiences during the Depression and what I was doing in college. One man told me, "I wanted to go to college like you are doing. It's good that you are. But for me the Depression came, we didn't have money, so here I am driving a hearse." Guys like that drove me to a doctor when my finger got crushed by a gear wheel as I was working to help set up the Frontier Days carnival in Cheyenne. Another guy, a man repairing a bus in Provo, Utah, insisted on giving me five dollars—a sizeable amount of money then—because "someone had given it to me when I was doing what you're doing so I'm just passing it on." I have recently been told that story was in someone's novel. I can't help that. It really happened to me, and I'm sure my guy had never read that novel. It was a very beautiful experience, one of many that have shown me the incredibly good side of humanity. Warms my heart just to think of it.

So, yes, I know the people described in the Dayton story, "working stiffs," as one guy said, not fancy executives or college types (like me, I know). They may be Trump people, but a lot of them are wonderful. And they're real people, who work, struggle, survive, and can be very kind.

In fact, I feel really at home with people like that. I grew up with them. I know them in a way that is very comfortable. When I'm in Erie, once every fifteen or twenty years, I feel that same sense of being home, knowing this place in a way I don't feel anywhere else (except Paris, but that's another story too), certainly very unlike how I feel in New Haven. I mean I love living here. It's perfect for me, not too big. Yale, which has some wonderful people (and a bunch not so wonderful), provides terrific libraries, museums, drama, music, and lectures. But New Haven has never felt like being home, like Erie. It's different. Yes, I live in a small house here, in a neighborhood of simple houses that is very like a neighborhood in Erie. I have chosen that and love it. Some of the people are very nice, but they're different from Erie people. They're just more East Coast, faster, more brittle. I wouldn't want to live in Erie now, but that doesn't mean that sense of familiarity, of feeling at home there, has left me.

Sometimes when I'm sitting in the Atticus Bookstore/Café here and I look out the window and see people walking by on the Chapel Street sidewalk, I am amazed that people can be so mobile, as though they have no intrinsic connection to the ground. Trees I can understand. They have roots. They sit there and grow, for years and years. These people just move over the top of things. They have no roots, in contrast, for example, to the ancient Greek hero Atlas, whose strength came from his contact with his mother, Earth. I mean how can these people exist without roots, without belonging? Of course, like trees, we are actually made of the stuff that surrounded us as we grew up. Trees, huge trees, are made up of the minerals they get through their roots in the ground, the water from the rain that lands on and around them, the air that surrounds them, the sunlight that shines down on them. We, too, our very bodies, are made of the air that has surrounded us, of animals and plants, many of which also grew up around us and themselves are made up of our immediate environment. And, of course, our language we have learned from those around us, how to think, how to say thank you, the days of the week, that one can even conceive that there is a week.

At Atticus this morning a young mother bent over with her hand on the shoulder of her lovely little daughter, maybe two and a half years old, to guide her as they walked by my table. The child stopped for a moment to look at me, I said "Hi," and she stood motionless for a moment, then raised her hand, smiled, and said "Hi." The mother smiled too as I said "What a beautiful, beautiful daughter you have." That mother is being absorbed by her daughter, as maybe even a little are people like me who respond to that tiny girl's incredible sweetness. These and, of course, many other experiences go into us, go into making us who we are, how we think, how we see the world. And this happens in not so different a fashion as the air, the sun, the water, the minerals, and the soil go into making what the tree becomes. That's really what "biopsychosocial" means, that and our taking in, processing, and acting on these things are what are involved in who we become. When Kant wrote about how we construct the world from our experience of it, that is the essence of what is involved. And, of course, there are Claude Bernard and Georges Conguilhem who help us reach from such consideration to the problem of "illness," including what we call mental illness, to teach us that you can't understand the abnormal unless you understand the normal.

Anyway, I understand the Dayton people better now. I think they've really been screwed by the vicious con artist, but a lot of them, maybe all of them, are mostly just trying to get along in this world.

The person is made up of the bio psycho and social. Those three components are like the two dimensions, height and diameter, of Piaget's test for how a kid gets the idea of volume, of quantity. Bio, psycho, and social are abstractions, the elements of which we see but we don't yet know how they constitute a combined thing, the person. Perhaps the person is the analog of volume. With the person, we're like the young kid who doesn't see volume. Like the slaves that Michelangelo saw in the masses of marble, the essence of what we're looking for, the person, is the complex reality, the construction that is constituted of bio, psycho and socio, each of which cannot exist in isolation as it contributes to the construction that is the person.

The Airport at Atlanta
[*11/28/06*]

So here I am at the Atlanta airport. I have a three-hour layover on my trip from Hartford to Los Angeles. The flight requires a change of planes in Atlanta since hubs like this are more efficient for the airlines than direct flights. The airport is huge. It looks and feels like a large prison, with long closed-in plastic-lined corridors, no doors to the outside, and few windows. The corridors seem to stretch for miles with small and large cell-like spaces off to the sides. I passed one of these spaces, fully enclosed by glass. It had a sliding glass door that opened electronically when a person approached it. Inside the room was packed with people smoking. They were like a mass of pale goldfish packed too tightly in a bowl with a sealed top.

Since I have three hours, I sit in one of the cell-like offshoots of a main corridor, watching people go by in both directions. Sometimes I see a person who has gone in one direction return in the other direction a few minutes later and then, after many more minutes, come back, going again in the original direction. Very few people are actually talking to others even if they seem to be together. Many have their heads tilted slightly, holding a phone to their ear, talking to someone who isn't there. Once when the crowd thins out for a few minutes, there is a man walking in the corridor pretty much alone, looking straight ahead and talking straight ahead. "Yes, I just left him and he seemed all right, but Nancy, who wasn't there . . .." I can't hear the rest because a man nearer me and coming in the other direction is talking into his cell phone: "Yes, we want to replace the 'Black for Style' line with the 'Brown for Casual.' We'll do that by . . .." He, in turn, is blotted out by a loudspeaker announcement: "Urgent attention. The Homeland Security Department has classified this as a level orange alert. Effective immediately, any liquids or gels, including toothpaste, over three ounces must be put in one-quart transparent bags and kept separate from other cabin baggage to be viewed separately by X-ray." I say to myself, "But that has been the situation for months." The male voice on the loudspeaker continues: "Be sure to keep your bags with you at all times and not accept bags from anybody else. Please report anyone behaving suspiciously. Have a good day."

Since my layover is at lunchtime and during my thirteen-hour trajectory from Hartford to Los Angeles only a "very light snack" (which turns out to be a tiny bag of potato chips) is being served on the plane, I decide to get something to eat at the Atlanta airport. They have an entire food center with the mixing together in the central area of small plastic tables and of the various smells from the surrounding restaurants: McDonalds, Blimpie's, Frankie's, Pizza Hut, and Oscar Meyers Custom Hot Dogs. Looking to see if there was anything else, I pass Hudson Books (funny how it is possible for even a bookstore to look like it was stamped out by a cookie cutter), Bijoux Incorporated ("gifts for under $10"), and Newscompany, and find a Domino's Pizza, a Chicken Licken ("real southern food"), and a Burger King. I finally decide on a club sandwich from Blimpie's that seems to have more real food in it than the other options. I tell the young Black woman working there who gets up from her stool for each customer saying "Can I help you" in a lovely way, not to bother getting up for me since I can get the sandwich and bring it to her cash register myself. She says, "Oh, that's okay, I need the exercise" and adds that if I want to take an extra packet of Russian dressing I can have it free. In fact, the few people in the airport who seem to be alive are some of the Black people who work there. One gives a friend a high five. A man calls across the corridor to a cashier talking on her cell phone, "Are you still talking?" and they both smile.

I go back to watching the treadmill of humanity. Almost all the people look serious, tired, busy, oppressed. People talk about an obesity epidemic. There are fewer fat people, really fat, than I expected. I start counting the fat people/nonfat people ratio. I don't think it is more than one to four. Then I start looking for attractive or interesting looking people. There are also fewer of those than I expected, maybe one out of thirty. Is it the context?

The people on the treadmill continue to pass. I am living the book *1984*, with the warnings to be careful of people. Or maybe it's the movie satire *Airplane*, where the copilot is a balloon that looks like a man and then deflates and the loudspeaker at the drop-off point for passengers says, "Park in the green area, don't park in the red area or your car will be towed," and then the exact opposite, "Park in the red area, don't park in the green area or your car will be towed." The treadmill of the thousands continues, and the male voice on the loudspeaker says, "Don't forget to take your vacation on Delta Airlines."

A Drop of Water
[*3/23/23*]

Have you ever noticed how a drop of water on a flat piece of glass forms itself up to its basic shape. Well, that's what I feel happens to me. On some occasions. I think I first noticed it at Pendle Hill. Pendle Hill is a Quaker center just across Crum Creek and the Crum Woods from Swarthmore College. Now, many, many years after I crossed that creek and those woods, that experience seems to have been like Alice going through the looking glass. I don't know exactly how it happened—perhaps someone had told me a little about Pendle Hill—but I had arranged to go there for a weekend, and here I was, approaching the large house at the beginning of my stay. I went in, introduced myself to the woman who seemed to be in charge, and she said, "Welcome, you're just in time for dinner." People, about eighteen of them, people mostly in their thirties and forties, were going up to the counter, taking a plate and some silverware, and helping themselves to the chili con carne, salad, and bread and butter. I did the same, and we all sat down at a large table. People started talking to each other and to me, and it was as though we all knew each other. Pretty much all of them were at Pendle Hill for a few days before going out to one country or another as part of the Society of Friends' outreach programs around the world. A couple of other people were just there, like me.

Now, seventy years later, I only remember one person, Gouri Bose. She was a dark- skinned young woman wearing a bright orange sari, and it just so happened that I sat down next to her at the table. It also just so happened that she turned out to be one of the most wonderful people I have ever met, and we spent much of the next two days talking together. We talked about India, a place I had previously hoped to visit, about life, about the Friends Center (Pendle Hill), about people, about everything. After that weekend we wrote to each other a few times, and I visited her and her new husband six months later in their tiny house in a small mill town near New Haven, where I was by then in medical school. I had just bought my first motorcycle, a used 125cc (very small) BSA, and rode out to her house to see her.

But a drop of water. It all felt so natural, my being at Pendle Hill, talking with Gouri, going up to the sink with my dishes after each meal and helping with the others to wash and dry the dishes and put them away. It was all so simple, so uncomplicated, so natural, and so wonderful. Now, in thinking about that weekend, I realize it was the first time I can remember feeling like that drop of water, having found my natural shape.

It happened again the first time I went to France. I sailed aboard the *Queen Elizabeth.* At first, things seemed strange, totally unfamiliar, and only a tiny bit as though I was going through that mirror. Strange, but, of course, there were lots of nice things. The third-class dining table to which I was assigned was occupied by people my age, and it was fun to meet them. By the time we reached France, like others on the boat, I had found my way around pretty well. But in France everything—the cigarettes, the gas, the food— smelled different, the people looked different, and the talk certainly was different. I couldn't understand a thing. Still, it rapidly began to feel okay, then better than okay, closer to perfect. I fell in love with Paris, a love that has lasted now almost seventy years and just keeps getting deeper, wonderful times and not so wonderful times notwithstanding. I mean how can you not fall in love with a place where a woman on the bus wants to get off at the back door and calls out, "La porte, s'il vous plait" (please open the door), in a voice that sounds like one of the most beautiful melodies from a Puccini opera, maybe *La Bohème*.

It is not that being that drop of water, having found a situation where you can learn how to be yourself, is wonderful all the time. No, not at all. Only that having found a place where you can do that is really very, very special—wonderful, in fact.

Birds Darting
[7/13/08]

So why are the birds so busy darting here and there without stopping? "Darting" is the word that always gets used, but what they really do is zoop, zoop, zoop all over the place—here and there, like I said. It's not spring any more. Their kids are all grown up and out of the nest on their own. They've moved to Hamden or wherever, so they don't have to be fed all day long like before. It's midsummer. It's the middle of a beautiful day, the sky is blue, the air is warm but not hot and humid, a lovely breeze is blowing. The trees are super green, my hydrangea is a deep, deep blue—my favorite color—the day lilies in their lovely orange are resting, and the raspberries dotting all the branches of my raspberry bush are waiting to get a little bigger and a little redder. The raspberry bush just keeps spreading, now it takes over about half of the rear part of the back yard. But what are you going to do? You can't tell a raspberry bush to stop growing. "Hold back, don't give me so many raspberries." No, you can't do that. That would be really dumb.

But, again, why are the birds darting so much, all over? They're not even sitting on my clothesline to rest a bit. They were doing that yesterday when I hung my white wash out. You know how a clothesline goes around pulleys at each end so that the line itself forms a sort of very long ellipse where there is a line on top and another on the bottom. You hang your laundry on the bottom line, which sags a bit from the weight. But the top line is pulled taut, and the birds like to sit on it. So that they can crap on the clean laundry, I suppose. They got two of my tee shirts yesterday, so I suppose today when there is no laundry on the line, it's just not worth their while to sit there.

Anyway, today, on this perfectly beautiful summer day, the birds are flying all over, like I said. Why aren't they just sitting on their nest, drinking a beer, watching the Red Sox game on television, or something? It's not like they have to carpool their kids to a Sunday soccer match, or get them ready for camp, or make sure they practice the piano. They don't even have to cut the grass, trim the bushes, or wash the dishes. Are they excited about the presidential election or that Senator Obama caved on the Foreign Intelligence Surveillance Act (FISA), allowing unprecedented surveillance, or the fact that the poor bastards in Iraq who should be doing National Guard service near their homes will now be pulled back out of Iraq, maybe. Not to go home, of course, but so they can be shipped to Afghanistan. I mean if you are part of a country that has troops in one hundred and twenty countries around the world—yes 120—you can't expect that the recruiters will tell you the truth when you join the National Guard: "Oh, don't worry. You'll just stay here in Kansas, you'll never be called to serve anywhere else." At least when you joined the French Foreign Legion, you knew you were signing up for pure hell anywhere in the world, but it was worth it to avoid a long prison term.

But the birds aren't even in the National Guard. Which makes me think also of the squirrels. Did you ever watch a squirrel jump from one swaying skinny branch of a tree, a branch about twice as high as my two-story house, to another swaying little branch on a neighboring tree, a branch maybe three feet away? Nothing but air in between—and below, until you crash into the ground. Sometimes I worry about those squirrels too. They don't have any disability insurance. Not even life insurance that would help their wife and kids if they missed that second branch. I would never have the courage to be a squirrel. But then I guess they don't have a choice. You play with the cards you're dealt, or not at all.

But back to the darting birds. This morning, Sunday morning, I walked to the corner store to get the paper. Then I came back home and turned on the radio to listen to Weekend Edition on NPR. Public Radio news is getting more dedicated to the trivial and the stupid every day so I turned it off, took the coffee I made yesterday out of the fridge and put some ice and milk into it, poured myself some orange juice, and put some something O's into a bowl with milk and sugar and started to look at the newspaper. Birds can't do that. They don't have a fridge to keep milk and orange juice and make ice. They don't have breakfast cereal in a box or a bowl to pour it in. They have to go looking for food every day if they're going to eat, if they're going to stay alive. Maybe that's why the birds are darting all over the place. I know that some birds fly around just to catch bugs in the air, but I don't think that's what these birds are doing. I think they're just fucking crazy. That's a psychiatrist's considered judgment, of course.

Collage
[*8/15/22*]

Wild Strawberries. The movie. The old professor is going to Lund to receive an award. He is with his son, who drives the car, and the son's wife. They stop to pick up a married couple who during the trip are always fighting and complaining about each other. They leave them before long by the side of the road, still arguing. The old professor recalls the various loves he has had, the places he has known, family holidays. He was betrayed by a young woman he loved but on this trip meets another version of the same woman who treats him with kindness. Her name is Sara.

Teaching my daughter Sarah to ski when she was about six: "Daddy, if you don't stop telling me what to do, I'm not going to ski any more." With Jeff when he was little, going to the hardware store on Saturday mornings to buy tools. Going to model airplane meets. Jeff became a good skier. Throwing the baseball over the Lombardy poplar and having Sarah on the other side catching it and throwing me "out." Reading *Night Flight* by Saint-Exupéry in French to Jeff as he was falling asleep and translating it on the hoof as I read. Making up stories about Peep Peep and Nutty for Sarah.

Falling off the sailboat up at the Island when I was in my seventies. Realizing that I was too old and incompetent to come back to this place I had known since I was three. Standing with Dad on the curb at State Street during the Decoration Day parade as a bunch of old guys were driven past in an open car. Dad turning to me and asking, "Do you know who those guys are? They are the last living veterans of the Civil War." Dad in the hospital bed in Cleveland. In a coma. I sit with him a few minutes then go out to the nurses' station and break down in sobs.

Skiing with other students from the "Uni" (University) of Geneva. With my wonderful skis—oh, what was their name, "DYNAMIC," great, huh? Swinging without effort from one side to the other as we slalom down the expert slope of Megève. Riding at dawn along the Seine with Traudl's warm arms around me, the fog lifting and the sun beginning to shine through, the soft sound of the 250cc BSA carrying us without effort. Or meeting—oh, damn what's her name, I know it so well, yes—Julie on the Paris Métro and commenting to her as she sits across from me reading a book in French by Paul Watzlawick, "I know him." I said it in French. It turns out that we get off at the same stop Odéon, so we go to my café and talk until two in the morning and become friends. It is she who introduces me to a family friend, Pernette, a painter who becomes a wonderful friend to me. I saw Pernette several times a year whenever I was in Paris until she died last year. Alain died one year—or was it two years—before that.

My sister died nine months ago, leaving me the last survivor of my nuclear family "of origin." Bob, my friend since junior high. died two months ago. I am having a birthday lunch with Sarah and two of Bob's daughters and the husband of one on Saturday. I had never met them before two months ago. They are really lovely. It is a very special connection. The five of us seem to have known each other for years.

Dry Cleaning
[*6/28/16*]

A couple of days ago, Friday morning, I put a bunch of clothes in the trunk of my car with the idea of taking them to the dry cleaners after breakfast with Larry. We had breakfast at Atticus as usual, and Mary Cruz waited on us as usual. Many months ago she had forgotten Larry's name for a second and called him "Rolando" by mistake. Since then he has been Larry Rolando, sometimes just Rolando. Mary Cruz knows what we both take for breakfast and, after checking with us briefly, brings it.

After breakfast, I drove over to Best Cleaners as planned. It's really nice. You go along State Street, and there it is on the right. When you drive into the driveway, there's almost always an open parking space in front of the door so you put your car there, get your cleaning, and take it in. On this day, as usual, the woman with the ends of her hair dyed red was at the counter taking care of something. Mike, the very heavy but very active owner, was at a table behind her and in front of the automatic belt from which cleaned clothes hang and that moves at the push of a button to bring a new group of clothes out. A sign hangs in front of the counter, saying something about this being one of the few places you can be out of your pants and nobody notices. The woman, efficient as usual, took my clothes and made out the chit. "Yale"? she asked. I asked if that was good or bad. She said "good," so I said yes and got a discount. Then Mike called out, "And 10% off for prepay," and I said okay to that too. I said something about his being so good, and he made a crack about coming to work to hear that since his wife was always the good one at home.

We laughed. I prepaid for the dry cleaning and drove to the Yale Gym, where at the desk in the entry, Vernon handed me a towel without even looking at me.

The Box
[*1/8/22*]

Today is Saturday. This past Thursday—it feels like years ago—David, Susan's husband Mike's brother's son, brought me the box. It was cardboard, big, about three feet square, and heavy. He was kind and thoughtful enough to bring it into the house (both of us wearing Covid masks) and lay it down in the middle of the living room. It stayed there untouched for over twenty-four hours. It carried with it the feel of Pandora's box, full of who knows what, possibly things toxic, even fatal, so it just stood there in all its bigness, in the very center of my living room.

Yesterday I finally opened the box. Inside were piled old notebooks, folders, photograph albums, and a little plastic holder for a picture. I had joked archly to my daughter the day it came that it contained the remains of my sister, who had died three weeks ago. It turned out that my bad joke was actually true. As I began taking some of the contents out, there she was, a picture of her when she was four. There she was, the announcement of her high school graduation, pictures of her early years in New York working at a day care center after she quit Antioch College before finishing her first year. And on and on.

I felt that she and I could talk about her situation, think about alternative pathways she might take. Then I remembered there were no alternative pathways, what she did is what she did. Her life is over. She is dead. It's all final. What is is what is. What was is what was. No more choices.

I will tell you about it. I am only about halfway through the box, and it feels as though I am examining her life, as an anthropologist might look at such a life in order to understand its meaning. Except that I am not an anthropologist. I am her little brother, and she is my big sister.

To begin with, I need to tell you that the box was not really three feet on each side. I decided two days after it arrived actually to measure it. That action felt a little bit the way it felt to skin the rattlesnake Marge, the hardy Canadian woman who worked for our extended family, had killed up at the Island years ago. It required effort on my part to make the snake real, to really know it was dead, and that I could manage its skinning. Like the snake, the box was in truth less dangerous than I had imagined—maybe. By actual measurement the box was not three feet per side but fifteen by seventeen by twenty-one inches. Still . . . .

Eventually I got a kitchen knife, cut the tapes, and opened that box that had been silently dominating the whole living room, even the house, and my life. Inside, at least to judge from the top layers, were a lot of loose photographs, some old dirty spring back binders, and some old-looking colored post cards.

I took one layer off, put it next to my chair, and started going through the stuff. It was pretty much what I expected. Pictures of Susan during her final high school years, often with a cigarette, slender, looking really nice, with friends, doing stuff. Not looking neurotic or anything.

But little by little, I noticed something happening inside of me. It was as though I had taken a slow acting drug of some sort and feelings were growing. There was stuff connected to Susan's husband, Mike. He died about five years ago from a brain tumor. He was nice enough. When I first met him I was in college and we would walk around New York together.

He would stop us in front of a store or something and begin explaining to me what was in the display window, where it came from, what its implications were. It was fascinating. Being with Mike was always an adventure. Then, over the years it was more like he was talking at me, teaching me something, that he was the one who knew stuff and I didn't. It started to become aggravating. When he and Susan came to Thanksgiving dinners at my house, he would be teaching us all. My friend Cele started hating it so much she wouldn't come any more. At my daughter Sarah's college graduation her history teacher came over for a while to talk with us, and Mike started teaching her history. He was never mean or aggressive, he just needed to dominate encounters. At the same time he was always kind.

The next layer of things from the box contained Sue's notes about a trip they took up along the Norwegian coast and over to Sweden and Finland—what they saw, what they ate, in detail. It had never occurred to me that she would write such a thing. She seemed happy and content from what she wrote.

Down another layer, Mike again. A book I never knew he had written, *Prize of War*, about the American Revolution. I knew he loved history and the sea, and that he had written about a medieval Scandinavian boy traveling the sea to Greenland, Finland, and around, but not this. His books were self-published but well written, interesting. There were newspaper clippings about exhibits he had mounted for this or that group, about the sea, about New York history, about fishermen. Clippings with pictures: Mike showing someone around the exhibits, lecturing to school kids. I had forgotten, but he did talk about the stuff like this that he did, not so much bragging as explaining. He had a life of this kind of creativity, this kind of knowledge, of productivity. He couldn't hold on to money, of course. Dad would often send some to them. Rather than saving it, Mike would plan a trip for him and Susan, to upstate New York or Stockmarknes, Norway, or wherever. I had stopped inviting them for Thanksgiving and had forgotten that other side of Mike, the interested, passionate, effective side.

In the next layer of the box was Susan's high school graduation yearbook. Tucked into the back of it was a loose picture, Susan at the piano. She was about eighteen. A beautiful picture. A serious but very pretty Susan. She played the piano very well, not as well as Dad, who was outstanding, but very well. And much, much better than me.

The yearbook contained pictures of each person in her class. Many Marzullos, Orlandos, and Pardinis. Fewer O'Haras and O'Days. Some Morrisons and Montgomerys, a couple of Krones and Vogels, including Sally and Sybil, Susan's best friends. Sally was kind of plain, but Sybil certainly wasn't. She said her name Vogel, which means "bird " in German, was really French and should be pronounced "vozhel" (with an accent on the second syllable of course). Susan, who when I was little had taught me how to ride a two-wheeler, and her friends were always good to me, even though I was four years younger, and I liked being with them.

There were almost no Black kids and no Asians in the school, but within the western European group, huge diversity. Funny, when I went to East junior high for a year there were many Polish and Russian kids. Not so at Strong Vincent, where Sue had gone. At East there were lots of Italians too, and some Anglos. All of this testimony to the diversity of families in Erie of western European roots. But at both schools there were almost no Hispanics or Asians and few Black people. For us, of.course, that was the world, and I suppose that world is still the expectation in many parts of the country, which is one source of the incredible schisms that are now so apparent. For that old group, my high school people, any status they had—and it was considerable—is now being threatened by Hispanics and Blacks and now even Muslims! My goodness, Muslims! I don't think there was even one Muslim in Erie when I was growing up.

Another scrapbook. This one apparently kept by Mike. Their marriage announcement and wedding pictures. The apartments they lived in on Manhattan's West Side and then in Brooklyn. Their Greyhound bus trips—to Gettysburg, San Francisco, cities and parks, hiking places, small towns, and God knows what else, all over the west. Mike had told me about a Catholic retreat place in New Mexico. When I hitchhiked out west I went there on his advice, slept in the hogan they kept for visiting Indians, and listened to the Gregorian chants in the morning. I met there a woman who had been a stunt person for the movies and then moved out there to become housekeeper, cook, and general helper for the monks. Mike's love of history, Americana, early civilizations, fishing culture, and on and on. I had forgotten how much he loved, was fascinated by, knew about (and taught you about) pretty much everything. He was wonderful and exciting in that way.

They travelled a lot, mostly cheaply. I think Susan liked it. So much was new to her, although we had travelled as kids with our parents—to Canada, Florida—and, of course, Dad loved history too. I had forgotten those early years of Sue's marriage, which were. I think, mostly good days for them. A couple of years ago, during that brief break in the clouds for Susan's spirit a few months after Mike's death, she told me that she didn't begin putting on weight, finally reaching a horrible almost spherical state, until our parents died in the mid-nineties (both the 1990s and their 90s). Once she became so fat, her life was reduced to sitting in an electrified wheelchair, watching the home shopping network, and being kind and interested to the women who came to look after her.

Another layer. Another "scrapbook"—it actually says so on the cover. Oh, beautiful, beautiful!! It is Susan's account when she was fourteen of our family's trip to New York in 1942. And such a wonderful, detailed account it is. The things we went to: the Statue of Liberty, of course, the Empire State Building ("Johnny almost got blown off the deck at the top"), Rumplemeyers, where we often ate. She had kept a breakfast menu, sixty-five cents for the most expensive breakfast, juice, ham, eggs, bacon, pastry, and coffee, tea, or cocoa. There was a program from Carnegie Hall, where she and Dad went to see and hear the famous pianist Alexander Brailowsky, a concert that she loved. Also ticket stubs from *Porgy and Bess* with Todd Duncan ($2.50 for orchestra seats).

We had gone to New York because Ruthie Markus, Mom's sister, was in hospital there. Eddie came to get her so they were already married by then. Was it when she had her leg amputated? Susan doesn't say why. Nanny came to New York, too. Susan and Dad and me and, I guess, Mom. Susan says that Daddy likes to go places by walking and Mom likes to take the bus or a taxi. That's the only mention of Mom. Visits to the Haydn Planetarium, the Bronx Zoo, the Natural History Museum. This presents a perfect picture of one aspect of our family. Dad, from Loudonville, Ohio, and all of us small town folk from Erie, Pennsylvania, nevertheless loved cultural things. And Susan expresses that love, except in the case of one French restaurant where she reports the food was awful. The whole scrapbook gives such a true picture of her and of us, including I guess, what she/we noticed and what she/we didn't. Here she is, at fourteen (and during the war, don't forget, though it is never mentioned), loving the trip, all the exciting, fascinating, and beautiful things she saw, and commenting on them. Wondrous, beautiful, beautiful!

Later, reflecting more on it, I think this scrapbook describing what she did is one of the few times I recall Susan using the word "I," and, even then, not much. Talking with her over the years, she barely used it either. If you asked her how she felt about something or what she did, she would use the word, but not often, and pretty much never spontaneously.

That early Susan, the Susan of the scrapbook, was very different from the more recent Susan, before she was the dead Susan, the Susan that is no longer here, the big sister I can no longer call, the Susan who, as Aeneas might have said, can no longer hear someone call her name, the Susan who in later years couldn't walk because she was so fat, who now had snaggly teeth. Two different Susans. But the essence of each, the kindness, was the same.

And the kids in the yearbook. A number of them are wearing military uniforms. Susan graduated from high school in 1946—remember, just one year after "the war" had finished.

The Great Waltz
[*1/3/18*]

Dear reader: If you can, please take two minutes (or more) to listen to a Strauss waltz. I suggest the "Voices of Spring" (there are many versions on YouTube), which is one of my favorites. Close your eyes, please, for a minute. Imagine that you have just entered a huge beautiful ballroom. Wonderful tapestries hang from the walls, magnificent candelabras shed warm light throughout. At one end of the room an orchestra is playing. If you are a man you are dressed in a pure white Hussars' uniform with gold braid. The medals you have won gleam on your chest. Your black boots make impressively solid sounds on the polished wooden floor.

If you are a woman your long black hair is piled in a wondrous winding nest on your head. You are wearing a full white silk ballgown, and you are beautiful. The hall is already full of handsome men and beautiful women all clothed in garments like your own and that of the man who now approaches you and requests that you join him in this dance.

It is the new year 1898, and both of you have been taught how to dress, how to converse, and how to act on such an occasion since you were young children. The orchestra now starts to play the "Thousand and One Nights" waltz, your very favorite of the waltzes composed by Johann Strauss, music to which all of Vienna dances these days. Your young man takes you by the waist, you place your hand on his shoulder, and the two of you, as one, begin to move, to step, to whirl, to slow, to move again. With brief pauses during which you stop to sip the finest champagne, you will dance the whole evening, lost in the music, in the feel of your lover, in being surrounded by others so like you, like the two of you.

Years will pass. In the Great War the fabric of your world will tear and fall apart. Fortunes will be lost. The aristocracy, although still rich, will no longer have these wonderful times. This wonderful world will only be a memory. Then Nazi Germany will take over your beloved Vienna.

It is 1942 now. Fifi and Joe sit in our living room at 1959 Lakeside Drive in Erie, Pennsylvania. They and my parents and I have just finished a fine meal in our small dining room. Dad sets up the card table, and my parents and Fifi and Joe begin to play bridge. Fifi and Joe are from Vienna. They were able to get out just before the Second World War started. Joe now works selling furniture at a local store. I don't know what Fifi does. They live in Edinboro, a little town outside of Erie. As they begin the next round of bridge, Dad calls to me, "Come over here, Johnny, and watch this." I get up from the couch and stand over them. It is Fifi's turn to deal. She shuffles the cards and then begins to deal them. With a single motion four cards leave her hand, each finding its place in front of each of the four players. Her hand moves again, again in one motion four cards leave her hand, each landing in the proper place. And she repeats this magic until all the cards have been dealt. She is amazing. It is what is left I guess of the magic world of Vienna, home of the Great Waltz.

Well, perhaps not all that is left. I have written elsewhere of going with my Austrian friend Traudl to visit her cousins when I was living in Paris in 1956. They brought out a small phonograph and a bunch of records, Strauss waltzes, to which we danced for hours. I have always loved this music. My mother and I sometimes danced to it together when I was eleven or twelve. I think maybe I was named for Johann Strauss. In my teens I had learned how to dance and managed well enough. But that night in Paris, dancing with real people from Vienna, dancing, waltzing reached a new plane. My partners were wonderful and turned me into an unbelievable dancer too, at least for the night. It was one of those things you couldn't even imagine was possible, sheer musical bliss in motion with another person. A tiny bit of old Vienna was still alive.

Stones on the Beach
[8/8/21]

I'll bet you've never heard of Beryl Markham. She was a pilot and a lover of Denis Finch-Hatton. "Denis who?" Denis Finch Hatton, you know, the lover of Karen Blixen. Yes, remember, he was killed when his plane crashed over Tsavo because he didn't know about the murderous down drafts there. "But Denis who?" you ask again. Well, never mind. But at least you know about Karen Blixen. "Well, not really." Yes, you know about her, maybe under her pen name of Isaak Dinesen. "That name is vaguely familiar." She was the woman whose life is depicted in the movie *Out of Africa*. *Out of Africa* is actually the name of one of her books. She lived in Kenya and had a coffee plantation there. She and Finch-Hatton were lovers, too. Both of them were kind of mythic people. He was an Englishman who become a hunter and adventurer in Africa. She was a Danish writer who began writing in the 1920's. She published collections of stories, such as *Seven Gothic Tales* and *Winter's Tales,* and wrote one story, "Babette's Feast," that also became the basis of a movie. These works are wonderful fantasies. *Out of Africa* is more autobiographical but, I think, heavily salted with fantasy as well. All very beautiful. She was a really big deal in the mid-20th century. Many people knew about her. So strange that relatively few do now, her life pretty much swept away.

    I don't know if you've ever been on the beach and, as a kid or even as an adult with or without kids, built a sandcastle near the water's edge. You know how when the waves come and then recede, bit by bit or even by large chunks your castle begins to disappear, disappear only to become part of the beach again. Within a few minutes it's just beach. You can't even tell that the castle was there, even if you had created a fantastically beautiful and elaborate castle. Beryl Markham, she's pretty much just part of the beach again, indistinguishable from the rest. Denis Finch Hatton pretty much too, although if you saw *Out of Africa* when it came out in the 1980's you may vaguely remember him. Even Karen Blixen, Isaak Dinesen. The movie and her books are remembered by some, like the stones you drew on to make your castle, but I'll bet that in another several years except for all but a few readers, these complicated people and their lives, their experiences, even most of Dinesen's books, will be just random stones on the beach.

So I Walk into This Café
[*11/12/06*]

So I walk into this café, the Danton, to have my morning cup of coffee. I sit down at a table by the huge front window, and I take out my little worn paperback copy of *Antigone*. Jean-Claude brings me my grand-crème, and we exchange views for a minute about the "nana" who's passing. So there I am reading and periodically looking out the big *baie vitrée* when the person sitting at the table next to me asks, "Vous parlez anglais?" To which, I reply, "Yes." "Oh, that's good," she says, relieved, and asks me if she can borrow my pen, just to make a note. "Of course," I reply.

W (woman)—You speak French very well and they seem to know you. The waiter just brought you your coffee without even asking you what you wanted.

M (me)—Well, I come here every morning. And Jean-Claude and I talk a little every time. He has a motorcycle, that one over there across the street, the big silver one, and I love motorcycles. Also, he has a great sense of humor and gets along with everyone. Everyone except the *patronne*. I'm not sure how long he's going to last here.

W—And you?

M—Oh me? Well, I came to France for a whole year in the '50's and fell in love with Paris. Now, fifty years later, I love it more than ever, if that's possible. There are some awful things about Paris and about some of the French, but wonderful things too, many, many wonderful things. Strangely, I feel as much at home here as I do in Erie, Pennsylvania, where I was raised. I come here now several times a year for a month at a time whenever anyone invites me to give a talk in Europe, so that's about three or four times a year. I just love it. I don't usually talk with people this much in English when I'm here. There's something about you....

W—Well, I don't come as often as you do. Not very often at all. I took French for seven years in school, but they didn't know how to teach it very well, so I never learned to speak it or even to understand much when someone talks to me. But I do the best I can. I did read *Antigon,* though. I loved that play. Life is so much like that.

M—I love it too, but I can read only a couple of pages at a time. I get so moved.

What do you mean life is so much like that?

W—Well, I'm married, and where I come from, I'm expected to start having children soon. But like you, I just love being here, and being free, to talk to people, to read. You know there's a large UN center here for international studies. I go to lectures there and meet fascinating people. Someone there said they might even be able to find me a job. It wouldn't pay much, of course. But I can't do that. There just aren't many possibilities or people like that where I come from in the United States. I suppose it's silly to say so, but in my own little way, Antigone reminds me of me. Situations where no one is really bad, but where everyone is stuck, without the possibility of escaping. You know, of course, that she dies in the end, after all the while just trying to do what's right. There's no way for her to escape from her impossible situation. As I say, it's silly to make a comparison, but it seems to me that a lot of the people I know live like that. Many don't really live at all, they just take care of their daily responsibilities. Then they die. Wow, that's sad, isn't it? Sorry, I didn't mean to say all that.

She smiles at me with an immense warmth and deep happiness, which seems strange since she was just talking about something so sad. Her blue eyes gleam with a beautiful youthful vitality. Around her head her curly light brown hair forms a soft puff illuminated by the morning sun shining through it from behind her.

She has finished her coffee and now puts out her cigarette, takes her purse off the back of the chair, and gets up to leave. She says, "It's been very nice talking with you. You seem very happy, and that makes me glad".

"It's been nice talking with you too," I reply. And then I add, trying not to sound too intrusive, "What's your name?"

"Augusta Rosenthal." And she smiles again.

"Augusta Rosenthal, that's very strange," I say. "That's the name of my mother."

"Of course," she says and disappears out the door.

It is a Quiet, Gentle, Pensive Rain
[8/13/13]

Sitting here on my porch at 50 Burton Street, Westville. No one is out. Nothing moves. The light of morning is softened by the grey clouds. All is quiet. Not even birds in the sky or in the bushes. "There are some things that cannot be expressed with words." So says the man commenting on Vermeer's woman putting on her necklace. He describes the painting, then we see it. He is certainly right. Strangely, I had never thought of that. "There are some things that cannot be expressed with words." Of course, the painting, the mad fury of Stravinsky's *Rite of Spring,* the quiet loving lilt of a Chopin Mazurka, this day.

Sitting on the porch at the Island, watching and listening to the gentle rain. One small, lonely rowboat way out there near the open. Two tiny people fishing in the rain. Hannah, this morning, certainly was beautiful, total lovely softness. The rain falls, making little circles on the boardwalk. Dianna is coming in from the boathouse.

There are some things that cannot be expressed with words. Love, fear, how it is that Alain must, or must not, feel as he sees his body dissolving with cancer? What should he have done with his life? I think he's wonderful, but does he? Should he have published more, made more trouble? Was he too passive? It's probably too late now. Just do the best I can.

The rain still falls. But barely. The birthday card from Carrie. It's been eighteen years now since we've even seen each other. *Les Parapluies de Cherbourg.* I saw it last night on television. Technicolor. They sing everything. The music. Haunting. Of course, I know the word "haunting" is used too much, but still. The last scene. He's at the Esso station where he works in Cherbourg. His wife and little child have just left for the store to buy Christmas presents. It's late evening. A car pulls up. A woman steps out. He and she were very much in love several years ago. They look at each other. They still are in love.

The rain keeps up. I have to go inside to write something for the writing group tonight. But I have nothing to say. Nothing that I can express with words.

Indian Dance
[*10/11/22*]

Ami picked me up around 9:30 as we had planned. She had never seen my house before so she came in. She glanced around the living room, with its piles of books on the floor and pictures covering all the walls. I showed her the small wooden statue of Krishna that I had gotten in Agra and told her that one day our Springer Spaniel Barney had noticed it up on the mantel and had begun to growl at it. It was the only time he had ever done something like that, as though he detected some spirit or other invisible thing there that we couldn't see. Then Ami and I left for the dance.

    The dance was part of a nine-day festival that Ami had told me about. I wasn't able to go last year when she first mentioned it, but this year I again said how much I would like to go and we arranged it. I no longer drive after dark so Ami agreed to pick me up. I usually only see her in her working clothes as a physical therapist, trying to help old folks like me maintain active lives as much as possible. But that night she was all made up, hair fixed, and wearing a beautiful bright red and bright yellow sari. And she had come for me!

    She helped me into the car, and off we went to the "temple." I had seen the temple before since it is next to the on-ramp to Route 15 and just a mile and a half from my house. A rather plain wooden building, from the ramp it looks like an underused hotel. Not tonight! We arrived to a parking lot stuffed with cars and to a crowd of brown people, the women all wearing elaborate dresses of bright colors and designs. It occurred to me that during the day I might have seen one or two of these women in an office or a business at their daily jobs. At the entrance was a pile of shoes, Ami indicated that I should take off mine. I don't usually do that because my feet are a mess, but I did this time. This simple gesture was my entry into a new land of experience. In a variation of Dorothy and the magic red shoes that helped her escape from Oz, taking off my shoes subtly signaled to me that I was entering a new land.

And was I ever! Surrounded by women of all ages in their bright beautiful saris, talking mostly in Hindi, men and women without shoes, and a few little kids some only two or three years old, Ami and I entered a large open, almost barnlike room filled with more people and with blaring recorded Indian music. In the middle a large open space surrounded some pillars in the center, around which a circle of women slowly revolved. Beautifully clad, with no two saris alike, each woman performed the same simple dance step, one two three, one two three. Outside the circle, men, most in Indian kurtas in dull colors of grey and tan, were seated talking or just watching. I was the only white person there, but people didn't single me out in any way. I loved that sense of belonging and not belonging. It reminded me of hitchhiking around the country when I was nineteen, meeting all the people who picked me up over the three months and nine thousand miles, being so accepted and yet so different. Here at the dance, off to one side of the Indian men watching the dance was an area with food and drink, but I never got close to it.

Ami ushered me to an empty chair and, having kindly occupied herself with my comfort, left to join the huge circle. And I? I was transfixed, transfixed by the colors, by the slow methodical repeated dance, by the diversity of women's appearances, their faces, their figures, their saris, and transfixed by the loud rhythms of the strange music. Gradually, a few men joined the circle, and progressively the circle became a mass, then several circles, then a single circle again. I was in Oz.

Where I stayed. Until an hour or so later, Ami came by and introduced me to her husband and her two sons of eight and ten, all of whom seemed lovely. She asked how I was doing. I said I would like to leave in about twenty minutes if that was all right with her. She said it was.

She came back in a while and all kindness, helped me find my shoes in the huge pile. She went to get the car, helped me into it, and drove me back to Kansas.

Solutions?
[7/9/17]

Do you mean that there are multiple possible solutions to how we think about mental illness and the people who have it? What kind of solution is that? Whatever happened to reaching the appropriate diagnosis and then providing the treatment that the diagnosis requires?

It is not clear that the mental health field involves that kind of unique specificity. And we are not alone in the world of science to reach such a conclusion. In its own way, much of quantum physics has the same kind of problem. Photons, after all, can act if misplaced as waves and as particles, and they can apparently be in two places at once. A related problem comes up in ecology. Why did the fish in the Yellowstone River diminish? Because of the wolves, of course. The wolves? Yes, when the wolves were considered a nuisance and were exterminated, the elk population flourished, and the elk ate the willows on the riverbanks, leaving the beavers with nothing to build their dams from, so the fish diminished. Oh!

The complexity and diversity of humans at the biopsychosocial level may require consideration of multiple points of view and/or multiple phenomena or sequences of effects to reach optimal understanding and intervention. Yes, stories can have multiple possible interpretations, can be viewed from multiple perspectives, and this does provide some deviation from traditional scientific thinking. But that may just be the nature of the reality with which we are dealing. If that is the case, trying to encompass all one needs to know about a patient in one traditional diagnosis may be a major disservice, a misreading of the nature of the phenomena with which we deal. The possibility of multiple stories about a person a Boris, the "Garbage Can Kid," or Mrs. Joyce, and multiple ways of seeing these people and their problems may add a greater richness to our understanding and our interventions. Did Mrs. Joyce get better by the time of our follow-up because people had started to like her better (because she had achieved some distinction by being involved in a research study rather than being just another "chronic patient" on that huge ward) or because of clozapine, or both, or something else, or some combination of things?

You Want Peer Support, I'll Show You Peer Support!
[*10/29/18*]

"Human beings are complex"— Lord Willoughby in the film *Captain Blood*

The title here is an adaptation from a *Far Side* comic strip of many years ago in which a beleaguered client cries out at an impossibly demanding bureaucrat. Sorry for the tone, but it is surprising how much people tend not to recognize the power of "peer support," something they themselves have almost certainly experienced and perhaps overlooked but never really forgotten. In fact, even in psychiatric disorders we tend to underestimate the incredible power of social contacts. If other animals require contact with their kind—horses, for example, are herd animals fundamentally relying on other horses—people too, in our way, are social animals, requiring contacts with other people for our very existence. In medical fields often, even in psychiatry, there is the idea that, yes, social contacts such as "peer support" are important, but not really that important, not as important, for example, as a medication or other medical interventions.

So let's consider the social part of "biopsychosocial" in the mental health field.

Why would a young healthy woman with a young child actually end her own life? She does it because she has been totally cut off from her social contexts by the actions of her husband. That is the story of *Madama Butterfly*. Why would a girl allow herself to be killed to fulfill her father's request?

That, of course, is the story of *Iphigenia in Aulus*, the play by Euripides. Those are mere stories. But they are stories found intensely meaningful over centuries in reflecting the human condition. My peer support experiences have not been that extreme fortunately, but they have been impactful, nevertheless. I think particularly of something I experienced sixty-six years ago.

As I have described elsewhere, after my second year at Swarthmore College, I had decided to spend the three-month summer vacation hitchhiking around the country. I don't know exactly where that idea came from, not from Jack Kerouac—it was still several years before he came out with his book. Maybe from Jack London or perhaps John Steinbeck, who so well, it seemed to me, described the "real world," the world of ordinary middle class or poor people and their everyday lives. Whatever the origins of my decision, my parents gave me their permission, asking only that I call them collect every Sunday morning to let them know I was okay and where I was. No cell phones in those days—1952—so in between my phone calls they would have no idea of how or where I was.

The trip began one Sunday when my father left me off on Route 5 at the west side of Erie, Pennsylvania. We kissed goodbye, he turned the car around, waved and headed home. I, with my fifty-pound army surplus pack on my back and wearing my Penn State T-shirt gotten when our high school swimming team won the state championships, hung out my thumb and waited. I had never hitchhiked before, never been west of Cleveland, Ohio. I spent that night in Hannibal, Missouri, the next day I passed through Belleville, Kansas, and soon I was in Cheyenne, Wyoming. The following Sunday, as promised, I called my parents from a pay phone in Cheyenne.

I gave them the news that I had gotten a job at a carnival

at the Frontier Days rodeo but had smashed my finger when a gear wheel from a Ferris wheel we were putting together fell and caught my finger against the bed of a truck. I did not tell them how scary it had been to see the white bone of my finger exposed or how much it hurt but reported that people had taken me to a doctor and that he had bandaged it up and I was doing okay now, selling hot dogs at the rodeo. I had had to wait a long time at the doctor's office. When I pressed the secretary, she told me the doctor had been up all night with a man from a car accident who had just died, that the doctor was really bothered by that but would be with me shortly. I figured I was pretty lucky considering and sat down to wait fifteen or twenty minutes more before being called into his treatment room. He washed and bandaged my finger with a splint, then sent me on my way. I didn't know why they didn't stitch it up, but it turns out you're not supposed to stitch up a finger so he had done the right thing. He hadn't given me any pain medication. It hurt like hell, but I had never thought to ask. That night, with a throbbing finger I didn't get much sleep lying in my sleeping bag at the small park in Cheyenne, but the next day was a little better, I went to the rodeo and got a job selling hot dogs from a tray held by a strap around my neck. They apparently forgot to hire anyone else to sell hot dogs in the crowd so I was mobbed. I put my back against a fence and sold my hot dogs as fast as I could make change. That rate of selling let up a little over the next several days. All told, I sold enough to make $50.00, money that carried me through my entire three-month trip.

Since I had done so well selling hot dogs I gave myself the special treat for the next several days of having a real restaurant breakfast at a Hot Shoppes—orange juice, pancakes, coffee. That's where I sat next to a guy at the counter who was reading the *Saturday Review of Literature*. When I let out an involuntary "hmmm," he looked at me, smiled, and said, "We read this out here too."

In the evenings I would go over to the Cheyenne Public Library, where I took the opportunity to read *Beau Sabreur*, the second of P. C. Wren's terrific trilogy (beginning with *Beau Geste*) about the French Foreign Legion.

That first Sunday morning when I called my parents, I told them a somewhat cleaned-up story about my travels, my jobs, my finger, and where I was. Despite the mishap, I was okay, I said. I'm not sure they were entirely convinced, but I reassured them several times, and we let it go at that.

Many weeks and several thousand miles later—after visiting Glacier National Park, a distant relative's dude ranch, the Grand Canyon, and many cities, mountains, other national parks, and farms—I had got a long ride into Utah ending at Provo. By then I had learned to shave at gas stations and had discovered that the bathrooms in these places had either a mirror or hot water but never both and that living on peanut butter from the jar in my pack and what bread that you could get here and there was not bad at all. I had had long talks with literally hundreds of people, people with many different backgrounds and experiences of life. There were no rich people, though, in all those miles, and only one guy from New York City. He was the only person to say he wanted me to pay for the gas. I said no.

So here I was in Provo, Utah, arriving late in the evening. When hitchhiking, you never want to finish a ride late at night. You don't know where you are. You know what city, of course, but not where you can find a place like a park or any empty lot to lay out your sleeping bag to spend the night. On the other hand, a long ride is a long ride, not to be sneezed at. My guy let me out in what seemed to be a residential area in Provo. The lights were out in all the houses around me, but finally I did see a light way off. I walked toward it and realized it was coming from a large plain building the side of which was open. It was a big garage with huge open doors. As I got closer, I saw there were buses inside, and, when closer still, a man kneeling, working on the wheel of one of the buses.

I coughed so as not to alarm him, approached, told him I was hitchhiking, and asked if he knew of a nearby park or somewhere I could put down my sleeping bag for the night. He got up, came toward me and described where I could find a park not too far away. I thanked him and turned to go. He called after me, "Just a minute." I turned back. He said, "Here, take this," and handed me a five-dollar bill. I thanked him and tried to hand it back. "I'm okay," I said, "I don't need it." (I had all that money from selling hot dogs, after all). He said, "No, you take it. When I was doing what you're doing, someone gave that to me. I'm just passing it on."

You want to talk about peer support? That's peer support. I have never forgotten that moment sixty-six years ago, as must be obvious from how often I mention it. Without having recognized it, I had been awfully alone. I loved talking with people who picked me up and others I met here and there, but I felt alone. I don't believe I had thought about it, but that realization now that there was someone who understood what I was doing, was in that sense with me, that there were even others besides him who understood, who had experienced the same thing—I mean, you just don't forget that. That was my peer support. I needed it, craved it, more than I would have ever guessed. I had been so much alone. But now I wasn't any more. And I would never be to that extent again. That's what peer support is.

I wish I could tell that man what he did for me. By now, sixty-six years later, he's probably dead. But maybe I can pass it on.

Biopsychosocial Fondue

Several disciplines, microhistory and anthropology among them, offer analogies to help free us from having only one conceptual model, the narrow disease model. Even the need to put together into one word the three domains bio, psycho, and social suggests that we tend to see them as entirely separate from each other. We focus on one (say, bio) or the other (psycho) or the other (social) to explain the phenomenon in which we are interested. But there are ways of conceptualizing the three areas as not so distinct. We can, for example, use an analogy from the novel *Bleak House* by Charles Dickens. He indicates how, through breathing, the London fog becomes part of the person, that the external and the internal mix in some special way. We could also borrow some ideas from chemistry. Perhaps in thinking about the bio psycho social interfaces we should wonder whether psychiatric disorders are in some ways like cheese fondue. I make a great cheese fondue, among the best to be found. I will not give you here the exact recipe, but in general it is made by putting together white wine and cheese. You heat them up together and then when all the cheese is melted you will notice that the wine and the cheese are both in liquid form, but they are not mixing! So then you put in a small amount of cornstarch, stir, and *voilà*, perfectly blended fondue!

What you have just done is add an emulsifying agent to substances where the two parts will otherwise not blend. Consideration of the various chemical processes in which two or more substances can interact may provide a way for considering bio psycho social relationships. With all colloids, for example, different emulsifying agents or processes are needed for different substances. With people and different social contexts the same specificity and diversity may be the case. In some instances, change in social context might be needed so that the blending can occur. But unlike, I think, colloidal systems, helping people and a social context interact more effectively may take considerable time. With the psycho and the social of psychiatric disorders there might also be the necessity for a stabilizing agent as in colloidal chemistry, something needed to prevent both parts of the system from reverting.

Sometimes what happens with people with psychiatric disorders is that they find, or the family or treatments help to provide, a kind of emulsifying agent so that the person and his or her social context that have not been able to get on well together begin to find a resolution for both. In terms of "treatment," for example, Larry Davidson's Program for Recovery and Community Health (PRCH) program has borrowed the motto from the Home Depot stores, "You can do it and we can help." This is a fascinating deviation from the usual concept of "treatment," where the professional provides the ingredient that cures the problem while the person is only required to "comply."

Why Do People Get Mentally Ill?
[6/24/17]

Or more to the point, why don't they? I was sitting out on my front porch this afternoon. It is an incredibly beautiful June day, a bit warm, but not nearly as humid as yesterday. A bird flew by and into the mass of tightly packed branches in the ten-foot-high rhododendron bushes in front of my house. How did it do that? In fact, birds do that all the time, flying in at perhaps ten or fifteen miles an hour without a problem. I can barely reach in there slowly without scratching my arm. I look around me. There are trees forty to fifty feet high around people's houses. All the trees are now in full leaf, so they are huge bundles of green. Did I say green? That sounds as though they're all the same color. We use that term, but I first realized when I was driving through the Pocono Mountains in Pennsylvania several years ago that there are at least a thousand greens. Looking around me now, I see the black green of leaves in shade, other leaves a yellow green, still others a light green, and yet others at the treetops directly under the sun a white green. The word "green" doesn't describe a single color after all.

But this is supposed to be about mental illness. Okay, one more thing, I have been going up to the islands (or the Island) belonging to my extended family in Canada since I was three, for over eighty-one years. When I was ten or twelve, I became interested in the three or four outboard motors we had. As the years passed, I learned how to operate and sometimes to fix them. They really weren't that complicated, a tube for the gas to go from the gas tank to the cylinder, points to regulate the timing of the spark, throttle to change the speed, spark plug, gas tank. I learned further that the Johnson Seahorse almost always worked and on the rare occasions it didn't, you needed to check if there was gas in the tank or, rarely, to change the spark plug. The Evinrude, on the other hand, only worked about half the time. You often had to adjust the spacing of the points or keep fooling with the readings of the throttle and the spark. Even then, half the time you'd be ready to come back to the Island from fishing, and the damned motor wouldn't start. You'd end up rowing that heavy boat for an hour. How could such simple things as outboard motors be so different, and sometimes so problematic?

Okay, so now we're back to mental illness. I'm looking at these trees and noticing all the different things we call green. I'm watching that bird and wondering how he (or she) manages to avoid clobbering him or herself on the branches while whipping in among them at several miles an hour. And then I'm thinking how I am able to think "bird" or "green" or ask myself these questions or notice the bird chirping up there on top of the front left corner of the porch roof or say "hello" to the black dog and his mistress as they come walking by, or think about all this stuff.

Okay, one more thing. I have a favorite television program called *Naked and Afraid*. I won't give you all the details, but in brief they put a man and a woman who don't know each other into the Peruvian jungle or somewhere, let each person bring in one thing, and then see if they can survive for twenty-one days. In one episode, the two people were trying to kill a small caiman (relative of the alligator) for food. (It's really hard to get yourself enough to eat in these places.) One of the people says, "You get on the other side of him, I'll stay on this side, and we'll . . .." I don't remember what they were going to do. I do remember that I felt sorry for the caiman, poor thing. These people were talking about killing him, and he could hear them but didn't have a clue what they were planning. What an advantage the people had! There were two of them, and they could talk together to plan!

So now, to mental illness. I would like to suggest that we have had the wrong focus. We humans are so complex that the issue is not so much why things go wrong but how is it that they can go right? What is it we do to survive as incredibly complex beings in this incredibly complex world? And how can those mechanisms go wrong? So yes, we're talking, for example, about defenses. Are they good or bad? Or, as seems more likely, are they essential? So, the question becomes more about how they go right or go wrong rather than only one or the other. Even something like a hallucination, for example, that is often assumed to be "pathological" is very frequently an important positive function. So, also frequently, we shouldn't be seeing "competence" and "pathology" as separate things, but as extremely closely related, often even different aspects, quantities, or applications of the same function.

A Little Bit of Schizophrenia
[*3/13/20*]

My grandmother was a terrific cook, especially gifted when it came to making German cookies. My mother, who could also be a terrific cook, inherited her mother's recipe box. When my mother died, I inherited those recipe cards. A typical card would have directions like "add a little cinnamon," so you would do that, whatever "a little cinnamon" might indicate. A month or so ago I wanted some good corn chowder. In the soup section of the supermarket I saw various brands of corn chowder in cans and in packets and so bought several different kinds. I didn't like any of them very much and so complained to my son, another excellent cook, how disappointed I was. He said, "Well, you can make it yourself." "Of course," I thought, so on this cold winter day set out to do just that.

    I had no recipe but figured it couldn't be all that complicated. I put some milk in a medium-sized pot, added some flour, and then from the freezer took out a bag of frozen corn. But how much corn to add to the milk? I knew that I didn't want to make corn with a milk sauce or milk with a few kernels of corn. So I started, one kernel, a few dozen, more, more, more. I began to wonder how many kernels it would take before the mixture became not just milk with some corn kernels but corn chowder.

    It reminded me of an experience I had just the day before. I had sat down with my hematologist to discuss the abnormal results of a blood test, followed by a bone marrow biopsy and further bloodwork to determine whether I had the (to me from my medical school background) dreaded multiple myeloma, an often-fatal leukemialike disease. My doctor very clearly wrote down the several criteria and the levels of the findings that would indicate, well what? Given my interest in psychiatric diagnosis, issues of discrete illnesses, continua of symptom levels, I listened carefully to her explanation. "So, on the right side of the paper, the higher levels of pathological findings for each of the criteria. that would mean multiple myeloma?" I asked. She said, "Well, it's all myeloma." "It's all a disease, both sides of the paper?" She clearly didn't want to get into this discussion, so I shut up, and she continued explaining the criteria and levels to me. Unable to contain myself, I said, "So it's a continuum from normal to pathological just like it is for symptoms in psychiatry?" She didn't want to get into that either, so again I shut up. I could see, though, that her page was divided by a vertical line, on the left of which she indicated acceptable levels of things and on the right levels at which treatment would be needed, and where I fell between those two sides would indicate whether I would need treatment or could just have repeated tests from time to time. So, I thought, do I have this disease or not? Fortunately, my findings were close to that line, but all of them were just barely on the left side, so I would not need to receive treatment. A great relief—well, mostly.

I have a good friend in Sweden who is a famous psychiatrist. He has a brother who is a successful and famous artist but who also has the diagnosis of schizophrenia. One day when I was visiting my friend, he asked me if I would like to meet his brother. I said, of course, and over we went to the brother's studio. I should add that neither my friend nor I see people with schizophrenia as being "schizophrenics," as being their diagnosis, so this was not a situation where we were going to see a "strange" person. In fact, it was clear after we arrived that my friend and his brother had great respect for each other.

We talked while the brother worked on painting a large canvas hung on the wall. I am not a great lover of nonrepresentational art so did not comment on it. I mentioned that I had taken some classes in drawing and painting when I was in my teens and then again when I was in my fifties and talked about the impact of colors. Although my stuff wasn't horrible, neither was it all that good. We talked about the artistic life, about life in general, the world, and about my visit to Sweden. As you may have guessed, our whole encounter was completely "normal," well, other than the fact that I had never had the chance to spend time with a well-known artist before. When it came time to leave, I thanked the brother for letting us see him at work. All in all, I had a terrific time. Where would he have been on my doctor's chart, to the left of that vertical line from normal to pathological? Was he "a schizophrenic," a painter with schizophrenia, a painter with schizophrenic symptoms? Or was he like my grandmother's cookies—did he have a little schizophrenia just as they had a little cinnamon?

When we got back to my friend Johan's apartment, his wonderful wife was starting to prepare dinner. We all pitched in, and then when we started eating our fish and potatoes and drinking the lovely white wine, she put on a CD of a Schubert sonata, a beautiful piece. After a long dinner that seemed very short, Johan prepared to take me back to my hotel and his wife gave me the Schubert CD, "to remember our evening by." I still have the CD and, of course, have never forgotten the evening or the entire day.

Methodology II
Putting Yourself in Someone Else's Place
[*11/1/09*]

I know this subtitle sounds very unscientific. In fact, I started out to write something about the importance of subjectivity as a crucial factor in the mental health field. But even the term "subjectivity" misses the point, like so much else we do that objectifies the concept and thus loses subjectivity. It seems to me unscientific to lose the very concept you are trying to understand, and here that would be particularly unfortunate since we are dealing with something that is central in understanding mental health and mental illness. So, for the purposes of this essay I will use the idea of "putting yourself in someone else's place." It's crucial in training mental health professionals and should be a major focus.

Methodology I has already been written. By many different authors. We have studied it in our statistics and science classes. It is the crucial methodology of measurement, hypothesis testing, controlled experiments, replication, reliability, validity, sampling, and statistics. But we need a Methodology II. It is also crucial in mental health/illness theory and research. but it is so commonplace, so mundane, that we don't even have a word for it, or a theory, nor is it a major topic of research. In psychotherapy research it has often been called a "common factor," a nondescript term if there ever was one, a concept without even a name sophisticated enough to arouse attention. Severe mental disorders such as schizophrenia have been given a variety of titles, "Praecox gefuhl" (Rumke), "Poor rapport" (Carpenter and Strauss), or "The impossibility of understanding such a person" (Jaspers). "Poor Insight" is another related concept.

People with severe mental disorders often use the idea of something strange in the their lives perhaps even more often than do professionals. But they, of course, state it differently. In our research on the course of disorder in schizophrenia, as we learned to have participants talk more freely and not merely pepper them with questions, we started to ask what was most important in their getting better or worse. The getting better answers were particularly striking. Rather than sticking to our prior focus on treatment, work, living situation, and so on, patients began to tell us things like, "The most important thing in my getting better was someone who took me seriously" or "... someone who cared."

Now, clearly, "someone who took me seriously" has not been a common part of scientific medical discourse, but if the people who are sources of data keep telling you things like that, it is even more unscientific to ignore such data systematically.

So, for the moment at least, let's continue with the idea of "putting yourself in someone else's shoes" until we can come up with an adequate word or phrase for what we're talking about here.

None of these concepts are what is usually considered to be subjectivity, the person's experience, but for the moment I would like to stick with the various categories and terms identified in the preceding paragraphs and, in fact, to note that none of them are within a person, they are all reflections of relationships. In the case of the professionally designated categories, interestingly, most of these phenomena are seen as "out there," the way the other person is. That may, of course, be accurate, but it is possible as well that it is also a phenomenon of the relationship, a relationship in which the professional is a major part.

I have been impressed by several of my own experiences that relate to this group of phenomena. Several years ago, my good friend and colleague Larry Davidson and I were invited to give an extended workshop on schizophrenia to mental health professionals in Madison, Wisconsin. We knew this would be a challenging task because that particular center had been the source of some of the major valuable treatment innovations for severe mental disorders. Not wanting to give merely a long set of boring lectures, we decided to start with a role-play, something neither of us had ever done before. Larry would be the doctor and I would be the psychotic patient coming to him looking for treatment. We didn't discuss the role-play further. At the event, Larry and I found ourselves in front of about one hundred and fifty mental health professionals. He began by asking me what brought me to the hospital. I told him that I was hearing voices, and without missing a beat, Larry began asking me the "voices questions": Were they men's voices or women's voices, did I hear them all the time or only on certain occasions? I could tell my doctor was going through a mental checklist, and although I wanted to tell him what my voices were like and tried to do so, he clearly was not interested in anything but going through his mental list. I became angrier and angrier at his lack of interest in me but stifled my feelings since I knew I needed him for my medications. After about three minutes, I couldn't stand it any longer, so we stopped the "intake" and began to discuss the interview with the audience. Interestingly, although the Madison people were not off on some theoretical island, I found it impossible to get them to understand how furious I had gotten (even though Larry was and is a very close friend). They, or at least those who spoke, just didn't believe it. Larry, not without some irony, said he was just being a "regular intake doctor."

That was for me a startling experience. I couldn't understand why the audience had responded in that way. A few years ago, many years after the Wisconsin incident, I gave some workshops in Stockmarkness, Norway. Although it was only the second time I tried it, I asked my psychiatrist host if we could role-play an intake interview where I would be a psychotic patient, for his residents. We did so. He was a great psychiatrist. Every few minutes we would stop to discuss the interview with the residents, and it all went beautifully.

A couple of years after that I did another series of workshops and lectures, this time in Tromsø, Norway. The psychiatrist from Stockmarkness was there, and we agreed that he would do a follow-up interview with me in front of the audience of one hundred and fifty or so professionals plus a few patients and family members. We started. He asked me how things had been going for me, and I replied that I still heard the voices but they weren't as bad as when he saw me before. He asked me if I was working, and I replied yes, I was working at McDonalds, that it wasn't a great job but it was better than nothing. He asked me if I had friends and I said I knew a few people but nobody who was really a friend. He asked me if I saw my family, but I found myself no longer wanting to talk with him. I answered his questions but minimally and became more and more troubled that here I was the visiting expert and I didn't want to talk. After a few more minutes we stopped, and the people in the audience, who again appeared to be skilled and compassionate people, asked me what had happened to me. I didn't know. Some asked me why I was being so difficult with my kindly doctor. Again, I didn't know. They seemed a bit put off by my "noncompliance." I was, too, and feeling a bit nervous. Then someone in the back of the room raised his hand and said, "I'm a patient and I've had the same experience as you." And then someone near the front of the room raised her hand and said she was a patient and had had that experience, too, with her psychiatrist. We then tried to explain to the rest of the group what we had experienced. We didn't succeed, but the other two patients helped me to understand. My very skilled and kind psychiatrist had just skipped over any details of my work experience, and I had that feeling again, that he just didn't care. The poor guy, how could he have known? But we three "patients" got it all too well.

Now an interesting sequel to these experiences occurred last year, when I told this story at a psychiatric center south of Bergen. One of the people there, before I even had a chance to explain, said, "Of course, you wanted to tell him more about your work, what it was like flipping burgers for eight hours a day or whatever." I asked him, with surprise, how he knew that, saying that no one before had ever made that comment. He replied that it was easy, he was a psychologist, but he also worked in the theater, where everyone knows, "The life is in the details."

Well, theater people may know it, also creative writing teachers and storytellers. But before I encountered such people in recent years—and I've had really good psychiatric training and interactions—I'd never heard that said.

So that gets me to where I want us to go now, the hypothesis that people in the arts, and especially theater people, know things about being human and especially about putting yourself in somebody else's shoes. After all, this is what theater people do, it's their life. These often very smart people spend their whole lives learning from other very smart and experienced people how to do it better. I took a brief acting course a few years ago, on the recommendation of a friend. The few times in my life I had tried being in a play I was horribly self-conscious and stiff. My teacher now, Doug Taylor, originally from the Actors' Studio, started us off doing exercises. We each teamed up with another student. One student would say, "You have brown [or whatever] hair." The other person would reply, "I have brown hair," and the two of you would just continue to repeat the same sentence to the other. I was doing that, and Doug says to me, "But John, you're not listening to him." I was perplexed for a moment but then realized that Doug meant we were supposed to pay attention not just to the other person's words but to his tone of voice, facial expression, everything. "World famous psychiatrist learns to listen." It made me think of the Yogi Berra saying, "You can see a lot by just looking." Yes, but learning to look (or to listen) is not so easy. Watching a baseball game, I wouldn't even see one twentieth of what Yogi could. We in the mental health field usually spend very little time learning to look or listen.

So, putting ourselves in another person's shoes, what has that got to do with the mental health field? How would we put it to use, in our practice, our theory, our training, our research? Remember the patients who reported that one of the most important things in helping them improve was someone who took them seriously, someone who cared. They only rarely said that that person was a mental health professional. The "common factors" so ubiquitously important in psychotherapy research? They are pretty much the same thing. Some in medical education are now paying more attention to these things, to learning to listen to the patient's story, to put oneself in the situation of the patient. But mostly these practices are seen as not part of the science of medicine or the theory, not even in the mental health field.

Doing Readings
[*10/16/21*]

I have started doing readings from my autobiography. It is a great pleasure, and much to my surprise, it is like entering a new world. It is a synthesis of two disparate things, the reading of a text and interacting with people. So, we have the combination of the psychological and social that the field of psychiatry has long sought, "psycho/social"! At last! I have given many lectures over the years and usually am viewed as a rather good speaker. I never read my talks but rather do them from notes and never give the same talk twice. But doing readings feels totally different. It requires attending to the text, of course, but it also requires looking at and interacting with the audience. I have been fortunate enough to find a wonderful teacher from the Yale Drama School who is helping me learn how to do this. But putting together the text and the interaction is a totally new thing for me. And I have been trying to understand how and why.

Is it because putting together the "psychological" and the "social" is both "more" and "better" than either one alone? In a way, it is a combining of thought and experience. How to explain it. I will tell you about an analogous experience that may help. A while ago a close friend of mine asked me if I wanted to listen to tapes that she and two friends had made to replicate the hallucinated "voices" that people with schizophrenia describe as a common, major, and often extremely troubling experience. I had been involved with treating people with schizophrenia and writing research articles on schizophrenia for thirty years. I had treated and studied many people who had such experiences, and I had published many papers on the nature of "auditory hallucinations" in schizophrenia. Yet I myself had never heard "voices." When I listened to the tape, I instantly realized that I had never really understood what "hearing voices" actually involved. Oh yes, I knew what the words meant concretely, but I had never realized how totally inadequate the phrase "hearing voices" was to reflect the complex experience it was supposed to represent. Even this shadow of the real experience was shocking to me, I had grossly underestimated the impact the real more complex experience could have on one's sense of reality, of being intruded on, even being taken over, the assault on your sense of confidence and how to operate in the real world. Of course, I knew the "voices" I was hearing were recordings on an audiotape, knew their origins, their nature, and how to turn them off. The experience was, nevertheless, almost overwhelming and such a revelation. "Voices" are not just voices, they are a major challenge to your entire sense of yourself and of the world! In fact, the label "voices" is an incredibly shallow, incomplete, and inadequate representation of the complexity and power of even this taped imitation of the actual experience.

Our words, words like "voice," are crucial, but at the same time they are a pale reflection of the experience. Many disciplines know this, such as drama, but medicine and often psychology attempt to be so scientific, so cognitive that they generally lose the nature of the reality. The bringing together of idea and experience may be both "more" and "better" for at least approximating that reality. So, when I am doing readings, attending to both the text and the connection to people, am I coming closer to dealing with the real thing, with the combination of cognition (psychology) and the experience of the social context? Does that more usefully and adequately deal with the nature and reality of the experiences I am trying to understand? It certainly feels like it.

So, from my teacher I am learning not to fold my arms when I am reading to people, to look up as much as possible to make eye contact with the people to whom I am reading, to register their responses, to ad lib if I become aware they are not understanding something, to smile and allow myself to make other facial expressions, to speak more expressively (as I do naturally when I am speaking French much more than when I speak English), and to gesture—in sum, to be there, to understand this is a social situation not merely one of mouthing the words written in my book. Is doing a reading a "more and better" way of communicating the reality of experience?

The Normal and the Pathological
[*10/3/09*]

Claude Bernard, the founder of modern physiology, stated that to understand the abnormal it is necessary to understand the normal. Georges Canguilhem, the contemporary philosopher, has elaborated on this idea that is such a basic postulate for all thinking about health and illness. For our discussion about "subjectivity" or putting oneself in the shoes of another, what is the relevance of this postulate?

The Preakness Stakes this past year (2009) was won by a filly named Rachel Alexandra. It was the first time in many years that a filly had won this race so there was much discussion with her jockey, the trainer, and horse racing experts. Among other things, the jockey noted that they had had a difficult time getting her to the site of the race. Like many racehorses, Rachel Alexander was temperamental and nervous, so they had had to transport her with her stable mate. The jockey explained (my paraphrase): "You know horses are herd animals. It is basic for them to take comfort from others they know, so transporting the two together was a no brainer and worked beautifully." We human beings are not herd animals. Nevertheless, as with other primates, being with others of our kind is and always has been fundamental to our very survival. No newborn baby would survive without prolonged connections with family or other humans. For us humans, language, customs, culture, and other social phenomena are a basic part of who we are. We are psychologically wired for that. This is probably one of the reasons that solitary confinement has always been such a powerful punishment and a contributor to some people going "stir crazy."

I have used the terms "putting oneself in someone else's shoes" and "subjectivity," to which I will now add "emotional connection" and "experience" as importantly overlapping terms. Although each has some different implications from the others, they all relate to the essence of experience and the ability somehow to know or share the experience with or of another person. In this way they are basic to who we are and our nature as animals, social animals. It was thus interesting and shocking to me when I saw in the program for a recent presentation of the history of theater that the list of "human sciences" included sociology and anthropology but left out psychology and psychiatry. It was yet another interesting glimpse of how we are seen and perhaps also of how we often see ourselves.

So, what is the connection among all these aspects of "subjectivity"? Well, we are talking here about complex interacting processes. If we start, for convenience sake, with "experience," we know that experience can influence brain structures and processes. On a psychological level, experience influences the meaning of situations, pain, need for avoidance, pleasure, implications, anticipations, and so on. Of course, it also affects body processes more generally (for example, hormonal processes, reflexes), but we won't get into that here. Part of experience depends on one's personal, social, and environmental surroundings (war, for example, contributes to PTSD). Moreover, a significant part of our experiences and how we deal with them is influenced by feeling understood or cared about by others. Hence, the very meaning and implications of our experience are influenced by our sense of what they mean to others (does my mother get anxious when we get on an airplane?) and also by what they communicate to us, intentionally or not. For example, when at the age of ten I was bothered by kids teasing me because I was wearing shorts, my father said, "What do you care?" I knew from his tone of voice and our history together that his words were shorthand for "What you are doing is fine, you can have confidence in yourself. What they were saying doesn't have to stop you from doing what you want to do." How different that is from an interviewer responding to a person who hears voices merely with a list of objective questions. After I had heard the "voices" recorded on tape and experienced their devastating impact on my ability to concentrate, when a patient would tell me about hearing voices my first response became something like "Wow" or "That could have been difficult." I felt this conveyed that I was noticing not just the symptom but the impact that might have on his or her humanity. My father's words, "What do you care," have pulled me through many experiences. My perception of his understanding my situation, being there, accompanying me, even though he has now been dead for fourteen years, is still with me. It has supported me, allowing me to do things that otherwise I might never have done, like writing a paper showing that people with schizophrenia could improve. I have described many times the negative reception that paper originally received. So, feeling that someone has put him or herself in your shoes, has grasped your situation and understood it, can be an extremely important "normal" experience.

Does it also relate to mental illness and its course? Well, people with severe mental illness certainly often say that it does.

Impasto
Understanding Human Development
[*11/27/21*]

Actually, I'm not sure there is a word that captures exactly the process I want to describe here, but "impasto" may be the closest. It's got to do with painting, the use of layers of paint one upon another, often for giving a three-dimensional quality to a work of art. In my adaptation of the concept I would like to indicate something where you start out with some important central thing. Then you add successive translucent layers that allow you always see the central thing but also the successive layers, and, of course, the whole thing involves the perception of an interaction of sorts among the layers that together constitute the totality. That's what I think depicts human development.

Take me, for example. Some of my basic qualities are perhaps stubbornness, intelligence, fearfulness, a tendency to explore, competence. Then add the early progressive school experience of freedom, creativity, intellectual stuff, being read mythology by Miss Ripley in second grade—all permeated by family and especially mother problems. Then the freedom of time in sixth grade with Douggy Young, the environment of the Second World War and Glenwood School. Then being a little *pischer* in Academy junior high and Mother being sick, and the fears, helplessness, and independence of a month spent as patient in the scarlet fever hospital. Then growing confidence and much time spent with my close friend Bob, absorbing music and literature. Being on the swimming and water polo teams and becoming captain of the State champion swimming team. A's in my classes at school. Debating awards, a driver's license and Swarthmore and Harvard acceptance. It's like that. Layer after layer after layer being laid down. Each translucent, leaving its trace. Then, of course, hitchhiking around the country, Bob still, the intense, often wonderful but often troubled connection with Ann. Graduating from college with high honors after experiencing really terrible anxiety around exams. Med school, Paris, breaking with Ann, being a student with Piaget, the wonders of having a family and children. That's how it is, layer after layer. In all this, in these layers there is the impact of the person's biology on how he or she acts and reacts, changes or does not change and, of course, the influence of the person's situation and surroundings, physical and human. Layer upon layer upon interactive layer.

Of course, I realize that such a layered construction is tragically inadequate, especially in contrast to the work of Piaget, Erikson, Levinson, Freud, Jung, Joseph Campbell, and so many others with more or less unitary models of development. But it is possible, notwithstanding the contributions of these major figures, that their models are too simple, too unitary, that they do not capture the complexity, the layering of the developmental process. Of course, it is extremely important to explore the development of thinking, sex, the hero's journey, and so on. But each one alone appears insufficient. Even a mix of two or three together is not adequate to capture the reality and the ways the components of these models interact to generate a human life, its vicissitudes, and the aspects of vulnerability and competence as they evolve over time.

One major aspect of this complex evolution is the way a person's competence and efforts, vulnerabilities and deficits, interact with the situation in which he or she finds himself.

In the *Aeneid,* Virgil captures an example of this interactive blend of active and passive when he describes how the ship of Aeneas, having escaped with Trojan sailors from defeated Troy, encounters a storm in which all the men except Aeneas "sink beneath the waves never again to hear someone call their names."

Biopsychosocial? We Have Barely Begun to Try
[*11/6/21*]

There is considerable agreement that the biopsychosocial model of mental illness is an important model for understanding the problem. So that takes care of that, right? Not in the least! The statement of the model is only the barest beginning. To start with, there are so many ways of trying to consider that model. Is it like how I dealt with having peas, potatoes, and hamburger for dinner when I was little, eating all of one, then all of another, then all of the third? Or is it like how I dealt with the same meal when I was a little older, mushing them all together? Or is it like a Brahms piano concerto, where each of the domains is developed in its own area while also interacting organically with the others, one domain perhaps dominating in certain instances or certain phases?

And if it is the last of these possibilities, the complex interactions of the three domains over time, how should we study them? How from a true biopsychosocial point of view can we prevent psychiatric problems from arising? How should we treat them?

There are many relevant recent developments in studying complex interactive processes in human functioning. Exploration of "the extended mind" (Annie Murphy Paul) is one in which, for example, riding a bicycle, a physical act, primarily is seen as a way of dealing with solving mental or psychological questions and states. The work of Davidson in developing the program describing "A Day in the Life" of people with severe mental disorders is another approach. The latter recalls the work of Brazilian theater director Augusto Boal (*Theatre of the Oppressed*). Boal used theater performances by the people involved to help indigenous people better understand their position and the roles of people in their environment. His work provides another example of using psychological and social processes to deal with what we have called mental illnesses with focus on the complexities involved by novel means. And, of course, there are approaches we could learn from other fields such as complexity theory and uncertainty theory, used as they are to study and deal with the complex fields of economics and politics.

Another approach is generated by the question, how is it that people who are mentally ill can also function successfully? A person with a broken leg cannot run a hundred-yard dash so how do we understand the differences? Important for our understanding of biopsychosocial are the many instances of nonsickness-related functioning that belie the possibility that sick people are only sick people. Good clinicians recognize, of course, that a person with a severe psychiatric disorder can also have major areas of competence and normality in their lives. This realization is less common in researchers and theory builders, however, where the complexity involved in that realization interferes with simple conclusions and hypotheses. Unlike a situation with a broken leg, for example, where the problem prevents a major area of function, there are numerous examples of the opposite even in people with severe mental illness. When I was living in Paris for a year, I came across one psychologist who was running writing groups for people with major psychiatric disorders. The focus was on dysfunction and discussing it. In a neighboring psychiatric hospital a worker called Ludmilla Elmassian was also running a writing group for severely disturbed psychiatric inpatients. Here the participants were invited to write anything they pleased. No one chose to write about dysfunction, and the writing was beautiful. In another part of Paris the same year I visited the "Atelier de Nonfaire," which can be roughly translated as the workshop of not doing. There I had a teaching session with a group of psychology graduate students who were visiting for a week. After all they had learned about the incompetence of people with severe psychiatric disorder, the students were shocked that here it was exactly such people who were carrying out all the tasks and were even importantly involved in organizing and running the workshop. In another instance, I conducted some follow-along studies in South Carolina, where I saw the same people with major psychiatric disorder every two years. One woman told me she had been in a psychiatric hospital since my last visit because of a recurrence of her disorder. I expressed my sympathy, but she disabused me. She said that that particular problem was relatively minor, but the big thing that had happened since our interview two years earlier was that she had divorced her abusive husband and now her life was so much better.

Our grasp of the meaning of biopsychosocial in the field of psychiatric disorder is still primitive indeed. Understandably so. Most of us specialize in only one or another of the three domains. Furthermore, dealing with one or another domain is already complex without attending to the others. And of course, funding, social pressures, changes over time in hierarchical relationships, and, of course, changes in beliefs and values from, for example, psychoanalytic to social, to biological—the hegemony of each in its period of dominance seeming absolute and the only rational solution—adds further to our tendency to believe and work in one or another of these areas to the neglect of the others and to their interaction. It does seem that we humans, at least in the mental health field, are like me at dinner as a child. We focus on one thing, the peas, the potatoes, or the meat, leaving the others for another time.

What Music Can Teach Us about Mental Illness
[8/12/15]

The biopsychosocial paradigm in the mental health field is like what people say about the weather: Everyone talks about it, but no one does anything about it. In mental health there are some who have mostly given up, those, for example, relieved by their certainty that "mental diseases are brain diseases." Others have not abandoned the biopsychosocial approach, and advances have been made in the field of PTSD, for example. Generally, however, progress has been limited, and the models used reflect only the simplest of possibilities, as, for example, in the diathesis stress paradigm which hypothesizes basic vulnerabilities set off by stresses. For those who deal with real people distressed with psychiatric problems, if we do more than diagnosis and med checks, it rapidly becomes clear that the real life of real people with psychiatric problems is far more complex than unitary or even simple explanatory efforts reveal.

I believe an understanding of music can help to provide some ideas about how we can think about the complexities of mental illness and even more broadly about how the human psyche may work. There are several reasons why music might do this. First, music is truly bio/psycho/social. Actually, music is even more basic science than biology since it involves basic mathematical concepts (Pythagoras). It also involves biologic processes of hearing and interpretation of sound, psychological processes regarding meaning, and social impact based on social customs, practices, and experiences. Another feature of music is that it can be extremely complex cross sectionally and temporally, involving aspects of harmony, what pitches or timbres do or do not go with others, and the importance of various sequences of pitches and various rhythms. And, at increasingly complex levels, we have the interactions of multiple instruments playing together as in chamber music or the orchestra, temporal subtleties like rubato, or the existence of themes that can recur as in the ritornello form or the development of these themes or, as in some modern music, the playing of more than one theme at a time.

So how might all these phenomena help us in thinking about human mental functioning in health or disorder?

Psychosocial Construction
[*7/11/20*]

I would like to propose that the idea of "social construction," although important in its own right, is not nearly as helpful for understanding what we call "mental illness" and its improvement as the concept of "psycho-social construction," the interaction of the person and the context in which that person lives. And the Program for Recovery and Community Health (PRCH) just happens to have an expert in that field, Pauline Bernard. In fact, I think PRCH has a unique collection of people who already are, or could, use such a model for their work.

The idea of psycho-social construction is not just that the person's social or other environment is crucial for our field but that the interaction of that domain and the individual is central. Thus, Larry Davidson's famous Edwina the dinosaur whom the experts have called "extinct" has the personal strength to ignore that stigma and to go on making chocolate chip cookies for children. In a related vein, Billy Bromage talks about providing "space" for his clients to act in new ways and develop new abilities and identities, a perfect example of the interaction of the environment and the person, and the construction of that environment and relationship to aid the person in the process of improvement.

Thus, I am suggesting that a considerable amount of the work at PRCH is not merely social construction, but is psycho-social, focusing not only on either the social or the psychological but on the interaction of the two.

Such a focus on psycho-social allows for inquiry into the

interaction of "constructions" in the person and the context of the person, rather than merely the social or the psychological. This is important because it gives another way of looking at the crucial processes. Let me illustrate this by a brief look at the history of western philosophy. John Locke, the empiricist, said that people's minds are created by their experiences of the environment. George Berkeley, on the other hand, said no, people's minds are created in themselves. It took Immanuel Kant to say, no, people's minds are created by their experiences, which are processed in specific ways by the characteristics of those minds. Thus, for example, in my back yard I see four-legged animals, and it is my mind that puts them into two groups, squirrels and cats. Obviously, the preceding descriptions are a bit rough.

A major reason for noticing all this in the context of social construction is that there are, at least, two tightly interacting construction processes. For example, Edwina experiences the social pressure of stigma but is still undaunted, going ahead to make chocolate chip cookies. And there are many viewpoints on how she is able to do that, invoking the involvement of entirely different processes, which in turn play a major role in determining what kind of interventions might be possible. Here are just a few of the most important theories: the learning theories of Skinner's behaviorism, with pigeons pressing bars, the stimulus/response theories of Neal Miller and others, Gestalt theories involving insight and creativity, Bergson and his interest in emergents, totally novel things like language that evolve over time, and, of course, developmental ideas like those of Piaget, Freud, Erikson, and Jung.

Implications of Complexity Theory for a Biopsychosocial Psychiatry
[*8/10/15*]

Complexity theory, like predecessors such as cybernetics, does not solve the problems of dealing with complex systems. It provides more of a model for thinking and acting than a method for demonstrating connections and relationships. However, that model is an extremely useful one and helps to highlight what we are not doing as well as suggest a way for how we might be more effective in understanding the relationships and processes of psychiatric disorder. By promoting the conceptualization of interactions among variables and among domains, complexity theory can be used to suggest possible paths for exploration and to identify gaping holes in our inquiry and understanding. It can, for example, be used to model how an individual and/or a family may attempt to adjust to a CNS (central nervous system) change, or how the CNS may attempt to help adjust the psyche to a major change in the family or other aspects of the environment. PTSD studies provide some examples of such changes in response to "stressors" or the presence or absence of "social supports." General adult psychiatry could learn from such conceptual models, notwithstanding the disadvantage of frequently not being able to identify a "stressful life event." Concepts like networks, thresholds, tipping points, positive and negative feedback and externalities, and path-dependent processes are readily considered. Even concepts like self-organization, agent-based models, adaptation, and emergence as identified in complexity theory, as evasive as they are to practical application, can be used as a conceptual tool for a more sophisticated approach to adult psychiatric disorders than we have at present.

So, let's play a little with the possibilities. In a paper published long ago I reported that, based on the descriptions by patients with schizophrenia, our concept of delusions and hallucinations as discrete events was inadequate, that for many people these experiences exist on a continuum. They may say, "Well, it was sort of like a voice but also like a thought," meaning that whatever it was lay somewhere between what we call a symptom and normal experience ("No, I don't really believe [or hear] it"). Recently, in a verbal report, Davidson has spoken about delusions as part of a tapestry of experience, that a thought in a person's mind is not an isolated experience but is part of a broader tapestry of cognitive and emotional experiences. But if such complexities are a necessary part of our field, how can we nail them down to describe "a disease like any other," perhaps like acute pancreatitis or pneumococcal pneumonia? Let's hypothesize that such a nailing down may not be possible. To carry these ideas further, as the psychiatrist Sarah Fineberg has suggested (personal communication), there is an infinite variety of tapestries based on our varied biologies, experiences, and social contexts. To accept diagnostic categories of such things is like "pinning a butterfly to a cork board." Yes, you can do that but in so doing you may be losing the very essence of the butterfly. What we may then need for our field is to have diagnostic categories and/or dimensions but to be aware that these are only rough estimations and that the reality of the person with the problem is ALWAYS also specific to that person and that our biological, psychological, and social interventions will also ALWAYS be at least to some extent specific to that person.

Years ago I and my family were at the Canadian island north of Toronto that belongs to our extended family. One rainy day I decided to make sugar cookies just like those my grandmother used to make. I didn't have the recipe but figured how complicated could it be, sugar, butter, and flour? Maybe two or three general combinations and I would have it. So I started. The first three or four batches, not so great, certainly not like hers. The fourth, fifth, and sixth, not so great either. I was rapidly becoming aware that even a "simple" system of three variables has an infinite number of possible combinations. I never succeeded with the sugar cookies, but I certainly learned something. And, unlike the situation with humans, the ingredients of sugar cookies do not even represent a "dancing landscape" as described by complexity theory, where each of the components is actively adapting to the others.

My hypothesis is that one very likely model for a true biopsychosocial view of schizophrenia and many other psychiatric disorders is to use SIMULTANEOUSLY a diagnostic approach and an individual approach in order to do justice to a rough typology (or dimensionality [Strauss Dx models) plus the infinite number of interactions that have contributed to the disorder and that can contribute to its improvement.

Of course, simple is best. That is, simple is best if it is adequate . I am proposing that it is probably neither best or even adequate, that we are dealing with complex systems and that to assume simplicity is like the old story about the drunk person looking for his keys under the corner lamp post rather than in the middle of the block where he lost them because the light is better at the corner.

The Story
Its Role in Medicine and Other Human Science
[*3/11/11*]

About forty years ago my parents were visiting my family where we lived in Rochester, New York. As we often did on such occasions, we decided to have a fancy dinner at an inn about twenty miles from Rochester where they had delicious food. And, as I also often did during those dinners, I ordered the lamb chops, which I love. For the main course they brought me two large double-cut chops. I ate one of these, but after the appetizers, the great bread, and side dishes and wanting to leave room for dessert, I asked the young waiter, probably a student at a local college, if he would wrap up the remaining chop so I could take it home. He was happy to do so and during dessert brought the bag with my double-cut chop to me. "I washed it," he said proudly. "Washed it?" I thought to myself, "What is that?" I looked in the bag and sure enough, there were the bones pure white, and the meat separated from them. I loved to chew on lamb-chop bones, but he had ruined them for me by separating them from their meat. I didn't know if I should laugh or cry.

When I see a first-person account of a person with severe mental illness published in a journal or as part of a book on mental illness, I also have a double reaction. It is wonderful that people make the effort and give respect to writing such accounts, but often they are like my lamb-chop bones, totally washed clean. Years ago, even before the lamb-chop incident, when I was at the National Institutes of Health, I took the opportunity on several occasions to make rounds with the noted specialist in epilepsy Maitland Baldwin. On one occasion, when one of his fellows recounted the history of one of the patients we had just seen, Baldwin said that you had to be careful accepting the history told by patients who had seen many doctors as these had. Patients begin to know what doctors want to hear, what they pay attention to and what they deem unimportant, and, without realizing it, tailor their accounts accordingly.

More recently, when I accepted (only briefly) the role of "medical backup," a "half-time job" in charge of two hundred and fifty psychotic patients, and began meeting with one patient after another, I was shocked at first with a common response to my question, "How have things been going?" Most of the patients had been in treatment for several years and were used to seeing "their" doctor for the standard five to ten minutes every six months. The patients often responded to me with things like "Well, I still hear the voices but they're not too bad, and I take my medications." "That's fine," I would reply, "But really, how are things going?" The person would usually reply again, "I still hear the voices, but they're not too bad, and I take my medications." "No really," I would say, "I'm interested in how things have been going for you, in your life. What are you doing, how do you spend your time?" At this point the person might start to believe me and begin to tell me the story of his or her last few months. Clearly, I couldn't meet the standard of limiting these encounters to five or ten minutes each, and shortly thereafter I retired.

To understand the potential role of the patient's story for telling us about the nature of the processes involved and their vicissitudes, we clearly need to learn to hear and appreciate these accounts. They are after all the basis for much of our data and thus essential for our concepts, our research, our theories, and our approaches to care. The "we do it already" or "we know it already" responses from professionals only demonstrate the degree to which we do not do it or know it already. Hearing a person's story without putting it in the procrustean bed of our own often unrecognized theories or time pressure is not all that easy. Novelists, theater people, and others, who are often pretty smart, spend their entire lives attempting to do just that, often learning and facing new demands and inadequacies at each step. In this essay we will describe some of the major issues and approaches to learning a person's story focusing specifically on the mental health field, approaches to conveying it to others, and possibilities for including the person's story in research and the development of more adequate concepts and practice.

Aren't the principles for a human science like psychology or psychiatry just like any other scientific principles? Not so fast! First of all, let's talk a bit about what a human science is, or at least how we see it.

So how can we approach teaching about categories but also about things that are human, that reflect complex feeling experiences, that make them work? The arts provide an interesting example. Several years ago I was in one of the Yale art museums and a woman was giving a guided tour of some of the paintings. As I passed by, she was talking about a copy of the *Oath of the Horatii,* a neo-classical painting by David. I stopped to listen. She described the history of the painting, the origins of the subject, the details of the style. When she finished, I knew a lot more about the painting, but that knowledge did nothing for my appreciation of it, which was pretty minimal. A few years later I was at the Musée d'Orsay during an exhibit of paintings by Van Gogh and Millet. Again, I overheard a woman giving a talk about some of the paintings and stopped to listen. This time the talk was wonderful. I felt I had "gotten" what the paintings were about and now had a much-heightened appreciation for them. What was the difference in my experience of these two museum talks? Why was one "didactic" experience so much more integrated with the "feeling" experience than the other? Well, artists and art critics probably know more about this than I ever will, but I have had this experience with teachers about literature as well. Two years ago a former professor of Harold Bloom's, the famous Yale professor, came to New Haven to give a lecture on poetry. It was like magic, like music! I think all of us in the audience were spellbound. He'd read a poem and then talk about it briefly. Such a contrast to the poetry course I had taken in college, where, as in the talk about David, I "learned a lot" but nothing that made much difference to me. In some ways psychotherapy may be similar, the difference between "You have an inverted Oedipal complex with counter-cathexis problems" and a psychotherapy that really gets at what's going on with you.

Undoubtedly, there are important variables in the "learner" as well as in the "teacher." This reminds me of what Ollie Remy said about fishing. Ollie Remy was an old French-Canadian guide who lived near the island that belonged to my extended family in Georgian Bay, Canada. Ollie, who was grizzled and getting on in age, would drop over to our island to tell stories and just talk. At some point he asked our kids, then aged around ten and fourteen, "So do you want me to take you fishing?" To which of course they excitedly exclaimed, "Yes!" Ollie smiled and then added very seriously, "Of course, you have to be ready . . . [long pause]. Because if you're not ready you won't catch anything. In fact, that's how you can tell if you're ready. If you're ready, you always catch fish. And if you're not ready, you never do." So maybe with teaching too, it's just that students sometimes are just not ready. Or maybe even the teacher isn't. In any case, it's a great way to explain whatever happens.

But there is another way to look at this, and the more I think about it the more lost I get. I get CDs and occasional DVDs from the Great Courses series teaching me about important things that I should have known about all along, like complexity theory, the evolution of ancient civilizations, and the intellectual history of the seventeenth and eighteenth centuries. Almost all the teachers for the Great Courses are good to very good, but the one (his name is Alan Kors) who lectures on the seventeenth and eighteenth centuries is incredible. In fact, the only reason I got the course was because he was teaching it. (I mean who cares about the seventeenth and eighteenth centuries?) I had heard a lecture by Kors in another course, and he was outstanding, so I bought this one hoping for the best. He's frigging incredible! Newton, Montesquieu, Locke, Voltaire, Rousseau, ho-hum right? Not at all! Their thinking is apparently the basis for all we believe and think about and struggle with now, to this very day! And here's this guy talking about history that could be boring, but it's spellbinding! How does he do that? He's the best teacher I've ever had. I think it's because he makes it live. And how does he do that? Well, partly, he makes it into a story, a story built on fact. Partly also, he really cares about it, loves it even, and you can tell that from the tone of his voice. But he's just telling you facts. Science and humanity, facts and feelings, has he then found the solution to putting them together? He also shows what these guys were struggling with as well as the context in which they were thinking and writing and their implications for their time and ours.

So why can't we do that, bringing science and feeling

together, maybe like that? And does that still count, I mean as real history? Could it count as real science?

So how does the data thing as science and the feeling/experiential thing as human fit together. Several possibilities:

One. It doesn't. There is the art of medicine and the science of medicine, and never the twain shall meet. That possibility seems total baloney to me, preposterous and ridiculous, even though that is how it is often taught and conceptualized. The doctor (if he or she is a good doctor) has to do both, almost always. The patient contains both, always. As a back problem or a person suffering from occasional anxiety, I am a statistic. If I get better, or don't, if I respond to a medication or don't, I am a statistic. If my back shows something on a scan or an X-ray, or not, I am a statistic. If lights go off in my brain scan when I am anxious, I am a statistic.

There is nothing wrong with all of that—in fact it is incredibly important, important for diagnosis, prevention, treatment, theory, teaching students, and advances in any of these areas. But it is never the whole story. Sometimes it is a major part of the story and the rest seems more or less to take care of itself, but "the other" part is always there as well. Very often, the other part needs to be attended to as well. It seems to me that in reality "the art" and "the science" are both always there, in the patient and in the treater, whether they are attended to or need to be attended to or not.

Two. The art and the science of medicine in the mental health field can be molded tightly together or combined into one indistinguishable unit. I have tried that in various combinations for over twenty years. Sometimes I have succeeded a little, or even somewhat, but never I think in a way that is completely satisfactory. Writing stories, first person accounts, along with more theoretical and traditional medical explanations is far from totally worthless. But it seems to me that always the explanation reduces, if it does not destroy, the impact of the art, of the story. Writers and storytellers say, "Show, don't tell," describe don't explain, and I believe that every time and every way I have tried to cheat on that by also explaining, the story or "the art" loses. There is something in the discursive that saps the power of the experiential. Perhaps literary theorists or others have explained how or why that happens. Is it that the pure story requires a certain attitude from the teller and from the reader or listener? Does it require that the listener participate actively by providing his own associations or images? Or is it, as some have suggested, that a story has many levels, many possible interpretations that give it its richness and power and that the explanation depletes these qualities. I do not want to go further into this here, but from my multiple failures, even partial failures, and those I have seen of others, I have come to believe that it is true. You cannot effectively combine the experiential and the discursive if you try to mush them together.

Three. Does this leave us with no solution? I think not. There is one, of a kind, suggested to me by a good friend, Ashley Clayton. I believe the best solution is to see science and art each as essential and yet impossible to mush together. As Ashley suggested, I think you must try to "hold on to" both of them at once, even if they seem to be contradictory or incompatible. I suppose one model would by the Yin and Yang concepts. If this is true, what would it imply? First, that you always have to do both, get the discursive piece and the experiential piece, and accept both of them as true, and evaluate the importance of each. Second, you have to try to figure out how they relate. And, finally, you have to figure out how you, the caregiver, and how the patient are going to deal with those two pieces.

"But we do it already." No. Well, maybe in the practice of a good treater, but not in our theory or our research, not in our concepts. Or is the "we do it already, we know it already" syndrome just a part of a larger and more buried complex, the "we don't want to go any deeper, it gets too gooey" syndrome. About three years ago I was in Paris, a city that I have loved for years and forms a major part of my life. I was in my usual small hotel, in the usual small room they reserve for me when I'm there, and feeling like the people who work in and run the hotel are like my family. I was listening to my little portable radio and heard this great interview with a woman who worked as a clown in an end-of-life-care facility for adults. She sounded bright and intuitive and thought in a very creative way about her role in such a setting. When the program was over, I went down to the front desk and asked Brigitte if she could find the website of the clown, Sandra Meunier. Brigitte found a website and on it a phone number. I called Ms. Meunier and told her I was a professor at Yale (a great introduction when you're making a cold call), that I was very interested in her work and could we perhaps meet and talk further at "my office" the café Rostand. We did that two days later, talking at length over coffee and an apricot tart. Finally, I asked her if I could come to the hospital to actually see her in action. She said it was fine with her, but she would have to talk first with the chief of service.

Two days later Sandra called saying it was fine with him also but he wanted to meet with me before I went on the ward. The necessary arrangements were made and the following Tuesday I met her chief and for the first time saw Sandra doing her remarkable work.

There's another aspect of the story, one that links it intimately to psychiatry and to medicine more generally. This past year I had the opportunity to participate in a program that teaches medical students how to evaluate and work with patients. I had been somewhat distant from the workings of the Department of Psychiatry and the more traditional aspects of medical education since my "retirement" a little over ten years ago. But when my French friends asked me what people in the United States were doing about talking with patients about their treatment and about death, I realized I had no idea—except for a fine course on end-of-life care given by the state of California. So, I decided I'd better find out, at least a little. When I returned to New Haven from Paris I called the head of medical education at Yale Medical School, whom I had taught as a resident, and he invited me to observe some of their programs on teaching medical students to interview patients. This I did. In the program they give the students different frameworks for talking with patients—for example, the initial "workup," talking with "difficult" patients, "bringing bad news" (such as a diagnosis of cancer), and so on. Then the student group of about thirty breaks into small groups of three or four and each student takes a turn interviewing an actor who has been briefed on his medical and personal history and what his symptoms are.

When I first learned about what the program involved, I thought that using actors was stupid and artificial. Fortunately, I didn't say anything because, boy, was I wrong! So, what's this got to do with story? Well, let me illustrate. Just this past week during a session with a small group of first-year students about to interview actors for initial patient evaluation, one of the students, a charming and shy young woman, said apologetically, "I don't think I'll be able to get into this, it's just imagination, not real. I'll probably laugh or something. It's so different from a serious discussion like this." I said something like, "Well, whatever happens. We'll just have to see. The beauty of this situation is that we can try things out. Mistakes or whatever, there's no harm done." It turned out that she was the first student scheduled to interview a "patient" (actor) in our small group. When the time came, she went to the door of the examining room we were in, with her white student-doctor jacket on, and said, as planned, to the actor waiting in the hall, "Hello Mrs. Zane, I'm the medical student who's going to be talking with you." We were all instantly involved. Just amazing! Start living the story, and it becomes real.

I guess the context makes the story real. It's all powerful. For one thing, it's wonderful seeing the young students put themselves for the first time in this life-changing position, working so earnestly and so competently, to be like real doctors. All my medical student days instantly came back to me, mostly as pure feeling. How much I loved doing that. How surprised I was that I was not a total fool. How equally surprised I was that a patient took me seriously and was kind! Wow! And we had had almost no training in how to talk to a patient. This today was so much better.

But the most moving of these experiences with medical students and their lived stories with "patients" was in the sessions of bringing bad news. These were third-year students now, amazingly so much more—what is the word—"competent," "cool," "mature" than they were the year earlier. It's amazing to see them grow, change. Anyway, bringing bad news. The format was the same as the others, starting with the actor-patient waiting in the hall. "Hello, Mrs. Lopez, I'm the doctor covering for Dr. Sanders. She had to have her appendix out. She's doing fine and will be back to work in about a week and will see you then, but I'm in the same medical group and am seeing her patients this week." Then the interchange begins. "What do you understand of your condition now?" Then, "Well, as you know, you had some tests done. The results came back, and I'm sorry to tell you . . . ." Even now, writing this, chills come up my spine. Tears start to form. The story between the medical student and the actor-patient has so much power. For them, I think it's the immediacy and seriousness and, yes, even the reality of the whole thing. For me, added to that are the many memories it brings back. Just a story.

Doing a Reading as Human Science
[*9/28/21*]

I had recently finished my autobiography after much travail when my friend Larry Davidson asked me if I wanted to do a reading for his group. I had never done anything like that in my life, so, of course, I said, "I'd love to." Actually, doing it was unlike any experience I'd had in my life, totally different for example from giving a lecture on research I had conducted. I learned tremendously from it, but what? how?

First, I learned that it was radically different from anything I had ever done. It was reading something I'd written, but as a participant with the audience, not as a giver of knowledge or anything like that. I was with them not at them. How do I know? Well, it was how I felt but equally in how they participated. For example, they made comments and then without hesitation described how something I had read connected with their own life, their own experience. They automatically did that, and it felt good that we were all in this together.

What else did I learn? Well, a great deal about my life through their connecting what I had written to ideas other than I had considered and to other experiences.

What else? That has taken me months to even begin to understand. Having felt overwhelmed and somewhat mystified by the experience, I contacted a woman who teaches at the Yale Drama School who I heard was a great teacher. She was. We focused mostly on the issues in giving a reading, issues that involved not merely communicating content but performance, the process of communication, including pauses, tone of voice, and so on.

I am not talking about performance in a prefabricated or manipulative sense, rather as the effective sharing and communication of feeling and the essence of experiences beyond the merely cognitive content. Now that raises a problem of which I have become increasingly aware and have tried to address in the last few years, starting from a presupposition in our field of psychiatry/psychology that we have tended to try to "be scientific." Being scientific about human experience can, of course, be very important. But it can also preclude attention to any data, any experiences, that do not fit scientific paradigms. Thus, for example, even the Gestalt psychologists who studied insight behavior in a chimpanzee who piled boxes on top of one another to reach a banana had trouble trying to explain adequately such behavior by traditional scientific study requirements. Discovering how low the banana must be, how hungry the chimpanzee must be, where the boxes must be placed, and other aspects that lend themselves to measurement may not help much in understanding how the hell the chimpanzee got the idea that this would work.

In stark and not trivial contrast, my dental technician recently was telling me of the lines from the Dr. Seuss book, *Oh, the Places You'll Go!*

> Wherever you fly, you'll be the best of the best.
> Wherever you go, you will top all the rest.
>
> Except when you don't.
> Because, sometimes, you won't.

How does such an important message get translated into

traditional scientific practice? I would argue only by loosening our concepts of science to let in such crucial notions. Qualitative as well as quantitative data? Of course.

One of the lessons that doing a reading might teach us is that to study humans we must decide on a vision of science that, while holding to standards of validity and reliability, is broader than has been acceptable for traditional science. If, for now, we table traditional notions of science in favor of starting with the data but then deciding on how we should study it, we need to attend first to how something like doing a reading of an autobiography gives us crucial information about human experience. Of course, more types of input don't necessarily provide different or richer experience. But, as a longtime lover of Puccini operas, I only recently realized how in even the simplest of stories—think, *La Bohème* and *Madama Butterfly*, for example—the combination of story, action, music (including singing), staging, and acting makes an impact not possible by just one or a few of these alone.

Dropping, for now, the prerequisites of traditional science, how should we understand the role of something like a reading? I suggest that it provides an important medium essential to any science that purports to deal with humans. As radical as it might seem, a reading offers the possibility of including important and sometimes subtle concepts and impressions as part of the equation.

How do we understand what a "reading" might be? For one thing, and perhaps most radically, it can be considered akin to the experience of reading to one's children, where the "performance" is an essential aspect. A reading where the reader is free to make ongoing comments on the content—"I wonder why he did that" or "Oh. that doesn't make sense" or "I was hoping that . . . " or "I did something like that once"—allows the listener to engage with the reader about the meaning or implications of a described event or sentiment. Such an approach permits exploration of the meaning and implications of a human experience or action such as in the Dr. Seuss quote given above. Although not definitive proof, such interactions provide inquiry into the more distinctly "human" processes and actions of human experience that are otherwise precluded by traditional scientific methods. Such an approach also permits feelings and intuitions to become part of scientific inquiry.

Everything is a Story
An Approach to Truth in the Mental Health Field
[*8/31/22*]

Concept: Everything is a story
So says my twenty-seven-year-old grandson Jake (or Jacob). Extrapolating from what he taught me, it seems to me that the idea of a story is like the universal solvent so vigorously sought in the Middle Ages. It is a way for the diverse and fragmented field of mental health to begin to put together our various methods and theories for understanding and acting. The biomedical story, the psychoanalytic story, the family dynamic story, and the rehabilitation story are tragically poorly integrated among themselves, yet most, if not all, of them address important aspects of life for many, perhaps even all, people with psychiatric problems.

The biopsychosocial nature of what we are trying to realize was clarified by a report I recently heard about the nature of monetary inflation. Such a process is often contributed to by beliefs and the realities of fiscal price changes interacting with each other. I am suggesting that in the field of human understanding, including the field of psychiatry, such important interactions occur as well.

But rather than pursuing that proposition from a theoretical point of view, I would like to focus here on one story that tends to be ignored or at least inadequately appreciated. It is the story that has neither a school nor a developed theoretical model nor a proponent to sell it and so tends to be overlooked. It is what I will call for the moment the people school, the experiences of ordinary people that have various major influences on their "mental" disorder. It merits an exploration, an understanding, even though it does not yet belong in an integrated way in any of the other schools.

A woman in her early twenties is discharged from the hospital after partially recovering from a psychotic episode that has been labeled as schizophrenia. She finds a job as a salesperson in a small store selling women's clothing. Still hearing voices, she is able to work but has difficulty in concentrating or paying attention to detail. Our person becomes friendly with another saleswoman and at one point confides to her that she still has some problems hearing voices. Her new friend suggests, "All right, why don't you tell me when you are hearing the voices and I will let you know if I hear them too, just to let you know." They do that, and our person's voices become less troublesome, allowing her to work more effectively and more happily.

Another patient, a woman who has the diagnosis of schizophrenia, has a major problem with concentration. Her thoughts jump around to different ideas, often delusional. This woman works as secretary in a very busy office, with many distractions and requests coming to her from the various people who work there. I see this patient in several follow-along research interviews over several months. When she reports to me after several interviews that she works in such an office, I ask incredulously how she is able to work in such a distracting place. She replies, "As I told you before, Dr. Strauss, when I am there, I HAVE to organize myself." I recall then that she has told me that in response to the same question at each of the preceding interviews. The reason, I think, that I did not remember her answer is that her explanation did not fit with what I had been previously taught, which included little about how people with symptoms often learn to manage them. This is an area of understanding psychosis that I would suggest is often as important as biochemistry, genetics, psychodynamics, and relationships, the area of what people (even very disturbed psychiatric patients) do to help themselves.

Method
"You can see a lot by just looking" (paraphrase of a favorite Yogi Berra saying).

And, of course, you can also hear a lot by just listening. In the early days of our research on diagnosis and diagnostic criteria we focused heavily on constructing simple questions to which we could make simple ratings of patients' answers. For people trained in psychodynamic psychiatry such simplicity and focus on inter-rater reliability was hard to learn. It is not that easy to break down complex concepts into simple questions and ratings, although once accomplished, it all seemed blindingly obvious.

For some time, we carried out extensive studies of psychiatric experiences and diagnostic criteria with these methods. However, we also had previously had extensive clinical experience, and our subjects, psychiatric patients, would often try to tell us more complicated things about their experiences. We tried patiently to listen but, I'm afraid, often gave the unspoken message that we were not particularly interested in all these details or issues and that we needed to get on with our long multi-itemed interview schedule. One subject, for example, tried to explain that the voices she and her family heard from the old grandfather clock they had brought over from England were different from the voices she heard that her family members did not also hear. But for us, that information was primarily a problem for us in making decisions about our ratings, not something we were interested in pursuing. We needed to get along with our multi-questioned interview.

But over time, it became increasingly clear that these "unhelpful" additions that patients were trying to tell us about were, in fact, potentially important aspects of their experiences and raised major questions about the nature of psychotic experience and related underlying processes. Thus, we became less satisfied with the rapid-fire method of "data" collection that we had been using. We gradually made our interview schedules shorter and left more time for open-ended questions and for just listening to patients' reports of their experiences whether they met our criteria for delusions, hallucinations, and so on, or not. For example, even at the simplest level, it would have been interesting to understand what was going on with that patient who heard voices that no one else heard but also heard voices that other family members heard as well—for example, what was the role of social factors in her experiences.

But the most significant aspect of changes in our data collection came from an entirely different—although, once again, in retrospect—obvious source. We were becoming increasingly interested in patient "outcome." This was another concept far more complex than often noted, because outcome when? After one month, six months, four years? So we began to conduct "follow-along," not just one-shot "follow-up," studies.

Simple enough, right? Observing trajectory, evolution of disorder or improvement over time rather than evaluating it at one more or less arbitrary moment. But not simple at all. We rapidly became aware that as we were seeing patients repeatedly over time (every two months, for example) they became more comfortable with us. (As clinicians as well as investigators, we knew, of course, that if we had the same investigator seeing the same patients over time, we would get "better" data.)

And as interviewee and interviewer came to know each other better and we were taking more time with fewer questions, patients began to tell us about things we hadn't known to ask. Remember Yogi Berra: You can see (hear) a lot by just looking (listening). But for that to work you need to know how to see, how to hear, and, in fact, how to be. If patients saw we were really interested in their experiences, they began to tell us more about things we hadn't known to ask. I've already described how I failed to hear the woman who had told me that her busy office environment forced her to keep her thoughts together. In another case, a man with bipolar disorder told me during one interview that he hadn't mentioned before that his wife also had bipolar disorder. When I apparently looked sympathetic, he went on to say, "No no, Dr. Strauss, that's a good thing, because when she tells me that I'm getting high, I know that she knows what she's talking about." So the changes in our research methodology led to very different relationships, which, in turn, led us to recognize new aspects of experience and experience context that we had no clue existed previously.

So
So, what you learn and how you learn interact, nothing new there. We knew that all the time. But I would contend that we don't know it enough, and especially in our human science we need to appreciate more fully what various methods teach us and what they hide from us. For example, after learning from patients some of the things they did to help themselves manage and to get better, in my clinical work I began to tell people who, for example, heard voices that I knew many other people who had that experience and could, if they liked, tell them some of the things those people did to manage their lives in case they wanted to try them out.

Finally, it is important to note that the way some researchers approach learning and the way some clinicians do may result in very different findings, experience, and knowledge. I noted a number of very different approaches, and the stories that emerge from them, at the beginning of this essay. I repeat my contention that we have been woefully incompetent in the efforts needed to see how much and in what ways these stories might be knitted together. In my autobiography I note how my father took a picture of me at the age of six trying to put together the large pieces of a picture puzzle. The photograph shows how I had completed the upper right half of the puzzle and the lower left half but had not noticed how the two halves could fit together. I think that we in the mental health field are very often in an analogous position.

Eighty-eight Years Old
[*2/17/21*]

I woke up at 7:30 this morning, as usual. What an incredibly beautiful day! The sun is just coming up. Everything is blue and orange and totally clear. I'm not sure I have ever seen a morning like this. The light, the whole atmosphere, seems unique. Such a strange time of a life! Yesterday, I had an echocardiogram. The technician kept quiet, but the expression on his face said, "I can't even find his heart. Does he have one left?" I walk gingerly so as not to slip on the ice with my unsteady feet. At morning physical therapy, I'm not even able to manage a fifth sit-up. I explain to my therapist that in college I was a wrestler and used to do twenty of these, She nods as though she hears this about twenty times a day. I stagger back to my car. But at least I can stagger. I know so many people who can't. Alain, twenty years younger than I, died of lung cancer four years ago. Malcolm, who was my age, died of prostate cancer before that. Sara Lee, my college classmate, died of ovarian cancer about forty years ago, Pernette, just this last year. Ralph Hoffman, Howard Blue, John Gunderson, Walter Clark, so many. I have one friend left who is actually one year older than I, Ralph Brown. My sister is four years older, but she is losing it cognitively. My wonderful secretary and friend Nancy, at least twenty years younger than I, is now totally senile. And, of course, my parents and grandparents are gone, even one of my cousins. Stuart was the first of the eight of us to die, last year, the youngest!

    It is all so weird and so strange. Dad, who lived vigorously until the age of ninety-five, used to say of his friends, "They're dropping like flies." I never asked him how that was for him.

I can still listen to Edith Piaf. I am still learning about the Greek playwrights from my CD lectures. In addition to the tragedians, there was Aristophanes, the comic genius. According to Plato, Aristophanes described how human beings were each originally a round ball that got split in half by the jealous gods and now spend their lives searching for their other half. I can learn all that and see this incredible morning light. I am very lucky.

Lucky, too, that I can talk with my wonderful son and daughter on the phone and with my friend Larry and my other friends. And my connections to these people who are so important to me have evolved in beautiful ways these past couple of years. As I have become older somehow there is a new reciprocity that is very special. I wish I could describe it more adequately. I experience it too in my wonderful writing groups! And I have also finished writing my autobiography, and it came out as a real book! The picture on the cover is a photograph of me that my father took when I was about seventeen. I was all dressed in my raggedy clothes with my crew cut preparing to go off to my summer job digging ditches for the gas company. Maria saw the picture on the cover of the book and asked, "Who is that?"

Getting Old
[4/25/22]

This getting old thing comes as something totally unexpected. It's not that I expected to die young. It's just that I never thought much about getting old at all. To the extent that I thought about it at all, for me aging was a process in which things just faded more or less, you slowed down, and then you died.

It's not that I didn't have lots of clues. Of course, I've seen a lot of people get old, and I've known tons of old people. In becoming a doctor, first in med school and then in medical internship and my year of medical residency, you see lots of them, and a lot of them die. It's just that it's not you.

I could have learned from the time I spent with my father, who died at the age of ninety-five. Boy, there were lots of clues. Mostly he was great. He joked about giving piano concerts to the "old folks" up until he was ninety-four, maybe even ninety-five. He joked about how easy it was because they didn't mind the mistakes he made because they were sleeping.

Sometimes he complained, a rare occurrence, about having to make so many doctor visits. And he would ask me, "Did you know Tom whatever?" And I would say, "No, why?" And he would say, "Well, he died." Maybe I would make a comment, but I never thought to ask about the man or what it meant to Dad. I just didn't have a clue. I wasn't interested. Or maybe I was afraid?

Whatever the cause, it never struck me to be interested in that stuff, so I never asked questions, never reflected on it.

Now, here I am, getting old, even being old, and what the hell, it's a whole new thing! It's not just slowing down, although that's part of it. It's not even being unable physically to do so much or last very long at a task, although it's those things too.

No, it's more complicated. The bad and aggravating stuff is certainly there, the shaky hands, the effort it takes to go upstairs, but there are also important new pleasures. People often offer to help me with something or to open the door for me or hold it open. It's gratifying to see in what seem to be trivial gestures that people can be so kind.

I also have a view of people and of life I never had before. It's hard to explain, but it's a broader view, a broader perspective, on what things mean, on how they fit together or don't, on what's important. It's like Robert E. Lee or Stonewall Jackson having a sense of the whole battlefield. Did you ever visit a Civil War battle site? You knew some details about the two sides at Gettysburg. You read the markers about the fight for Little Round Top, but when you're there and actually look around, you can't see shit! Everything is just trees and hills and fields, These features all blend into each other, and there's no way you could get a sense of where the Union cavalry was or even your own tenth Tennessee regiment. But Lee and Jackson and a few others like them could. Well, when you get older, you get more intuitions about where stuff is and how it fits in or it doesn't.

But it's losing people that's hard! I've lost four important people in just the last couple of months! That's a lot. It's like they've all slid off the game board or something. And they won't be back! Ever! And if you include the last several years, I've lost a real ton of people. A lot.

I know, of course, that although the loss is huge and forever, in some ways it isn't total. For example, I think of my father quite often these days, and he died twenty-seven years ago. I remember some of his jokes, some of his advice, how it was when he sat at the piano and played something, then stopped for a minute to turn to me and say, "Johnny, listen to what Chopin is doing here. He changes one little note and the whole piece goes from tragic to loving." Then he'd play that part over and continue.

Still, losing people you really care about is hard, and there's no way around that. I go back to the *Aeneid* where Virgil says of sailors who have died at sea, they will "never again hear someone call their names." He might have added that the people who call the name of someone who has died will no longer hear an answer.

Becoming an Old Man
[4/8/23]

I want to remind you of the story of Pandora. In this Greek myth Pandora was a girl who was always too inquisitive. One day, some mysterious person left her a large box with the instructions, "Don't open this." Pandora tried hard to obey, but by the next morning she couldn't hold out any longer. She lifted the lid of the box, and all the evils of the world flew out, pestilence, pain, greed, illness, and so many more. Pandora slammed the lid shut, but it was too late. Then she heard a little voice coming out of the box. At first, she thought, "I am never going to open it again." But the voice kept calling, "Let me out. Let me out." Pandora, who had a warm heart, opened the lid just a little, and out flew hope.

We are going to need that story because at least at the start of this essay I am going to recount some of the hard things that come with getting old. You may have thought of some of them, but hold tight because I'm going to tell you about a whole bunch. It is important that I do so.

Perhaps it is the physical things that start to go first. Running becomes difficult, perhaps a few years later, walking, and then you might need a cane, then even a walker or a wheelchair. Mentally, of course, things will happen as well. I have noticed that it is hard to remember some nouns, although they do arrive perhaps two to five minutes or hours later. Gradually, the various body systems falter. Sight, hearing, and balance are particularly notable, and perhaps the digestion, the heart, and on and on. You may have never used many medications, but after a while you will have a little bowl that you will carefully refill every morning with eight or more different pills. Or you may have to resort to a pill box divided into each day of the week. And so it continues. Doctor visits become more common, then much more common. You stop driving at night and eventually by day as well. Travel inevitably becomes more difficult. And friends and relatives begin to fall ill and die. So yes, many grim things so that managing becomes more difficult and at times feels almost impossible and overwhelming.

So where does the Pandora story fit in? I am now ninety years old. About twenty years ago, I was in Paris. I was on a bus to go to the apartment of a wonderful French woman, a good friend, for dinner. It was the evening rush hour, and the bus (number 47 to place d'Italie) was very crowded. Unable, like many others, to find an empty seat, I was standing in front of a seat occupied by a young girl of about sixteen, who got up and offered me her seat, "S'il vous plait, monsieur?" I was fine standing in those days (only seventy, after all), but this was such a totally unexpected and beautiful gesture that I thanked her profusely and sat down. Tears came to my eyes. Can people really be so kind? I had never before been offered a seat in a bus. Yes, the indication was that somehow I was no longer perfect, but at the same time I learned that the world could be much more gentle and kind than I had realized.

Over subsequent years, I have had many experiences of both the bad and the good. The former caused by the decay of my body and of my mind and the latter by acts of kindness, such as people holding doors open for me as they see me with my cane or putting my bags of groceries in my cart at the checkout counter. Two days ago, when I was wrestling a large case of bottled water into the trunk of my car, a middle-aged woman who was walking past stopped and said, "Here, let me take that." With grace and ease she carried the heavy case to the trunk of my car and fit it in with the groceries I had already put there. I thanked her, of course, saying to her husband, who was smiling at her as he came up to us, how wonderful she was.

But what I am most grateful for is my connections to my children, who are in their fifties. While I have, of course, a long history with them of being guide, teacher, and director (as well as many other things), progressively, especially in the last five years or so, there has been a steady shifting in our roles. While they still take me seriously, they have also taken to giving me advice and counsel. They have also provided much practical help, bringing me food I love, ordering a movable chair for my bathtub, arranging things with various people working on my house, assisting me with my computer and telephone, and so much else that has never happened before. This shift has been so gentle and kind that our relationship has evolved into one of more equality and reciprocity of care and advice, and now they are doing much more for me than I do for them, all with great warmth.

The story of Pandora has taken on new and greater meaning for me. Yes, there are some awful things that occur now, but there are some incredibly beautiful ones as well.

What Can You Do When Someone Is Dying?
[*10/15/13*]

What can you do when someone is dying? This whole thing of life and death is a bigger deal than I had ever realized. How come it took so long to notice? Because it's too big to see? Too scary to manage?

If death is difficult to deal with, so is the appearance of a life. I remember when my son, our first child, was born. I was so overwhelmed with this new being that all I could manage was wonder about what to do when he cried, this little new thing, how to change a diaper. When my daughter was born, I did a little better. I was amazed at this new life, arriving, just like that! She didn't exist before, and now she existed, this person.

But now, I see people dying. Of course, I saw that before. But at first, as with people being born, it was just something that happened—everyone knows that. Now instead of going to the hospital, you go to the funeral. Everyone stands around or sits around, cries a little, or not, and then it's over. The person who died is no longer there, of course, and the loss may be big. But it happens.

But now I'm beginning to think about Henri Bergson and the *élan vital*, the life essence. Life, coming and going. Coming from nowhere and then at some point, poof, just leaving.

For the doctor caring for a severely ill patient, one minute there she/he is on the bed in front of you, alive. The next minute he/she is still on the bed in front of you but no longer alive.

Life just inhabited this body, but now it doesn't.

The body is there, very much as it was before, but now there's no life in it.

A person comes from nowhere and goes where? Probably to nowhere, but not exactly. Like slugs, we leave our trail after us. But usually, although not always, what we leave is nicer than the scum of the slug, and sometimes it is really incredibly beautiful. Think of your mother, your dad, your grandfather, your uncle Herby, your uncle Raymond, even Alice, your grandfather's second wife.

Life is something really incredible. There are things all around us, of course, but then you have the things that are alive. That's so different.

But what do you do when one of those living things is dying or, as the French say, is disappearing and will soon be *disparu*, will have disappeared? What do you do especially to help them through this, their process of disappearing, of being no more, *en face du néant,* facing nothingness? A person appeared, just like that, and now he/she is going to disappear, just like that. With Alain facing death, I offered to talk about it with him, but he, with his advanced metastatic cancer, said no. Severe illness and death he finds boring. He's not a complainer. He's terrific. So I sent him links to some incredibly beautiful music on YouTube—Shostakovich's fifth piano quintet, Rachmaninoff's third piano concerto, played with so much feeling by Olga Kern.

You can't stop the process of dying. You can't make it disappear.

People say it—and it's true—we are so fragile. The *élan vital* comes, and it goes, just like that.

Death and Stuff
[*7/16/09*]

Sandra and I were sitting at the café Rostand, and I criticized her, saying, "Why didn't you know me before my father died?" I was joking, of course, but at the same time I was serious. We had met for the first time only a few weeks earlier, as I have described elsewhere. Sandra is the French woman who works as a clown in a geriatrics ward and who had arranged for me to follow her around as she worked. On the job she wore a white puffy organdy blouse, red clown nose, braids wired out horizontally from her head, and at her waist an mp3 player playing bird songs. While following her around, I noticed that a few patients avoided her, but many were delighted when they saw her. The same was true of the staff. I asked myself if I had been head of that unit whether I would have let her on. Shamefully, I decided, probably not. After all, a hospital is a solemn place and decorum must be maintained. Afterwards, I asked if she had written up any of her encounters with patients. At first, she said no, but after further conversation, she said yes. She took some papers out of her bag and lent them to me.

In her writings Sandra described, for example, entering the room of one woman who told Sandra that she heard the bells last night. Sandra is not the kind of clown who juggles or does somersaults. Instead, she does the thing that is really hers, which in this case was asking without missing a beat, "What did they say?" The woman replied that they asked her if she was coming and she said, no, not quite yet. I know I have to come soon and I'm in a lot of pain, but I'm not quite ready."

In another encounter, Sandra entered the room of a man with a severe neurological problem who had been mute for many months. Soon, for the first time in ages, he was starting to talk. You see, Sandra is like that. As the clown Annabelle, for many people she is fantasy, feeling, childhood, and they meet her in that part of the human experience. I found her writings so beautiful and moving that I wrote a draft introduction and conclusion to the group of them. When Sandra and I met again at the Rostand, I told her how impressed I was with them and asked if we could try to publish them with my introduction and discussion. She was eager to do so, and we did.

So, here we were at the Rostand again, talking about a conference in which we were both going to be involved and about life. That's when I said, "You have your nerve, why didn't you find me before my father died?" You see, although I am a psychiatrist, I am also a doctor, and as a medical student and later as a medical intern and resident, I saw many people die. Even though that was years ago, I still remember many of them very clearly. But no one ever talked to us about dying. No one taught us about it, about the feelings surrounding it. At that time, and very often still, getting into medicine was like joining the marines. You just do what is expected of you, learn the skills. But feelings, of patients or your own, you just suck them up. You suck them up so well that no one even has to tell you to suck them up. Not talking about feelings is a central part of the training. You do what you need to do, and the other stuff doesn't exist.

And that approach works. Sort of. When my father was dying at the age of ninety-five, fourteen years ago, I was still in that mode. He had a brain tumor, and there was nothing they could do to treat his illness. We could have talked about it, but I had never talked with anyone about death, and it never occurred to me. I was nice and reasonably attentive to him, and then he died. But after meeting Sandra and seeing her work, damn do I feel terrible.

It's not just me. Three weeks ago at a French palliative-care conference (care *en fin de vie,* at the end of life), one young woman recounted this experience: While visiting her very sick mother at the hospital, the doctor took her aside and said, "Your mother is going to have to go to a palliative care unit, please let her know that." The young woman replied, "How can I tell her that, I don't even know what it is." The doctor said, "Okay, I'll have you meet with the social worker." The young woman met with the social worker, who told her that patients received palliative care when there was no hope of cure but added, "When you talk with your mother about it, don't talk about death." You see, I'm not the only one.

So, Sandra was like a ray of light to me, but she came into my life too late to help me talk with my father, about life, about death, about whatever, all the obvious stuff. In his *Six Memos for the Next Millennium,* Italo Calvino quotes Hoffmannsthal, "Depth must be hidden. Where? On the surface." Over the centuries, great writers and thinkers have repeatedly said that the obvious stuff is the most important, and it's what nobody sees.

Not just death, sex too. When I was an intern, I spent half a day a week in an outpatient clinic. One patient, a young man recently married, said to me, "And oh, another thing doctor, my wife and I have been having sexual problems." I had no idea what to say, we never talked about sex in medical school—oh, some lewd jokes, of course, the anatomy and physiology, pathology, and treatment of the sexual organs, but never anything about sex!

I guess some of that has changed now, but there are still a

lot of people who never dealt with those things in their training—like me, and like the French doctor who said, "You will need to talk to the social worker." Wild, isn't it!

Just as Calvino talked about the obvious, Yogi Berra did too. "You can observe a lot by just looking," he reportedly said, and it's one of my favorite quotes. You may have noticed that! The problem with not noticing the obvious is true in the mental health field as well as in baseball. Years ago, I read a report written by Susan Gottschalx a nurse in Moab, Utah, who did a study of people with severe mental illness. Among other things she asked patients how their illness had affected their lives. Nothing striking about that question is there? Yes, there is. I was terribly impressed by it and never forgot it, but it was only years later that I began asking patients I was seeing the same question. When I did, almost always they would perk up immediately and often say something like "You know, you're the first doctor who ever noticed that I have a life?" The relationship might change notably after that. We physicians are trained in all kinds of things related to illness, and there is so much to know that we have always more to learn. But, as with death and sex, we often miss the obvious stuff. It's not just us, of course. Bill Clinton's campaign slogan "It's the economy, stupid" reflects the same idea. As Calvino notes, the obvious is often the most important and the most unnoticed. Sandra, why didn't you come along before my father died?

Death
[*9/28/20*]

Joe died a couple of weeks ago. That's been hard. Death looms larger these days. A lot of people have been dying. Of course, a lot of people have always been dying, but it didn't seem so ominous then. My grandfather died when he was eighty-three. I felt very close to him, but I didn't especially feel his death. He was old after all. My father and I went to his funeral together, and it was good to be with him. I just kind of followed in Dad's wake. Then my lovely aunt Ethel, the youngest of Mom's sisters, died. She was a really good pianist. Then Herb, Mom's brother, died, but that was several years later. I had spent a summer living with him in Cleveland just after I graduated from college. He had been terrific, let me borrow his car, gave me full independence. When I quit the course for which I had come to Cleveland, learning that it was not after all necessary for medical school, Herb sat me down, worried, he said, that since my mother had left college even before the end of her first year, I might be doing something like that. I reassured him that after all, I had graduated from college, was now going to enter med school, and had learned that I didn't actually need the course I had been taking. He said, okay, he just wanted to be sure. And that was that.

When Herb died about eight years later, I was already in my thirties. I went to the funeral, of course, and was fine until he had been laid in his grave and we were returning to the cars. Then, suddenly and unexpectedly, I broke down in sobs. I guess I was really missing him. Strangely, about thirty years later the same kind of thing happened to me. I was about sixty years old and spending time in Paris. It was summer and some French friends who had a place in Normandy invited me out there. I went, and one day I asked if we could visit some of the war memorials from the Allied invasion. They said sure. The wife of the couple with whom I was staying took me, along with her son aged about nine. We drove down along the coast and came to a kind of museum. It included a domed building showing movies of the invasion. The images were all around us on the walls and on the ceiling, where planes dived. It was very impressive and lifelike! Further down the coast we came to the American Cemetery. We went in and came to a little cabin with an old guy inside, behind a counter. I had recalled that a friend of our family, Walter, might have been buried there. He had been a German refugee for whom my father and some friends had signed affidavits in 1938 so he and two other Jewish young men could come to the United States and escape the Nazis. Walter became our friend and was the only one to volunteer for the army. Before being shipped over to Europe, he had left for me his table radio and his sergeant's stripes. A couple of months later we learned that Walter had been killed on the beach during the Normandy invasion, on the day after D Day.

I asked the man in the cabin if he could tell me where Walter's grave was. He paged through a huge handwritten book with thousands of names in it and found Walter's. The man, who had a bunch of little maps, took one, marked where the grave was, and handed it to me. We used the map to find our way among the thousands and thousands of American graves, marked with crosses mostly and a few stars, to Walter's grave. As I was reading the gravestone, suddenly, without any warning and in total shock, I broke down in tears. Fifty years after he had been killed, fifty years! And during all that time I guess I had harbored my sadness!

Anyhow, Joe died a couple weeks ago. Ordinarily I haven't paid a lot of attention to deaths, but somehow they are now registering with me. At our fiftieth high school reunion someone told me Jim Smithers was dead. Jim Smithers was kind of wiry and was on the golf team. I never knew him very well, but we did know each other. (There were three hundred kids in our class, and we were together for six years, so naturally we all knew each other.) Jim was totally confident and always knew how to get along just fine. When I heard that he was dead, I found myself thinking (as I never had before), "I can't imagine this person ever dying. He was just too with it, too much up to whatever life had to offer." At the sixtieth reunion I learned that Monica Howard had died. Monica wasn't at all like Jim. But she did come from an upper-middle-class Protestant family, and in Erie and at Academy High School such people were the kind of the top group. I mean we all were fine together, but you felt that some kids were finer than others, and Monica was maybe the finest of all, the most fine with herself, with her friends, with us all, the most confident and competent.

People like that don't die. I learned at that reunion that Monica had been a diabetic, even took insulin. What?! Jerry Burrow was like that too. He was in my class in med school. A very good student, very competent, very nice. Years after graduation Jerry became dean of the med school. A few years later when we were members of the group of retired professors, he would recognize me and and say, "Hi John." Nice guy. He was another person who clearly would live forever. Now at that point it wouldn't have occurred to me to talk with anyone about such a sentiment. I didn't even know I had thought it. I felt it without noticing. But Jerry died.

Well, of course, a lot of other people have died too. Most I didn't know as well. But some I did: my father, my mother, my aunt Ruthie, my grandmother, tons of people. Alain died, though much younger than I. We were very close even though we only saw each other a couple of times whenever I visited Paris. (Of course, I was often in Paris four times a year.) Terrific person. Alain would walk over through the Jardin du Luxembourg from his office on boulevard Montparnasse to lunch with me at the café Rostand, and we would eat and drink and talk for a couple hours about absolutely everything. He was like a colleague and son to me. I was shocked when he told me one day that he had been diagnosed with lung cancer and was told he would be dead within a year. The next time I was in Paris, Claire, Alain's wife, called me one day to say that he was having chemo and needed someone to sit with him, would I do it. Of course! I asked him if he wanted to talk about death, something I had never done with anyone before but had just learned to do from my friend Sandra, the clown. Alain said, "No. Death is boring." So we didn't, which was kind of a relief. He died soon after.

And wonderful Pernette, iconoclastic Parisian painter, lovely Pernette, the only person I knew who was older than I, even if only by one year. She died in her sleep a couple of months ago, and her daughter sent me an e-mail in the U.S. to let me know.

And Sonya, married to Jim Fowles. Well, I've talked about her elsewhere.

So that's it. Joe died a couple of weeks ago. We had been in the same class at med school, when I had not known him very well. Then a couple of years ago we discovered that we had gotten lockers at the gym not far from each other. We started talking and decided to have lunch. Then we decided to have lunch every month. We'd establish the date for the next lunch at the end of each meal, and early on the morning of the planned lunch Joe would call me just to remind me. The lunches were wonderful. We could talk about anything, things we were trying to figure out, work we were doing, illnesses, experiences, life. No matter what, it was always fascinating. Joe had novel ways of looking at any topic I might bring up. I guess he liked meeting that way as well. Maybe despite the rigidity of the arrangements, or because of it, we felt almost complete freedom.

A couple of months ago Joe was invited to give a retrospective show of his sculptures in Bridgeport. There were all kinds of complications surrounding it—arrangements, transportation of his works, publicity—but it came to pass, and I went down to a presentation Joe gave, explaining his work. He was very good, and there were a lot of people there. It was great for the attendees and for him. But at lunch a couple of weeks later he wasn't doing so well, experiencing shortness of breath and other things. Four weeks later, a day before our planned lunch, his wife, Susan, called me. Joe had lost his short-term memory, she said, and couldn't drive. Could I come over to their house and pick him up? Of course.

Loss of short-term memory is not just a neurological category, it's a horrible thing. Joe couldn't drive because he couldn't remember where he was going or how to get home. When he ordered lunch, he couldn't remember what he had ordered. Although anything that did not require short-term memory, like our conversations, was fine, anything that did was lost. He had become a kind of slave in the world of reality.

Two weeks after our second lunch that way, Susan called to say that Joe was in the hospital. When I called later, it wasn't clear what was wrong, but apparently many things were. Covid had come, so visiting was impossible. Not long after that he was home again and asked me to come over and take him out to lunch. I explained that with the virus now, that was impossible. Several days after that he was in a palliative-care facility, and in another few days Joe was dead.

Apparently, he had a kind of fulminating amyloidosis, a situation in which a strange protein called amyloid invades all the organs of the body. It so happens that I have amyloid cardiac disease, but mine appears to be stable and to have been stable more or less for a couple of years.

Joe is dead. We only met once a month, but I miss him. We understood each other amazingly and connected in a very special way. His death is totally not fair. It is a real loss. It is certainly not fair to him, and it has left a hole in my life.

Nothing to Write About
[*11/28/17*]

I have waited for some muse or inspiration these last several days, but none has appeared. That is unusual for me, but the reason is not a lack of things to write about, rather it is the overwhelming amount of them.

With all the news I wonder if our democracy is disappearing. Most of them in the past have, you know. Governmental systems do change sooner or later, all of them. Although I have been pretty critical of ours, I do not want to lose it. But it does seem to be going, in dribs and bits, or in huge chunks, like the polar ice caps are.

At another level, people are getting sick with major, possibly fatal illnesses.

And less significant, things are breaking. My alarm system just went out, and within two days my water heater died of old age. At least, those are both fixed now. Some things you can fix.

But as terrifying, sad, or just plain annoying as these things are, I can take comfort in the people I meet everyday. The guy who replaced my water heater works in the evenings with a companion who he says is wonderful, capable, always available. I gather they both have day jobs. My guy, Bill, has a daughter in college. He says she is doing great, wants to be a psychologist, a professor. He thinks it would be better if she was a school psychologist because she could find a job near here rather than leaving for some distant place in the country. He says she's a terrific girl.

On Monday, at the Yale gym, I ran into the fencing coach

again. We are the same age. He is in terrific shape but congratulates me for walking up the stairs to the locker room rather than taking the elevator. Still, he says, laughing, it would also be good if I paid more attention to my diet. The fencing team is okay this year, he reassures me. I guess they really don't start serious practice until after Christmas.

I was at Edge of the Woods today to buy cider, cashew nuts, and peanut butter. The latter I make right there by pouring nuts into the grinder, then holding down the "on" button. Leaving, I passed a young woman giving away samples of something. She smiled as she said good-bye to me. I said, "What a great smile." She said, "Yours is too."

The amazing thing is that in such troubled times there are so many people who can be so great. Maybe especially the people leading workaday lives.

Il me manque
[*3/29/22*]

"*Il me manque,*" he is missing to me. The French phrase has especially the sense that something is missing. Perhaps one's intelligence, the ability to remember something, a basic thing like a leg, or a person. It conveys the possibility of a whole range of things, from the most trivial to the most fundamental, the very deepest. The French phrase carries with it an immense range of possibilities in contrast to the English "I miss you." I miss old-time movies, I miss going to the beach. But these aren't big things, not severe hardships (depending on the tone of voice maybe), and that's in keeping with the idea of a stiff upper lip or narrow range of feelings that is acceptable.

As I've mentioned, my friend Bob died three weeks ago, on Sunday, March 6. Now that's a strange one. One of his adopted daughters, Lili, called the day after, March 7, to tell me. Bob had two adopted daughters. He had had a vasectomy before or early in his second marriage, but then his wife and he decided they wanted kids. They arranged to get one from China, went there, and spent some weeks there to get her. That was Lili. Later they wanted another child and went to Argentina, I think, to get Ani. Lili had some problems with her feet. Ani had other, big problems—with her vision, I think. I don't recall ever meeting the daughters or even hearing their voices until Lili called at the end of Bob's life. But she, on the phone, acted as though she knew me. I feel partly like an old guy who has just heard about her and partly as though she is almost my own daughter.

I guess that reflects how it has been with Bob and me these last years. Partly, we knew each other very well, having shared so much since we first became close friends in junior high. Partly, we had drifted apart since he left Erie for Cornell and I left Erie for Swarthmore. We had been together almost constantly in junior high and high school, taking the same classes, spending afterschool time at his house or at mine, going to movies on Saturday afternoon and afterwards to Polako's for sundaes, at Sunday school bugging our teachers there, latching on to our teacher Frank Fox (who taught us about Buddhism, Spinoza, and Montaigne), listening to Brahms or Ravel or Prokofiev on records that we bought at the music store where Bob talked knowledgeably with the owners, sometimes on Saturdays going to WLEU (the radio station), where we had made friends with the disc jockey and sat with him and talked together while he was playing a record. Even when I made the swimming and water polo teams, Bob, who wasn't a great swimmer, became the team manager. We were both on the debate team and did well in the competitions. Since he was Rosenthal, RO, and I was Strauss, ST, and the classes weren't that big, we often sat next to or behind each other in class—in Latin, German, or English, where we had the Victorian, statuesque Miss Winifred Mong. Bob was often talking or drawing, anything to avoid paying attention, and often being very funny. One day in Latin class Mrs. Ryder was trying to teach us grammar and turned to Bob with a question. He didn't have a clue what she had asked, and I, sitting just behind him, whispered what I thought was the answer, "Absolute, ablative absolute." He spoke up, "Ablative absolute." Mrs. Ryder turned on her heel and said sharply, "Bob, I'm disappointed in you. There is no way this could have been ablative absolute." I sank into my seat, ashamed and chagrined, but said nothing, feeling that if

I spoke up that would just make everything even worse. Poor Bob, too, said nothing. But "ablative absolute" became a code phrase between us when I was giving advice. Before we graduated from high school, Bob had already published a poem in *The Atlantic*, "To Tame a Fox," based on the St-Exupéry book *The Little Prince*. Bob may also have published something in *The New Yorker*, I don't remember for sure.

Our connection was much more erratic after we separated to go to our different colleges. Yet in some strange ways, not. I guess during those teen years we became attached a little like with protons. One such proton could be in California and the other in Connecticut, but if the configuration of one changed so did that of the other—instantly. While away at our separate colleges Bob and I had almost no contact. Yet when we did see each other during holidays or summer, we were like those two protons. Once I was concerned I might have gotten a girl pregnant. That is to say, I knew it was physically impossible, but the girl was worried. Bob and I were in Erie on vacation, and he said, "Don't worry, if she's pregnant, I'll marry her," even though they had never met. And weirder still, even though I knew that was totally ridiculous, I felt relieved.

Over successive years we continued to see each other but only intermittently. I would get tired of his constant joking or his never seeming particularly interested in what I had to say. His life seemed to be full of dramatic things: He had a girlfriend who was the daughter of a genius professor at Cornell; he married a brilliant woman who had escaped from the Warsaw Ghetto as a child; he was involved with the Blackstone Rangers racial justice group in Chicago; or whatever. Yet we never failed to talk with each other when we were in the same city, or on the phone every month or so, or for birthdays. Then his wife, Kris, died, and he remarried, His second wife, Mary, was a kind of new age psychologist but very bright and impressive. She took a job in California, so they moved there, to Santa Barbara. When I visited my son, Jeff, in Los Angeles, Bob and I would meet for lunch in a small restaurant halfway between. Later he moved to LA, and we would see each other there. I often felt we had become distanced from each other, and getting together was not much fun. Yet, at the same time, it was still special. Like two protons, we were attached, no matter what. We had all this history together. And it was somehow very lovely, though very strange.

Bob stopped work when he moved to California with Mary and never got his psychologist's license there. I had no idea where he got the money to live on and never asked. They adopted the two girls, then got divorced. He continued to be busy with stuff, although I was never clear what or even aware I didn't know since we always had much to talk about. One thing, he was writing a version of "The Grand Inquisitor" from Dostoyevsky's *Brothers Karamazov*. Bob worked on that year after year, but although he said he would, he never sent me a draft. In his mid-eighties (our mid-eighties!) he fell down and was unconscious for a while until one of his two sons (by his first wife, Kris—both now in California) found him. Bob seemed to be okay but moved from a regular apartment to an assisted living place. We continued to talk on the phone every month or so and always on our birthdays. He would ask me to send what I was writing, which I did, including my autobiography, *To Understand a Person*. He sometimes made comments that seemed often a bit dismissive. I would ask him how the Grand Inquisitor was going, and he would say he was making small changes and would send me a draft, which he never did.

One day I called and left a message, but he never called back. That was the first time that had ever happened. Then

Lili called me. Bob had gotten very sick, kidney problems and other things. He went to a hospice place, and then on March 6, he died. My Bob died.

I called Lili a week later, just to talk and to see how she was doing. When I told her how hard it was to lose him, though sometimes I was okay, she said, "I know. It comes in waves." "Yes," I said, "I hadn't thought about it that way, but that's exactly right. It comes in waves."

D Day
[9/3/14]

I just had an afternoon snack and thought I would sit down and write this. The snack was a half bowl of cornflakes with milk and sugar. I rarely have an afternoon snack, not like when I was a kid and had one pretty much every afternoon. When I was in sixth grade, I had transferred to Glenwood School, a public school, from the Erie Day School, a private school but which my mother now thought was just becoming a socialite plaything.

Glenwood was much closer to home, only a mile away. Douggie Young and I walked there every day. We walked home to lunch at noon and then back to school to play baseball with the other kids before the afternoon started. At first when I went to Glenwood the kids teased me because I had been to a private school that had long vacations and ended early and where, they said, we didn't learn anything. But after a couple of days they saw I knew as much as they did and stopped. Douggie was there. So was Jim Thomas, who was later on the Academy High water polo and swimming teams with me. The Brown boys, William and Robert, kind of country kids and William not too bright. Barbara (Bobby) Ann Smith, tall and thin, who liked me (and still did when I saw her at our fiftieth high school reunion). Joyce Cooley, small and full of life, whom I also saw at the fiftieth reunion. And, of course, there was Patty Baker who was beautiful and with whom I fell in love, although we never saw each other out of class. She lived with her parents in a trailer in the woods and disappeared after sixth grade.

In those days we lived on Cherry Street, 4524 or something,

the right side of Cherry Street as you go up the hill. Next door lived Milton, who Dad said was involved with the black-market meat business and whom we didn't like much. Kitty corner across from us lived George, one year older than I. He was kind of preoccupied with himself, like his father, Ralph. A couple of years later when Bob and I joined the Boy Scouts, George was the patrol leader. We impeached him, but we didn't know that if you impeached someone you had to plan to have someone else elected to replace him. George was quickly reelected, and Bob and I quit the Scouts. George's mother, Hilda, was such a contrast to George and his father. She was ravishingly beautiful, tall and slender. I think she was Hungarian. They had had to flee Europe. Dad told a story of one day seeing Ralph and saying, "Would you like a ride downtown? I have my car." And Ralph replied, "You have a car! I have two cars!"

Douggie and I spent a lot of non-school time together. We played games of hide and seek with other kids in the neighborhood in the evening well after dark—home free was the tree in our front yard. As I mentioned, we walked together to and from school. Sometimes we filched a golf ball off the seventh hole of the small city course since that hole was over a hill from the rest of the course and the players couldn't see it 'til they got to the hole. In the summer we had water fights at his house, which was one block up the dirt road from ours. Each of us had a hose, and used garbage can tops for shields. Their dog, Tippy, a middle-sized slender animal with smooth black hair and a white tuft on her tail, would run barking around the yard with us. Douggie's younger sister Marilyn was very pretty. (Shortly after we started junior high, Douggie and his family moved to Olympia, Washington, because Douggie's father was transferred there.)

My family was often visited on Cherry Street by the "three boys," Walter Strauss, Fritz something, and a third whose name

I can't remember. They were actually young men, German refugees for whom Dad, Milton Schaffner, and Bernie Gottlieb had signed affadivits (whatever they were) so they could leave Germany and come to the States. Walter was our favorite. He was short and lovely, kind and bright. The other two went into business and, I guess, did all right. Walter, though, thought he should try to repay the country that took him in and joined the army. He became a sergeant and, before he was sent overseas, gave me his sergeant's stripes and his small table radio. I kept the latter next to my bed for many years.

On June 6, 1944, Douggie came to our back door in the morning and shouted out, "Hey Johnnie." He always did this. I think we had a back doorbell, but he never used it.

Douggie had a paper route, and sometimes I would go with him, even on collection days. He would go to each front door, ring the bell and say "Collecting," and people would bring him the thirty-six cents for a week of the *Erie Dispatch Herald*. On this morning of June 6 Douggie was really excited. "Come on, Johnnie, I've got extras to sell. It's D Day, and they've put out a morning paper for it." We went down the five blocks to the corner of Peach and Cherry, a major intersection one block away from Glenwood School with a drugstore where you could get comic books, two-for-a-penny fireballs, and MaryJane caramels on the way to school in the morning.

We shouted "Extra, extra, special D Day edition!" The papers were all gone in no time.

It just struck me, having my snack of corn flakes today, that at the very same time that Douggie and I were shouting "Extra, extra" on the corner of Peach and Cherry, Walter Strauss, who had been shipped to England, was lying dead on Omaha Beach.

We found that out later, of course.

I still had his sergeant's stripes and the little radio.

X14-598
[*1/10/23*]

X 14-598, that was the phone number of Rose Trimble. Rose was my first real girlfriend (unless you count Alexa Collins and Barbara Pixler in second grade). We were thirteen years old and in seventh grade. Everyone had moved from their elementary school to junior high. In our case this was to Academy High School, which was an imposing building "high on the hill" at Erie's south end. Its big football stadium was used by all the city's high schools. As seventh-graders, we little kids had to be careful in the halls not to get run over by the football players and other senior high kids who seemed monstrous in size. They were not mean, just unlikely to notice us scurrying around under foot. Like them, we went to the Friday morning pep rallies in the auditorium, where the cheer leaders and the band were already on the stage to cheer for the football team. Those of us in seventh grade were there to learn the cheers and the songs. "Oh, we're loyal to you, gold and blue, and to you we will always be true," songs like that. I remember Rose first from Miss Brailey's geography class. Slender, blonde, and blue-eyed, she had, like Bob and half our class, came to Academy from Jefferson Elementary School, not Glenwood, where I and Barbara Smith and Joyce Cooley, the Brown brothers, and many others were from.

Rose was beautiful, very smart, and very shy. I remember one day she left class in the middle looking very wan. I think she was sick. I don't remember exactly how it happened, but I started calling her from my house after school, and we would talk. A couple of times we saw each other outside of school. I would take my bicycle to her house, which was in a newly developed area on the south edge of town, and we would go bike riding together. When it came time for the annual junior high prom, I invited her and she accepted. I bought her a gardenia corsage, and she had a beautiful white, or was it light blue, formal gown. Her mother pinned the flower on it. We danced together, waltzes and foxtrots, which I had just learned in dancing school, newly admitted since it now accepted some Jewish kids. Somebody, maybe my parents, must have driven us to the dance and then taken us home afterwards. I never kissed Rose. Never ever.

Over the years Rose became friends with Patty Ulrich and Emily Albright, and I started spending time with other kids and got onto the swimming and water polo and debating teams. Other than in a class or two, in the cafeteria, or in the hall, Rose and I rarely saw each other.

Much later, at the fiftieth reunion of our class, Rose and I danced together. She said something along the lines that she was more than just an Erie girl, meaning, I guess, that she was more than I had recognized. I think she probably was. I certainly had fallen in love with her. X14-598.

Gute Nacht
[*9/28/11*]

My brother-in-law, Mike Cohn, died two weeks ago. He died of a glioblastoma, a horrible invasive brain tumor that grew very fast. He went downhill and died much more quickly than was predicted so at least had a very short period of disability and no pain—a silver lining of sorts.

When you called Mike and Sue, Mike would answer the phone with an intimidating, Teutonic "Mike Cohn." He had come over from Germany in the 1930's to escape the Nazis. He and his older brother traveled with his mother, "Mu" (for *mutter*, mother). His father, a Communist, had come a year earlier. So far as I know, the father more or less disappeared from Mike's life after that. The brother went on to become very rich. Mike became the errand boy for "Mu." She was tough but a survivor, probably the model for Mike's saying about mountain climbers: "No matter what difficult and hazardous mountain you climb, three German women will always have been there before you." Mike became a curator at the Brooklyn Children's Museum and, after retirement and up to the month he died at the age of eighty-eight, a writer of self-published books. They were historical novels, carefully documented stories about young people: a Norwegian boy of the twelfth century who becomes a merchant and sails around the North Cape to trade with the Russians; a southern girl from a Tory family during the American Revolution who, in transit by American boat to the British occupied city of New

York, is taken prisoner by the British; *Black Men of the Sea;* subjects like that.

Mike didn't finish college until helped to do so by my parents when he was in his forties. He never went further, but he knew everything. I first met him when I was in college. When I walked the streets of midtown Manhattan with him, he would look in store windows and tell you the origins of one or another object, a shoe or a particular kind of watch, and its historical significance. At first, I loved being with him, as, many years later, did my son. But Mike had a problem. He had to show off his knowledge in every situation. When my daughter graduated as a history major from Amherst, at the college graduation lunch Sarah's history professor came over to meet us and congratulate her, and Mike began lecturing, teaching history to the history professor. Mike's need to dominate all conversation was so bad that after a while, no one could stand being with him. It was sad. He wasn't mean. He was very kind and very smart. He just couldn't control his impulse to dominate.

Our father, Susan's and mine, was also a dominating presence. He loved to tell stories, even if it meant interrupting someone who was also talking. At his ninety-fifth birthday party and a reunion for our extended family of about fifty-five people, I got up to say some nice words about Dad, but I had barely started when he stood up and began telling a story. Maybe he hadn't heard me, I don't know. It was okay but nothing new. Dad's own parents had come over from Germany to settle in Loudonville, Ohio, where their aunt Nanny lived with her rag-seller husband. They came when they were young adults. Dad hated his father, who, he said, shouted and yelled and never accomplished anything. This was not entirely accurate because that same father, having started as an assistant to a rag dealer, became co-owner of the town general store, then the town banker, and eventually town mayor. He was elected mayor even though his was the only Jewish family in Loudonville.

When I was in seventh grade, I got a C minus in math. Dad looked at the report card and said, "How did that happen? Should I talk to your teacher?" I said no, that wasn't necessary and after that got all A's for the rest of junior and all of senior high. It wasn't fear he wanted to instill, rather the idea, "If you're going to do something, do it right." That was a very serious idea for us. When I cut the grass, Dad would look at it and say, "You missed a part there." I would fix it and never miss it again. The message was clear, uncomplicated, and seemed basically very important.

Dad hated Germans, not individual people just the conglomerate. "They eat with their fork in the left hand and never put it down, shoveling food in their mouth." "They don't take baths more than once a week or even less." But he liked to tell German stories that came from his family. A favorite concerned the name of the underwear company BVD, which, he said, stood for *Besser Wie Drek* (better than shit). The V had to be considered a W for the story to work, but no one cared. Dad also loved thick sliced ham and *Kartoffel Salat* (potato salad). When I was little, after I got into bed, Dad would come into my room, put his hand on my shoulder and say softly in his Loudonville version of the German language, "*Gute nacht. Schlaf gut*" (good night, sleep well).

When I was in Europe for the year in 1956, I and my friend Mubahat Turker, a lovely, bright, and soft-spoken Turkish girl whom I had met at the Alliance Française, went by motorcycle to visit my friend Traudel in Vienna. I had avoided going to Germany until then, but crossing part of Germany was the best way to get to Vienna from Paris. At the border, a brutish German border guard talked to us roughly in that guttural language (which I had studied in high school and college and really liked learning). I thought to myself, "Listen buddy, we won the war, not you." A few hours later my motorcycle had engine trouble. There had been problems before, and I had taken it to a Paris mechanic who did a terrible job on it. In a small German town a local mechanic fixed it rapidly and without fuss, and from that day on it ran beautifully. Mubahat and I went to a small restaurant, where they had *Kartoffel Salat* and *Speck* (ham) on the menu. I ordered it and felt very much at home. How weird was that!

I had a dream last night. In the dream my father had just died (in fact, he died sixteen years ago), and our family friend Randy, who also happened to be our rabbi, came into the room and sympathetically said to me how difficult it was to live as a man without an older man to guide you.

Mike, you were a good kind person, impossible to spend much time with but lovely and very smart. And you wrote some great books.

I bid you, "*Gute nacht. Schlaf gut.*"

"It's Not the 1940's, After All"
[*6/8/15*]

As I was going down the stairs to the Bass Library at Yale recently, a young woman passed me as she was coming up. She didn't look at me, at the beautiful blue sky above us, or even at the stairs. She was staring at the little rectangle she held in her hand. I have gotten used to that, of course, or at least have tried to. My friends tend to put their little rectangles away when we meet for coffee or breakfast or lunch. I think it's because I blurt out unkind things if they put them down on the table when we get together. I know "it's not the 1940's, after all," but much as I try, I can't get used to it.

It was Tommy who first said that to me. It's strange that of all people he was the one. Tommy is pretty much in charge of Aquilla Motors now. It's a small but very successful auto repair place in the center of Westville, about four blocks from my house. It's a wonderful place. I first started going there when I moved to Westville over thirty years ago. Bill Aquilla ran it then. He was small, wiry, no nonsense, I think a first-generation American of Italian descent. He really knew cars and ran a tight shop but always had kind words and some wise observations about the world to share—plus a great smile.

Bill died of cancer of the pancreas about six years ago. He wasn't all that old. Then his son Tom, Tommy's father, took over. The place still ran well. Tom's wife, Mona, or daughter Stephanie often worked at the cash register and made out the bills and receipts. They were all efficient, but never too busy to smile broadly when you came in, say something about the weather, how the business was going, or make a nice comment about how you looked.

Tom ran the place for several years but somehow seemed to like talking about cars or the business rather than running it, though he never complained—well, maybe a little. Young Tommy worked there too and in his early twenties seemed to be increasingly taking over. And he was good. Still fun to talk to and greet like his father and grandfather but clearly interested in running the operation. None of the Aquillas were ever too busy to explain to you what they were doing, what your car needed and why, or even occasionally to offer to drive me home if the car had to stay at the garage. I started buying all my gas there just so I could see them and pass the time of day for a couple of minutes.

About two months ago when I stopped in for gas, Tommy told me that they were going to take out the gas pumps and only do repairs. He said that the state required that they replace the underground gas tanks because of their age. That was going to cost many thousands of dollars and it really wasn't worth it since they never made money from selling the gas anyway. He had told me before about not making money from the gas.

Soon after, when I passed by, I saw the diggers, the holes in the ground, the absent gas pumps, and the flat ground that replaced them now covered with cars to be repaired. Of course, I couldn't go there for gas anymore, but last Friday I called to make an appointment for an overdue oil change.

I went in on Monday, and of course Tommy and I got to talking. I said I missed coming by for gas and talking with them and asked him how things were working out. He said, partly as though he were teaching and maybe just a little defensively, "Things are going great. As you can see, we've got more business than we can handle. And now we don't have to go out every few minutes to give someone five dollars worth of gas or something. (Although the gas was self-service, someone always came out to work the pump for you. It reminded me a bit of the Atlantic gas station in Erie where Dad had an account. We always bought gas there, and the guy who came out to pump it always said, "Clean your windshield?" When I was sixteen and had just started to drive, I was coming home from a date when the car died not far from that Atlantic station. I was scared, had I done something wrong? I called home from the payphone on the corner and Dad said, "No, it's fine. Go to the Atlantic station, tell them who you are, and they'll take care of you." Wow, talk about a reassuring Dad. And they did take care of me. They put a new battery in, and off I went.)

I told Tommy I totally understood why they got rid of the gas tanks but said I missed the old days anyway. "It's not the 1940's anymore," he replied in a kindly voice, still teaching, "Now a guy sits in a little box and never comes out and handles the money and the automatic pumps. That's how the world is going. There are hardly any of the old stations left." "I know," I said, "and I know in a lot of ways it's better now, but I still miss it." "It just isn't the 1940's anymore," he said again, still trying to teach me but still maybe feeling a little wistful himself. He hadn't been alive in the forties, of course, but I think in that family he got the idea.

When I was going down the stairs to the Bass Library the next day and saw that girl looking at the little rectangle she held in her hand, I repeated Tommy's words to myself, "It's not the 1940's anymore." It was impossible to say "Hi" to her.

Im Spital ist im Spital
[*9/3/19*]

I had a patient when I was a third-year medical student on my surgery rotation, an older German guy. Lean, pleasant, clearly sick, he was being "worked up" for a thyroid problem. I went off the rotation before they came up with a diagnosis, but someone told me they had found that he had a thyroid cancer. Then I saw him on a stretcher in the corridor and told him I had heard about the diagnosis. "*Im Spital ist im Spital*," he replied in a kindly way. I have never forgotten his words.

These last few days they have come to me more and more often. What exactly do they mean? The literal translation, of course, is "In the hospital is in the hospital." But I think he was telling me that some things you just can't fight, you need to accept. Now that may seem like a pretty mundane notion, but the more I think about it, I believe he was trying to teach me (and maybe persuade himself of) one of the most crucial principles of existence.

Oh, come now! No, really. You see, one of the big things I have seen in my own family is people, good people, who have given up. My father is one. He quit college in his second year when his mother died and his father was hospitalized and settled more or less into working for his dictatorial father-in-law. Much later he gave up the possibility of getting his college degree at the University of Pittsburgh extension because he would have been required to leave Erie for six months to spend time at the Pittsburgh campus, and my mother threatened to move back to Cleveland if he did that. So, he didn't.

My mother quit college before the end of her first year. She got married, moved to Erie, which she hated, and had kids. She tried again and again to engage in political action and artistic creativity, each time facing major odds.

And my sister, too, quit college before the end of her first year. She married a guy even more assertive in his Teutonic way than my father, becoming more and more passive, then more and more fat, then virtually immobile without an electric wheelchair.

As I write this, I am overwhelmed. I have never put these facts about my family members all together before. Now you see why, for me, fighting (in my quiet way) has been a question of survival. I saw giving up all around me and the devastation that it involved. I couldn't let that happen! I have worked very hard, often against anxiety, sometimes without sleep, to make sure it didn't. I have never accepted the idea of giving up.

But now, of course, I am dealing more and more with the inevitable. My physical abilities are lessening, I have problems with walking and shortness of breath. I am still very lucky. I can drive, unlike Bob. I can walk without a cane or walker, unlike Bob and my sister. And my head is reasonably clear. I can think creatively, write papers and comment more or less wisely on people's work. Sometimes I am unable to remember names and nouns when needed, but you can usually slide around that, and the words often come to you later.

So that's the lesson of *Im Spital ist im Spital* that is most important for me now. Sometimes you really do have to accept that fighting against fate can be dumb. There does come a time when *Im Spital ist im Spital* must be accepted. Of course, it is not always so clear when that time has come.

Humanity
[7/25/17]

In a sense, "discovering" humanity was even more difficult than "discovering" science. I think I had always been pretty compassionate and sympathetic and to my knowledge had never gotten into the "I know what you're thinking way down deep" that is often a problem with learning psychoanalytic theories and psychotherapy practice. Well, maybe a little, but never too much. Sometimes, on an airplane I begin talking with my neighbor and am asked what I do or did. When I answer, "I'm a psychiatrist," the other person often comes back with "Oh, oh, you can read my mind." To which, I reply, "No need to worry. I can't even read my own." And I mean it. We both laugh. Relatively early on, I wrote research papers with titles like "The Person with Hallucinations as a Person." I meant that too.

But even though I think I was more a humanizing than a dehumanizing psychiatrist, it was still a shock to me when a young woman with schizophrenia with whom I was conducting a follow-along research interview asked me, "Why don't you ever ask me what I do to help myself?" My research group had already gone beyond the common process of focusing only on questions about symptoms and treatments to add questions on work, living setting, and friends, so I was especially surprised with a question signaling that we had left out something so basic as the capacity of the person him- or herself.

I was into my forties by then, with many years of psychiatry research and practice behind me. How could I have never thought to ask about her own active role in her life. Even today it is hard to believe we could have been so blind. You see, as I discovered progressively over the next years and am still struggling with, she was raising the question of subjectivity, her own actions, which necessarily reflected her own decisions, her feelings (not just "affects"), and her way of seeing the world. How could we have missed it? One reason, I think, is that medicine tends to be an objectifying field. This is not necessarily bad. It provides a way of trying to understand very complex phenomena, illnesses, by focusing just on the "facts." The implicit assumption is that a person has something wrong with them that can be clearly identified and that comes from a problem, genetic, bacteriologic, traumatic, or whatever.

A further problem connected to missing something so basic as the role of the person in working to solve their issues is that many of us have the "we know it/do it already" problem. That is, as experts we believe we look at the illness objectively, and that gives us the approach and skill to know how to think about it. I later learned about a philosophical article, "What Is It Like to Be a Bat" (Thomas Nagel, 1974), that deals with the problems of putting oneself in the place of another being. And it is that kind of subjectivity to which my follow-along patient's question leads. Over subsequent years I have learned how much literature, theater, film, painting, even music, contribute to answering her "Why don't you ever ask me" question. One of the basic problems is a physician, or a "professional" of any kind, an expert, is supposed to know stuff, and what the issue of subjectivity raises is the issue of not knowing. By not knowing I mean learning how to know you don't know, and thus how you need to listen, ask questions, reflect, feel. An example: Around the time the young woman asked me that question I had already treated and interviewed at least a hundred patients who had auditory hallucinations, heard voices. Then, while on a sabbatical in Toronto, I came to know an occupational therapist who had collaborated in developing one of the very earliest, "voice hearing" tapes. These were tape recordings of "hallucinated" voices. She and two colleagues had produced these tapes by having one person record what he thought might be the kind of "voices" that a person with auditory hallucinations might hear. They then asked people with auditory hallucinations to listen to the recordings and suggest what would make the voices sound like "real" auditory hallucinations. They revised the tapes accordingly. My friend asked me if I wanted to hear the tapes and I said, "Of course." Sitting in a living room, I put the earphones on my ears and started listening. The voice would start, go on for a while, and suddenly stop. Then it would come back but at a volume so low I couldn't understand what it was saying. Then it started making comments about me, criticizing me, then fading away, coming back, and continuing along the same lines. Around this point, my friend asked me to select a movie we might go and see that evening. I found myself resenting that she was interrupting my voices and wished she would stop talking. Finally, I started looking through a guide to what movies were on but couldn't find any movies, not just movies I wanted to see, but any movies at all. I was that distracted by my voices. And all the time, of course, I realized that my "voices" were on tape that I could turn off at any time, they were not inside my head and beyond my control. It was a very shocking experience. It was the first time that I began to have a sense of how much I didn't know about the experiences my patients were having.

Several weeks later I was back at work and conducting a research interview with a young man who had auditory hallucinations and whom I had interviewed before several times at regular intervals. Now, his voices notwithstanding, he had started to go back to college for the third time. Rather than proceeding to what now seemed to me to be our canned questions ("Is it a man's voice or a woman's voice?" "What does it say?" and so on), I felt tremendous admiration for his courage and effort, something that had never occurred to me before my own experience with "voices." As a result, my attitude toward him and my reactions were entirely different from our previous interviews when he had described the same sort of things.

So, subjectivity. One problem in our field, as I mentioned above, is that we are experts and thus "know" and "understand" and have not learned to not know. And apparently, assuming that we know or should know is not limited to us mental health types. At one point I was interviewed for a psychiatric newsletter by a reporter who specialized in our field. He started out by saying he understood that I was interested in subjectivity and then rapidly followed up with the comment, "But you've been working on subjectivity for quite a long time." Seized with a mixed feeling of guilt (Why is it taking me so long to solve the problem of subjectivity?) and anger (Damn it, this is complicated!), I responded vaguely in an attempt not to be rude. Days later, I thought maybe I could have said something like, "Well you know, humanity has been trying to solve the problems of subjectivity since well before the days of Euripides," but, of course, that thought was far too late.

Not knowing permits, rather requires us to listen, reflect, and try an approximate understanding of how it is for another person. In that quest, our own experiences and the arts are a crucial contribution (uncertainty theory).

So, you see, we have now gone from learning to appreciate

science, the beauty of measurement, research design, data analysis, to dealing with the profound and diverse mysteries of subjectivity.

But why make such a fuss about this vague subjectivity stuff? Because a central aspect of our field is to realize what an experience of another person is. When, for example, we ask the question "Do you hear voices when there is no one around?" We need to know that our concept may be "voices," but if the person answers yes, the experience for them is almost certainly not just "voices" but may include terror, shame, fury, despair, or some complex combination of feelings. And the possibilities for the compound experience are extremely diverse. One person I talked with during a research interview said that she hallucinated the voice of Barbara Streisand. Barbara Streisand turned out to be her favorite singer, and for that person, her voices were a real pleasure. Although that kind of thing is not very common, it is not rare either. At the first "voice hearers" congress, which was held in Maastricht, Netherlands, in 2009, many participants showed no evidence of psychiatric problems and described their voices as being helpful—for example, making helpful suggestions about what they should do—and some people even wondered how people managed to get through their lives without hearing voices. That conference had been called by Marius Romme and Sandra Escher, who went on Dutch television to invite anyone who heard voices to attend. That method of "sampling" meant that there was no assumption that voices were always pathologic and thus attracted people for whom "voices" represented a whole range of experiences. It demonstrated the degree to which assuming "voices" were necessarily pathological might need to be seriously questioned. It thus raised questions about some of the very foundations of psychiatric thinking.

Scenario One
[4/21/08]

(Based on a role play with Raquel)

Darkened stage. Barely visible a figure seated in a straight-backed wooden chair facing the audience near front stage left. An empty easy chair a few feet away with a small plain table between the two chairs.

Moderate light. Enter stage right a young man dressed in sport jacket and tie, short haircut, looking like young eager professional.

Light comes up full.

D (*young doctor*): Hello, I'm Dr. Strauss. Have you been waiting long?
P (*person in chair; a young man, a bit disheveled, long hair mussed, four-day beard*): It's all right. I've been talking with my friends.
D (*looking around, seeing no one*): Did they come with you?
P: Oh, they're always with me
D: Oh (*sitting down in easy chair*). Well, what brings you to the clinic today?
P: Well, certainly not my friends.
D: They don't help with transportation?
P: Are you kidding?
D: Well, how did you happen to come here today?
P: I took the bus.

D: I mean why.

P: Well, I've been pretty upset.

D: Yes.

P: What do you mean yes? Everybody seems to think I'm going out of my mind.

D: I'm sorry. I just meant go ahead.

P: Oh.

D: You were going to tell me why you came to the clinic.

P: Well, I have these neighbors on Skiff Street, and they have these two dogs who are always barking. I think they're dealing drugs

D: The dogs?

P (*looking at D like he's kooky or stupid*): No, not the dogs, the neighbors. But I hear the neighbors talking a lot. Sometimes they seem to be talking about me. They look at my house, sometimes even point. I'm worried they're planning something.

D: Planning something?

P: I don't know, maybe they think I've been spying on them.

D: Have you?

P: Well, a little. They scare me. I hear sounds at that house all times of the night and hear their voices.

D: And that brings you here to the clinic?

P: Yes, because no one else seems to be paying attention or care. There are never any police around or anything and the other neighbors never do anything.

D (*fidgeting a little in his chair*): So you think the problem is yours?

P: No, not really. I've called the police a couple of times, they came once and then just went away, and the next time I called they just said, well, they hadn't found anything so if I heard any gunshots or anything I should call them again.

D: Have you had any experiences like this before?

P: Like what?
D: Well, like bad neighbors?
P: Well, once I lived near a college, and they had parties all night long that kept me awake.
D: So you moved?
P: Well, I complained to the police then too, but that didn't do any good so, yes, finally I moved.
D: How has your health been generally?
P: Why do you ask?
D: Well, you came to the clinic so I thought maybe you were having some problems with your health.
P: No, I'm okay.
D: Haven't seen a doctor for anything or gone to other clinics.
P: No, but my mother says I should go and get a checkup.
D: A checkup for anything special?
P: No, just a checkup. She worries a lot.
D: Does she have any health problems she sees a doctor for?
P: Oh yeah, arthritis and stuff like that. She's always complaining about something.
D: Any other people in your family with health problems?
P: Well, I have a sister with SDHD or something.
D: And you, what do you do? How do you spend your time?
P: Oh, I'm a drama student at Yale University.
D: How's that going?
P: I just had a play produced at the Cabaret. It didn't go very well.
D: That's too bad. Well, I'm not sure what I can do for you. Just let me ask you some other questions, though, since you came to this clinic and it's a mental health clinic. Do you get depressed?
P: No.
D: Trouble sleeping?

P: Only when those cars come by and the people are talking.
D: Do you think you're going to do anything about that?
P: Well, I'm not sure I can do anything. They scare me so I don't want to get them mad. The police won't do anything. I may just have to move again.
D: Do you have friends that can help if you need to move?
P: Oh yeah, a couple of people would do that.
D: Are those the friends you were talking with before?
P (*looks at D strangely*): What friends?
D: The ones you were talking with when I came in.
P (*laughing*): Oh, I've had those friends since I was little. They're not real. Just people that are with me all the time, in spirit mostly, and they help me when I have problems.
D: Oh. Well, I'm not sure what I can do to help you with your neighbors, but I'll think about it and why don't you come back in a week, and if they're still causing problems maybe we can figure something out.
P: Okay, but don't talk with anybody else about it. Okay? Because I think they could really cause me trouble.

Scenario Two
[4/28/08]

Setting: A small, barren interviewing room off an emergency room waiting room, furnished with two chairs, a desk, and a few dull pictures on the wall.

D (*doctor*): So what brought you here to the hospital?
P (*patient—a middle-aged woman, slightly obese, nice looking, well but simply dressed*): Well, I was feeling anxious.
D: Has that happened often?
P: No, but it does happen sometimes. I was in the hospital once before for it.
D: It gets pretty bad?
P: Yes, I don't sleep well, it's really hard for me to work, and it doesn't go away.
D: Is there anything you can do for it?
P: Well, I stop drinking coffee. I lie down even if I can't go to sleep. But neither of those things help much, and there's nothing else that helps at all.
D: So you come to the psychiatrist at the hospital?
P: I don't see what else I can do.
D: Of course. Is there something that sets it off?
P: Well, sometimes I fight with my husband. He gets annoyed with me when I get this way. He doesn't understand very well, even though I try to explain to him. He goes off the deep end pretty quickly, wants me to see a psychiatrist and stuff. Then he storms out of the house, and he's gone a couple of hours.

That scares me. But then he comes back, and he's okay for a while.

D: The last time this happened, you came to the hospital. Did that help?

P: Yes, I stayed for a few days. They gave me some medication, I got some sleep, then I was okay.

D: Any other illnesses?

P: Well, I had my appendix out when I was seventeen. I get the flu occasionally. Nothing else really.

D: Any family history of problems like this?

P: No, not really. Oh, my mother would fly off the handle sometimes. My father could be so aggravating. Then she'd get upset and go up to her room and stay there for hours. But she'd get over it.

D: Well, I'm going to see if I can get your last record, see what medication they gave you and things, and I'll be back in fifteen minutes or so.

P: Okay.

Half an hour later

D (*entering the room after knocking*): Well, they're still looking for your old record, but I wanted to talk with you a little more.

P: Haven't I seen you before?

D: Well, we talked here about a half hour ago.

P: No, in Chicago.

D: Well, I have been to Chicago a couple of times but just to visit family. I don't think we met there.

P: No, I mean at my cousin's house.

D: What is your cousin's name? I don't think so.

P: Walsh, Bill Walsh. It was last year, and you were there. You were arguing with my cousin, and he got really angry. Then you turned on me and started shouting, and they called the ambulance. Then they came and took me away, and it was because you got angry at me. I don't know why you would have done that. Now here you are again, and you're asking me all these questions. . ..

D: Now, just a minute. I have a very common face so maybe it was someone who looked like me, but I haven't been in Chicago for about four years. I think the first time we met was here just an hour or so ago. I was asking you a lot of questions, that's for sure. You came in, you said, because you were anxious, and I was trying to see if we could figure out why you were anxious and the best way for you to feel better.

P: Oh.

Taking Someone Seriously
[*11/9/16*]

On Monday night, attempting to avoid any more election eve predictions, I turned to my favorite escape channel, Turner Classic Movies, where they were showing the black-and-white movie *Love Me Forever* (1935) with Leo Carillo and Grace Moore. Leo Carillo, I thought, he's just a bit player not a leading man. But there he was, a bit paunchy, little thin black mustache, talking with a lower-class Italian accent. And there, also, was the opera star Grace Moore, tall, slender, looking stylish, and speaking beautiful American English.

In the story Carillo is a guy who runs a restaurant in New York City, and Moore is part of the show, singing beautifully. But while she sings some customers are talking loudly, others playing with their spaghetti, and Leo, furious, stops the food service and chases all the customers out of the restaurant. He decides to start a new and more classy restaurant, named after his mother Margarita, where for the shows they do scenes from opera. Carillo falls slowly in love with Grace Moore, but she is going out with a young, handsome, slim man from Boston who appears to be well educated and very well brought up. As the story continues, the restaurant is a success, and she keeps going out with the Boston guy. He repeatedly asks her to marry him, but she says no. In a conversation with Leo she reveals that she is unhappy because she wants to try out for the Metropolitan Opera but doesn't see how she can get an audition. A couple of weeks later, she tells Leo she will be going to Boston for a week. Afraid of losing her and increasingly in unspoken love with her, he says he will get her the audition and also pay for the best singing teacher in New York.

He does. The head of the Met comes to the restaurant and is amazed by Grace (who does have a beautiful voice) and wants to sign her up. Leo Is very happy for her. He declares his love for her but also says he's just a poor immigrant and knows the two of them are so different that she could never be serious about him. He walks out of the room.

Well, it turns out she's a success at the Met. (It's hardly a surprise since we've seen her doing scenes from *La Bohème* at Leo's restaurant.) Thinking he has lost her to the Boston guy, Leo has been drinking heavily and gambling and has huge debts and he wants to see her perform one last time before the gamblers kill him for nonpayment. He goes to the opera where he knows they are waiting for him, but Grace Moore has arranged for the Met to pay off Leo's debt. She sings the opera, they wave to each other during the curtain calls, he goes to her dressing room afterwards, and they decide to get married and go off together. The movie ends.

Me with tears in my eyes, I know it will never work out. Their backgrounds are too different. She is too upper class, he too much of a peasant Italian immigrant.

This thing about some people being acceptable and others not goes way back, for me and perhaps for everyone. When I was about seven, my grandfather was owed some money by someone who had some cabins in Miami Beach. The latter repaid his debt by allowing us to stay free there. On the long drive down, we would stay at "tourist homes," large houses that were kind of like bed and breakfast places. (No motels in those days.) They advertised themselves by signs on their lawns out front. Often the signs had the word "restricted" on them. My parents told me that meant "no Jews" so we couldn't stay there. In those days, of course, at gas stations and restaurants there were "Whites Only" signs all over.

At that time, too, my friends at school would go to "Sunset Camp" during the summers. I couldn't go because Jews were not allowed there. When I was thirteen many of my friends went to a dancing school. I couldn't go because they didn't allow Jewish kids. A few years later they changed their policy, and I went. One boy made a nasty joke about me, but otherwise it was okay.

Things got better. I had no further experiences of that kind. I went to a large ethnically diverse public high school, and things were fine.

About ten days ago, a man called me from Atlanta to arrange some things for my upcoming trip there to give a talk. I could swear I heard the tone of voice familiar from my childhood: "I will talk with you politely because we like to treat you people as though we respect you because that's how we are taught to behave as upstanding good people."

I think one of the problems with having, or having had, a serious mental illness is that it carries a stigma like being a Jew in the 1940's or, much worse, being Black over a much longer period of time or being the girl from high school I knew who got pregnant in her junior year and was ostracized by the administration afterwards or being a frumpy Italian immigrant like Leo Carillo, maybe as bad or worse than all of those. Some of our follow-up study patients have said how important it was for their improvement to have "someone who took me seriously" or "someone who cared." I think we are talking here of the human condition and something that is very important for most of us, whether we have psychiatric disorders or not.

Nurses
[*4/1/20*]

Yesterday, while I was watching television to reassure myself that the rest of the world really did exist, the news programs were stuffed with stories about COVID-19: how many people had died from it today, in the United States and in the world; how many people had it in the world and in the various countries; how we in the United States didn't have enough masks, protective garments, or even ventilators to stop people from strangling to death, things like that; plus information about how generally at the state and local levels governments were being effective and at the national level people were making excuses and blatantly lying, saying things like "there is no problem with ventilators, we have plenty of ventilators." Then the channel I was watching aired brief interviews with a couple of nurses, nurses who were asked to describe what it was like to work in these conditions of plague and the incompetence of people charged with managing the system.

The nurses didn't say a lot, and that reminded me of my experience working on medical wards as an intern and then as a medical resident. The nurses rarely said much. Oh, one might come into the office and say, " Dr. Strauss, I think you will want to see Mr. Jonas." Things like that were always said quietly and calmly, but it didn't take me long after becoming member of the house staff to know that they were just being who they were and you had better get your ass down there because if you didn't hurry, Mr. Jonas might be dead before you arrived.

I loved working on those hospital wards. I remember a movie where there was a scene of the whole community getting together to put up a barn. There were no orders, no apparent organized plan, just all those people coming together spontaneously because something needed to be done. They were all in it together, doing their job. The ward was like that. There was not a lot of talk, although we had many friendly encounters, but the ethos of the place was, well, we have a lot of sick patients to take care of, we are in it together, and you just do your thing.

The nurses on television were like that. They didn't complain about anything, they didn't even have much to say. One got a little teary eyed when she said how sick some of these COVID patients were, how sad it was that their relatives were not allowed to come in to be there with them, how complicated it was to keep more or less sterile when there were no new gowns and masks. But mostly, they didn't have that much to say.

But you could tell what they were feeling and how they were working to exhaustion to care for their patients. At a lower level of intensity and demand, I have always seen that on medical wards. "Dr. Strauss, I think you will want to see Mr. Jonas" was like a poem by Shelley or Matthew Arnold, saying so much beneath the words. It said, "I, a nurse, have seen a lot and I can tell that this man is in severe distress and in danger of death." It said without saying it, "You will want to see Mr. Jonas right away because you need to see if you can save his life." It said, "We are part of a system that works together and cares for each other and can count on each other to do all we can for our patients." It said all that without saying it.

That way of working and being together was especially beautiful at Boston City Hospital. Boston as a city was known to be famously corrupt at the time. At "Boston City," you were always short on supplies, staff, and funding. We were still using the original Wangensteen suction devices, two bottles connected by tubes on opposite ends of a rack so that water flowing from the top bottle created a small suction in one of the tubes connected to that bottle. We had no electric suction, no suction nozzles in the wall to help us to care for patients. We knew, however, that there was a full-time elevator operator hired in one of the buildings that didn't have an elevator. We knew that a mildly retarded aide was disliked and teased by the other aides because he didn't realize that when he was given a task to do like pushing a patient on a stretcher to X-ray, he was supposed to take a long way around in order to go by the cafeteria and stop for coffee; he just accomplished the task he was given without using up extra time.

But the nurses were incredible. On our ward we had forty-five beds, almost always full. About a third of the patients were on the danger list and so might die at any time, but even the patients not on the "DL" were severely ill. You couldn't be admitted as an inpatient to Boston City Hospital unless you were very ill. So the nurses on their shift were working all the time without let up. There were never enough of them. Yet, on those rare occasions when they had accomplished all their "meds" and "vitals" and other tasks, they would start giving patients back rubs. I never even knew that as an assistant resident on the ward until one evening when I needed to see the nurse Patty. Someone told me she was in the second room. I went to find her, and there she was giving a patient a back rub. I said, "What are you doing?" She said, "Oh, we always do this if we get our meds done early." My heavens, I thought, how lucky I am to know such people.

So, when I saw the two nurses being interviewed on

television and having so relatively little to say, I marveled once again at how incredible nurses are. I mean they are the people who actually do the work, now more than ever. I was also a little sad that everyone doesn't realize that, in this world that we live in.

Human Nature
[*3/25/08*]

I grew up thinking all people were basically good. My Dad would say things like "See Bill? He goes around all day picking up trash from the Apartments with his big two-wheeled cart. He doesn't make much. He was an alcoholic. But he's a good person. He does his work. He's nice to people. He's conscientious." And when Dad or I saw Bill, we would say hi and talk a little. Learning to read at school, I found the same world in the Alice and Jerry books. "Alice goes up, up, up, Jerry goes down, down, down. Alice and Jerry go up and down. See Spot jump. Jump Spot jump. Alice and Jerry and Mother and Father see Spot jump." I grew up thinking like that about people. Even Mrs. Moorhead, Dickie's mother, who could be very stern when telling me to "Run along home, Johnny" after Dickie and I, aged four, had played cars for several hours on his front porch, which was right next to mine at the duplex house where we lived, even though she would often give me and Dickie a lunch of soup and a peanut-butter sandwich. Ron, who worked for Dad, was an amazing worker. He knew how to do everything, fix machines, make things out of wood—he built a fine big bookcase for us in a couple of hours—paint buildings, everything. He had a drinking problem, as did Jim, the painter, and Bill. but they were all good reliable people, except, I guess, they got drunk, but that didn't happen often. Without even knowing it, I thought like that about people. That's just how things were, how the world was, how people were.

Not only were people basically good, but good people

always won. Jack Armstrong the All-American Boy, Captain Midnight, the Shadow, Superman, Batman, the Flash, Hawkman, Captain America, of course. But also the Allies when they creamed the Nazis, and later, the United States in its struggle with Communist Russia. The world was basically good, and so were people.

I knew, of course, of the concentration camps, of the six million or so of Jews and others killed there, of the history of slavery and the almost extinction of American Indians, of crime and murder, and bullies and rape and brutality. But somehow I was like a duck, with all that water pretty much rolling off my back.

Later, I hitchhiked for three months and nine thousand miles all around the country, and then for two months and I don't know how many miles around Europe. When I talked about those experiences, I said that the people who picked me up were a select sample since nasty people wouldn't stop to give you a ride. Well, there was that one guy (from New York City, of course) who in Kansas wanted me to pay for the gas. And there was the other guy outside of Chicago who said he was gay and leered at me, but he let me out of the car without a problem when I said I wasn't. Often while I was hitchhiking, people would insist on giving me money even though I would try to give it back, would pay for me at a diner where they wanted to stop for lunch, would invite me inside their house for a pancake breakfast after I had been sleeping in a neighboring field. Twice, people even invited me to sleep in their house. People would indicate or even say, "I met many people when I did what you're doing who did the same thing for me that I'm doing for you. I'm just passing it on."

And, of course, when I went to medical school it was even worse—-or better. You didn't pay attention to whether someone was a crook or a saint. They were people, people with problems, and you were there to help them. "Does this hurt? How long have you had that? Do you know what might have caused it?" Their morality just wasn't part of the deal.

But the last eight years has begun to help me learn better. Finally, something is beginning to get through to me. Lying to get us into a war? They've killed over a million people, four thousand Americans and around a million Iraqis, thousands of Americans wounded, probably well over a million Iraqis, several million Iraqis made refugees with homes, lives, families ruined. I remember staying up all night when I was a medical intern to try to keep <u>one</u> person alive, trying to find out what the infection was or the nature of a metabolic problem. Old George Bush doesn't care about millions. Nor Dick Cheney, or old Condi Rice, or Paul Wolfowitz. Or the rest of the crew, FEMA: "Oh, are there people there dying under the bridges and from need of food, water, and medicine?" HUD: "Well, maybe the trailers for the Katrina catastrophe do have toxic formaldehyde in them." The people at the top are supposed to keep our food, our air, our water supply uncontaminated, but the rest of us are getting sick and dying because they don't care. And how about global warming: "Oh, that's just a big fairy tale." Slowly, it's getting through to me. There are people who are evil. Oedipus put out his own eyes to punish himself for something that wasn't even his own fault—he had no way of knowing the guy he killed in a fight was his father. So far as I can tell, the people in charge now feel no guilt or even concern while they go about making themselves and their buddies even richer than they already are.

So was Dad wrong? Were Alice and Jerry wrong? Was my medical school and psychiatry training wrong? Were all those people who picked me up when I was hitchhiking wrong, and my kind aunts and uncles, my grandfather and grandmother, my teachers and my classmates, who were all nice or at least not evil, were they all wrong? One time Ray Greeves, the toughest kid in eighth grade who could beat the crap out of anybody, and I got into an argument. I think he'd bumped into me in the hall or something, and damned if I was going to back down. So we started to square off, and I knew I was going to end up a bloody pulp, but someone said, "Oh Ray, let it go." And he backed off. Even Ray Greeves wasn't evil. That year Teddy Grabinski got caught throwing a wadded-up paper ball at a kid at the back of the classroom by our teacher Joan Brownly, who looked up for just a second from the movie magazine she was looking through sitting behind her desk with her legs spread wide apart while we were doing the class assignment that she had put up on the board. Teddy Grabinski said, "I din't do nothin', teach." He lied, of course, but he hadn't killed even one person and he didn't act like he had just granted a huge gift to this not too bright bunch of people in front of him.

But these guys now. They're teaching me something. And still, after all I've learned these last years, after all I've rethought about concentration camps and torture, slaves and slave ships, and guys running factories where toxic fumes and materials kill or maim their workers, even after seeing the cruelty of the guys with whom I worked digging ditches for the gas company who would find a frog and place it so it'd have to breathe the gas and die—even after all that, I have to really struggle not to think that people are basically good. "Baboons, baboons, baboons," I repeat to myself. "I belong to a species like baboons." But I still barely get it. I think the problem is the diversity. How can you put your soul around the huge concept that some people who don't have much money give you five dollars (in the days when that was a lot of money) and others don't even notice if they kill a million people?

Ich Weisz Nicht
[2020]

Ich weisz nicht was sol es bedeuten,
Das ich so traurig bin;
Ein Mährchen aus alten Zeiten,
Das kommt mir nicht ausz dem Sinn.

Die Luft ist kühl und es dunkelt,
und ruhig fliesz die Rhein;
Die Gipfel des Berges funkelt
Im Abendsonnenschein.

I learned this poem, "Die Loreley," by Heinrich Heine in Helma Flugel's twelfth-grade German class at Academy High School in Erie, and it comes back to me now. And, in fact, *Ich weisz nicht was sol les bedeuten* (I know not if there is a reason), meaning I don't know what it means that it comes back now.

There are two parts to me. One is the man who says, "Now, now, logic tells us that it's not all that disastrous. Life goes on. No need to be so emotional." The other says nothing. He just sits there, quiet, knowing almost, that it's not quite so easy, that you're just being naïve with all your logic and reassurance.

My father was someone who always struck up conversations with people wherever he was, at the barber shop, the bank, a restaurant. And when I went out with him as a little kid, he would always joke to any new person we met that I was born at the depth of the Depression. I always suspected that maybe he was saying that I was part of the Depression, but

I don't really know what he meant, and all the people of his age who knew him that well and maybe could tell me are now dead, Maybe he meant I was a bright light that came during dark times, I don't know. But it didn't feel that way. I never took it too hard though. It was just Dad and his jokes again.

But ever since the time just before our invasion of Iraq, I have had this growing concern, worry, I guess, that something bad was going to happen with the political situation in the United States. And that growing feeling is still growing. I find myself wishing that it would happen so at least we would know what it was, wouldn't have to worry about the unknown, and could figure out how best to deal with it.

When Delphine, who taught me how to write in French, and I were having breakfast one morning a few years ago, we were talking about something and she said, "But you have to realize, I have never known a war, never experienced a depression." That shocked me. I have lived through how many wars, World War II, Korea, Vietnam, and smaller ones, and I grew up in the midst of the Great Depression. To me, that was the world, how it was.

I am amazed now when I see the kids' rooms of friends of mine, even friends who have very little money, that the rooms are full of stuffed animals of all sizes. I had one, a bear, and it was enough. What are the kids doing with all these bears and rabbits and dinosaurs and things? This isn't going to be a long diatribe about how tough things used to be. They didn't seem tough at all, just how things were. What seems so strange is that people have so much stuff now and to them it seems that is just how things are. Growing up, I never knew a family that had two cars. If they had a garage at all, it was a one-car garage. We knew people at all social levels so, again, that was just how it was, the world.

And then immediately following the world of the Depression came the Second World War. Gas rationing—we had a B card, not as bad as an A card but not enough to take long car trips. Friends going into the army, off to war, some not coming back, friends who had escaped Germany just in time and were called refugees. You finished everything on your plate and never threw out food, not only "because of the starving people in China" but just because.

My model airplanes first had cardboard formers that bent and fell apart, then thin pine strips that didn't fall apart but broke and splintered easily, and finally balsa wood that you could cut precisely and could form. And, of course, there were no televisions, no computers, no cell phones—well, you know all that. We didn't even have plastic—did you know that? The first kind came out in my late childhood. It was called bakelite, and it broke into a thousand pieces if you dropped it.

So now, when everybody has so much that we don't even notice it is so much, there is the thrum thrum thrum of our soldiers going into Afghanistan, into Iraq, and coming back with PTSD. Explosions and bombs over there, a million refugees in Iraq. At home Hurricane Katrina brings devastation and the sight of people standing on roofs waiting for help that never comes. Billions of dollars in no-bid contracts go to friends of the White House, and the money is lost somewhere. The dollar drops, securities firms go bankrupt, the stock market falls. There are billion-dollar bailouts for large corporations but not money for education or roads. Now, the Secretary of the Treasury, a former CEO of Goldman Sachs, says they will create a committee later to see how the financial meltdown (of which they were at the center) happened. For now, though, just give me $700 billion (at least), and I'll take it over and give it to the securities firms. No oversight nor judicial review of my actions will be permitted. Jawohl! When the Reichstag, the German parliament building, burned down in 1933, Hitler blamed someone else and seized more power. He was always blaming other people. Before he shot himself at the end of the war, when all Germany was in ruins, he said that the German people had let him down. Naomi Klein wrote a book entitled *The Shock Doctrine* about how many regimes use (and sometimes cause) a crisis so they can seize more power and grab more money.

Ich weisz nicht was sol les bedeuten. Perhaps it's just life, but I sit here not being so sure.

My Self
[*3/17/19*]

So here I am a big-shot—well, medium-shot—professor of psychiatry emeritus at Yale University School of Medicine, working on my autobiography and trying to figure out how to understand and describe a person, when all of a sudden I find out—in a very unlikely place.

It all started this morning, when I had a dentist's appointment. My previous dentist, the very nice Dr. Berman, had retired and it was well past time for me to find a new dentist. Dr. Tagliatiri had been recommended. So, because I was having some vague aches in my jaw, I made the first possible appointment, which turned out to be 8:15 this morning. I went in expecting he would find some horrible cavities requiring immediate treatment. He seemed very nice. He reviewed the X-rays that he had received from my periodontist, peered into my mouth, and said everything looked pretty good.

I had left the whole morning open for the dental work I thought would be required and so had all this free time ahead of me. I called my personal trainer, with whom I had cancelled an appointment, to see if she was free, but I only got her answering machine. So, what could I do? I had skipped breakfast, thinking I shouldn't eat before seeing the dentist, so now I decided to go to my office/play area at the Atticus Bookstore/Café and treat myself for my good fortune.

I found several new wait staff there that I had never seen before, perhaps because I don't usually go on Thursdays. A lovely young woman, small, thin in her Atticus t-shirt, black haired, with a round face and a kindly smile, came to my table. We talked a little before I ordered. When she brought my coffee, we talked a little more, and then, as she often passed my table, we talked for a minute here and there. Her name was Adelida. She was from Albania, twenty-one years old, spoke English very well, and had been here for three years, with her mother and her brother. Besides working at Atticus and another restaurant, she was going to school two nights a week, "but it wasn't enough." In the course of our talking, I asked if she missed Albania. And she said, "Yes, I miss my self." She went on to tell me what her self was. "I miss my language, how people think, the way people are, the people I know, our customs, the way the city is . . .." I don't remember what else she said because here I was, a professor of psychiatry from Yale, trying to figure out how to understand and describe a person and their connection to their world, and Adelida had just told me.

My self, a sense of who a person is, in the context of their language, their usual people, their usual surroundings, an amalgam of person in context. And now I understood my self much better thanks to Adelida. Me in Erie, me in Paris—yes, of course, being in those places is so special for me because my self is inextricably woven into them. They are where I feel really at home, where I am me, my self. My goodness, thank you, Adelida. Thank you to that young woman from a small town not too far from the capital of Albania who hopes to become a party planner.

Still a Brahms Fan
[*1/7/23*]

At my high school our yearbook was called the *Academe*. It had individual pictures every year of the 200 or so graduating seniors each with some pertinent quotations such as "loves Jim's hamburgers," as a way of remembering the people who had been such a major part of our lives. Next to my picture was the statement, "Brahms fan."

And I still am! Seventy-two years later! Yesterday, I was listening on YouTube to Brahms' two piano concertos. God, I love them! The unique combination of power, majesty, and periods of subdued absolute loveliness. He wrote that famous lullaby, after all. In his works he has passages of kindness, love, and understanding and others with the passion of Hungarian dances. And he loved the lilting melodies of waltzes by Strauss. No one, no one ever has been able to create music with such a mixture of total beauty.

I have recently turned ninety years old, and that's what I want to be like when I grow up. No, I will never be able to write music. Somehow, I was always a total failure with my many attempts at piano lessons and flute lessons, from the age of seven until during my first year in medical school, when I practiced for my weekly piano lessons on the top floor of the Woolsey Hall concert building. Of course, with much pain, I could learn the notes of my Bartók piano music for beginners, beautiful little tunes. But it was always such a struggle for me. When I stayed on one of the smaller islands belonging to my family in Canada, people on the main island commented that it was lovely to hear the sounds of my flute coming across the water. That was the high point of my music career. It was a mostly blighted career that limped along until it disappeared altogether.

But my love for Brahms never disappeared. As a child, he played the piano at a Hamburg whore house, and he went on to become a huge success in Germany, in Vienna, and then worldwide. He never married the love of his life, Clara Veeck, the widow of Robert Schumann, but they did remain close friends. And he wrote incredible music. The two piano concertos are my favorites. In these the music seems to have two instruments, the piano and the orchestra. Each is treated so that their separate parts are beautiful, and together they are truly magnificent. Of course, his double concerto and requiem are also incredible. And the chamber music pieces, well, I just don't know enough about music to appreciate them. That's sad, but still, going through my day with snatches of the piano concertos in my head, and even singing sequences from them to myself. What a gift!

Oh yes, absolutely, I'm still a Brahms fan, after all these years.

N Dimensional World
(N=Indeterminate)
[*3/23/17*]

Who would have ever thought there would be a 2017? I mean really, if you were born in 1932 you would realize that the year would always be 19 something.

Julie Legrand is having an exposition and book signing in Paris starting tomorrow. I met her on the no. 4 Métro in the late 1900s, so at least eighteen years ago. Sitting across from me, she was reading a book (translated into French) by Paul Walklawitz, whom I know. I asked her how she liked it, and we began to talk. At the Odéon stop we both got up to leave. I invited her to have a coffee at the Danton. We talked there until 2 that morning. She lived on rue Dauphine, my favorite street in Paris since I first got there in 1953. She was soon to defend her dissertation at the École des Beaux Arts and invited me to attend, which I did. The subject was a tube of striped toothpaste. How did the stripes get there. Were they put in the tube like that? Did they come from the cap? Did the light in the room bring them out since if you made the room dark you couldn't see them. People asked her very serious comic questions. It was lovely. She passed. So, tomorrow Julie is having her book signing. She now lives in a tiny government-supported apartment for artists and has had many shows. Julie, with whom I chastely slept, through whom I met my good friend Pernette, who has shown in Paris museums, and keeps going even though finally broken up with Ming. Julie of the no. 4 Métro.

Or Robert. We met on a train too. But only a few months ago. Robert is an old Jewish guy. (When I told my daughter, Sarah, that, she said, of course, "and what do you think you are?") He's an old Jewish guy who lives in the Village (Greenwich, of course). He, too, invited me to a book signing. The signing happened four days ago. Sarah and I went. It was even better than I expected. Many of the sixty or so people there looked as though they might be setting out in a few days to join the Lincoln Brigade and fight for the republic in the Spanish Civil War. They were radicals of all stripes and genders and colors, mostly old but not all. A couple of the women had blue hair. Some others, older, looked like Jewish grandmothers. My goodness!

Or Donald Trump. (What these days can be written without mentioning him?) Supported by a couple of multibillionaires, he is in charge of the most powerful country in the world but has no clue about governing. Worse, he is surrounded by people who also know nothing about governing, or if they do, want to wreck the departments they have just become the heads of. Donald Trump, who somehow got elected, tweeting all the while, leading us as in a train descending a mountain at top speed, leading us all—and maybe the world too—perhaps to jump the track at some curve and end crashed and burned, totally destroyed, at the base of the mountain.

Or Eliza, from Brazil, a music lover, her research asking mothers what it's like to sing to their infants. Eliza, whose father was taken to the ICU, received her doctorate, and learned that her husband would be transferred to Texas, all within three days.

Or Jennifer. Originally from Lexington, Kentucky, but who grew up in Appalachia in North Carolina. Lovely Jennifer, nurse practitioner student, in her third and final year, to graduate in May. She shyly asked me nurse practitioner questions at my cardiology visit yesterday. Lovely smile. In the spring she will be going with her husband to live in Illinois and start work in family practice.

N Dimensional World
Alice and Jerry for Mental Health Types
[*10/24/18*]

Now we go up up up. Now we go down down down. Now we go up and down. Watch Jerry go up! Watch Alice go down! Watch Alice and Jerry go up and down! I don't know how kids learn to read now, but certainly they don't start with *King Lear* or even *Macbeth*. Yet, that's sort of where we mental health professionals start when we learn our profession. There is so much basic stuff, especially concerning people's social connections, that we ignore almost completely.

In considering human interaction, for example, take the word "nonverbal." I had a patient once who was from Nantucket, the small island off Cape Cod with a population of a few thousand people. She divided people into two groups, those who lived on Nantucket and "offislanders." So, a couple of thousand people in one group and a couple of billion in the other. We do something similar with the word "nonverbal" in human interactions. There's the verbal stuff and then there is the other stuff. Except that if you're an actor or a singer you spend a huge amount of time, maybe most of it, with that "other" stuff, the tone of voice, the pacing of speech, the gestures, the position of your body, your actions, your inner feelings, your basic sense of identity, and so forth. If you are a performer, you spend most of your professional life working with and learning about those "nonverbal" things.

Consider also the concept of "social relations." Or the simpler one, "relationships." Or the more general one, "We are social beings." What do these terms mean? For one thing, they're all part of the "social" piece of "biopsychosocial." Now if you took all those thousands of people studying brain function or even bodily function more generally, and told them, "Okay, we are going to fire a lot of you until you get to be the same number of people as those who are studying social aspects of mental illness" you'd probably be investigated not just by the university and business, but even by government. Well, you say, the "social" isn't as complex as the brain, is it? You've got to be kidding! What does it really mean, for example, to say, "I felt so alone (or different or isolated or defective) that I could barely stand it"?

What do we need, what have humans had or evolved to, that makes us "social" animals? What does it even mean to be a social animal? It is said that horses, for example, are "herd" animals. The implications of this statement are fairly clear to me. These are animals that stick together because the mountain lions are less likely to eat you, maybe being in a herd is helpful for finding food, and so on. But what about us? The word "social" seems vague and not very helpful, like Nantucket's "offislanders." What do humans get or lose from that ballpark characteristic of being social? What does it teach us that in the mid-19th century "mountain men" would exist alone hunting and trapping in the Rockies and then get together once a year to drink and I don't know what else together with one another? How about monks, people living in isolated Montana homesteads, people in big cities, and how about the evolution of our being (more or less) social over the centuries in families, tribes, chiefdoms, states? Specifically, how have we done that, what does it imply?

So, like my person from Nantucket lumping together the several billion "offislanders," our concepts of "nonverbal" and "social" hide and allow us to hide the complexity and the importance of the "nonverbal" and "social" aspects of our work. What is underneath those global, vague terms?

Hi Annie, I'm writing to you as my anthropologist friend, and I have a question. I have gotten increasingly interested in what relationships are all about. My thinking about this began with watching one of my favorite television programs, *Naked and Afraid,* in which two people, a man and a woman who don't know each other, are plunked down in some remote place to see if they can survive for three weeks. They can take one object each, like a machete or a fire starter, but otherwise nothing, no clothes, no shoes, no weather protection, nothing. Although this is a partially artificial situation, it still gives a picture of what human survival involves, including the need/possibility of co-existing with another human being. For example, if one person gets sick or injured, he or she would just die without the help of the other, having no way to get food or water. And if the two don't get along, that situation can result in non-survival. For example, one woman got furious and threw their machete into a lake. So starting with this and then listening to some courses on archaeology and the evolution of families, tribes, chiefdoms, and states, I am wondering how humans developed psychologically and socially first to co-exist with each other and then in increasingly complex societies, how they learned ways of getting along, co-existing yet retaining identity, and so forth. I am familiar, of course, with the developmental theories in psychology, but there must be anthropological writing about these issues that is more empirically based. We know that infants can't survive alone, but that seems often (always?) true of adolescents and adults as well. Do you know of any anthropological writing on biopsychosocial evolution, on the needs, behaviors, and so on that have made humans "social" animals?

A Strange Thing Happened
[*2/19/14*]

A strange thing happened. Two months ago I was asked to review an article for the *American Journal of Psychiatry*. That happens sometimes, and I did it, sending in my judgment of the article. Six weeks later I get an e-mail from the editor of the journal, asking me to write an editorial related to the article that I had reviewed. Now the *American Journal of Psychiatry* has perhaps the largest circulation of any psychiatric journal and a large international circulation besides, and this has never happened to me before. Oh, once, about twenty years ago, the editor of a much smaller if still respectable journal asked me to write an article on subjectivity, which I did. My article included a recounting of some strange experiences of my own, and after he received it the editor wrote to say that my submission was somewhat unexpected, but they decided to publish it anyway.

Needless to say, I was delighted to get this request from the editor of the *American Journal of Psychiatry* and, of course, accepted. That night I awoke around 3 am with this great feeling, "I don't have to be a good little boy. I can write whatever I want. And, well, if they reject it, that's life." So, with the same delightful feeling of freedom the next day, I began writing. I introduced the piece by saying that it was going to have the form of theme and variations. Bach, Mozart, Beethoven, Brahms, Rachmaninoff, and others had used this form, and it had the special beauty of taking a theme, or an idea, and then looking at it from several different perspectives. And that is what I did.

I agonized for a week about it, being both delighted in my affrontery and creativity and worried that it wasn't very good—it wasn't Mozart and or even variations on "Twinkle, Twinkle, Little Star." But it was the best I could do, and I had never seen anything remotely like this done in psychiatry or any mental science field.

I sent it in. I thought there was about an eighty-seven percent chance of it being rejected. "Dr. Strauss, this is the dumbest thing we have ever seen, really stupid and inadequate, and besides totally unfit for a scientific journal like our own, or any other really. Please don't ever send us anything again."

But no, three days later, an e-mail came from the editor: It's spot on, and besides it reflects your important contributions to the field for those of us who know your work and instructs the next generation on these valuable approaches" (or something like that).

Wow! I was delighted, of course, overwhelmed. No person had ever written me such a letter. For several days I expected a follow-up e-mail. "Dr. Strauss, you received the last e-mail because of a clerical error. It was really meant for someone else. Please discard that e-mail and never send us anything again." But day followed day, and that e-mail never came. Instead, I received an e-mail from an editorial assistant saying I could send my piece in any format and she would convert it to the format required. That had never happened to me before either.

Now, here's my problem: I feel as if I have reached some wonderful apex. I mean that's it, I have it all. That means I have no need or desire to do anything further—I mean, like psychiatric writing. I am well aware that with my editorial I didn't really solve anything, offering no big solution to a major psychiatric need. Still, I have that feeling, "Let's just go out and eat ice-cream," or something like that.

But there is still a glimmer of hope. I received a small book from Swarthmore with information about its one hundred and fiftieth anniversary. In it I found a quotation from somebody named Marjorie Garber '66, who, it seems, teaches literature at Harvard: "The humanities and the arts are not decorative embellishments, they are at the heart of any complex attempt to understand and appreciate our world." YES! And she has lit a tiny flame that may be the center of how I might proceed, a kind of neo-Gestalt approach to our field using the arts in the process.

Another Strange Thing Has Happened
[*12/9/20*]

Another strange thing has happened. I never would have expected it. Nor have I ever seen it reported by anyone else. At the age of eighty-eight I have finished writing my autobiography. The process started strangely, but even more strangely, the book having now come out, the process seems to continue on.

It all began when psychology post-doc Sarah Kamens asked if she could interview me about my life and work. I was thrilled. So we started. The interviews were conducted in my dining room and after each—there were three in all—we went to the diner for dinner. Sarah recorded the interviews and had them transcribed. I was sure I had been impressive, but when I saw the transcriptions I was appalled. They were often incomprehensible and mostly very dull. Certainly, I could do better than this.

So I set to work actually writing out my autobiography. After a couple of months of work I sent the manuscript to my kids, Sarah and Jeff. They were very polite. So I read it myself. They had been polite. It was really quite dull. I tried making major changes. Still dull. Okay, I would try to get an editor who could revise it. A consultant gave me a long list of editors to try, none of whom I knew. I pretty much gave up, or at least tabled the whole thing.

Until one day I was having lunch with Stan Possick and mentioned I was looking for an editor. Well, it just so happened that Anne Ranson, the stepsister of his wife, was an editor and that she had edited the autobiography of her father. I got in touch with her, she agreed to try, and within a couple of months she had rejiggered the whole thing, had asked me to do things like please write something about your mother, to explain other things like about my father as a community leader (I never saw him that way), and what was this thing about me as a Jew going to Sunday School?

Clearly, Anne was terrific, asking me just the things I needed to be asked so that I could clarify and add. But even more important, she juggled the chronology I had written to intersperse it with the detailed accounts of experiences that really brought the whole thing to life.

But I failed in my efforts to get a commercial or academic publisher. They said they weren't doing such works any more or there would be a year or so delay. About that time, a friend I hadn't talked to in several years called me, and during our conversation he told me that his wife had "self-published" a novel she had written and that the publishers were very good. So, I called Paul and then Collin, they consulted me often, and a few months later copies of the book came to me in large boxes.

I was excited, of course, but I also realized something strange was happening. It had actually started many months earlier. In writing the autobiography, questions came up. Why wasn't it a simple story, a simple progression? What should I do about the fact I was leaving out huge chunks of my life (like anything about my mother)? Why was I paying so much more attention to the summers during my college years and so little to the college experience itself. And in the process of talking about these things with friends, I began to learn so much, about myself, about them, and about life more generally.

So anyway, the boxes of books arrived at my house. I loved seeing them and treasured the book they contained. But it wasn't just that. Somehow, though in a way I didn't understand, I found that arrival was more part of an ongoing living process than an event.

And that process continues. My cousins and I make up an extended family in which we had a lot of contact early in our lives as we grew up. Now, although the seven of us who have survived live in different parts of the country, with the advent of the coronavirus we have started meeting every three weeks on Zoom. Often the content seems fairly vapid, being about the weather (really), vacation plans, and so on, although it is still nice having the connection Once the book came out, though, several of them got copies and made comments, talking about their own experiences, and we have woven a more solid web among us about who we are and how we connect.

I have also given copies of the book to people with whom I have been close at some time in my life, and here too, the ongoing process feels like spinning a strong thread that draws in not only the past but also reconnects in a very living way. Thus, I mailed a copy to a girlfriend from seventh grade and her husband, with whom my daughter and I have had dinner when we have been in Erie this last couple of years. I have sent another copy to my best friend from high school at his request (we have talked periodically over all these years on the phone), to a woman with whom I had a very intense relationship in college, to a good friend in Paris who is the sister of a very close friend of mine there who died two years ago, to other people of whom I am very fond, including one in Texas, and, of course, to my son and daughter and to my granddaughter, who had made many helpful comments during the writing process. In each instance, it is like—to change the simile—casting out a line that brings us closer together, making the past and even the current situation more real, more present

When I started, of course, I had no idea of anything like

this happening. What a great pleasure to have this awakening! It is like the spring. A new feeling of being alive.

But I'd really like to go further to help you to see how it feels. "Show, don't tell." That's what the writing teachers say. And they are right. But how? When I took a course on opera two years ago it was pretty much worthless, mostly gossip about the sopranos. Except for one thing the teacher said: "Because of the needs of the music, the arias and things, everything you try to show takes longer, though if the composer is good, it's amazingly intense, the feeling is really powerful." I was just listening to *La Bohème,* and, damn, when Mimi and Rudolfo get together again before she dies and sing that incredible duet, you feel it down to your very core. But that's music linked to drama, which goes straight to your soul. I can't do that. So let me try something else. I'll borrow from Charles Dickens in *The Christmas Carol.* Playing the ghost of Christmas Past, I'll try to help you look back in your life just as the ghost did for old Scrooge by showing him scenes of his childhood. And as I have done in working with this thing, this autobiography.

Think about a really meaningful experience or time in your past. I'll give you a minute.

Okay, have you found one? Now look back at it from where you are in your life now. Really look back at it. Look around. Look at other people there at the time. Look around at the place. Maybe look at what happened just before, what happened just after. Now try to think by looking back what it might have meant to you and what it means now.

Now do that with another time or event.

Does that help at all to get some sense of how it might feel, what it might mean, to look back in your life and see the spread of it, maybe to try to understand it from where you are now?

That's all. Thanks.

Doing the Humanities
[8/9/20]

I suppose there are many ways in which the humanities can be useful in the mental health endeavor. But rather than focus on what people can learn didactically from the humanities, I would like to look at what "doing" the humanities has to offer the mental health field. Let's start with an example. Margery (not her real name) was a young woman in her late teens hospitalized for a severe psychiatric problem that had received many diagnoses, schizoaffective disorder, personality disorder, and so on. I was her doctor. Margery was an "impossible" patient who often required seclusion to manage her outbursts and general negativism. One day she came to me and said she had learned that the church next to the hospital was looking for actors to be in a play they were going to produce. Margery wanted to try out for a role. Many on our staff thought she was too disturbed to participate, but in the next several days we worked out a plan by which Margery could go over to the church for try-outs accompanied (as unobtrusively as possible) by a staff member. She did so and won a major role.

Following extended rehearsals, several weeks later Margery approached me and asked if I wanted to attend a dress rehearsal. Of course I did, and the following day I was able to do so. Following the rehearsal, Margery brought the play's director over and introduced me as a "friend." The director told me not only how well Margery was doing with her part but also how helpful she had been in settling people down when things on stage began to get difficult. Margery was clearly "doing" the humanities and the interaction had been a major plus all around. (Margery had become an exemplary "patient" on the ward as well.)

So, what is going on here anyway? Another example may help to clarify. The year I took out of medical school to be in Paris I spent some time at a psychiatric hospital learning how they worked with patients with severe disorders. Two people there led writing groups for patients. One, Mrs. Elmassian, worked with inpatients. I attended one of her groups. She had people write about anything they wanted, and then the group would discuss the writing. The writings were impressive, as was the group discussion. I couldn't detect anything particularly "psychiatric" about either. The other group, consisting of outpatients, was led by a psychiatric nurse with an advanced degree. The writings focused on psychiatric problems and how to deal with them. This group seemed much more scripted to me and much less effective than the other.

One more example. My friend, the professor of psychology Larry Davidson, set up a project for a small group of people with severe mental disorders. They were to interview another group of people with severe mental disorders, produce a report, and then read it to a group of professionals. I had the good fortune to attend this presentation about "A Day in the Life" of people with long-standing severe psychiatric problems. It was a beautiful and moving description of what the presenters had learned, an enthralling narrative. The audience of sixty or more professionals was as impressed as I was. It seemed to me that in this project the participants had accomplished the almost miraculous task of acknowledging psychiatric problems but rather than digging into them had transcended them to be active and competent, experiences that could form a base for self-esteem and competence in their daily lives.

What have I have learned from these and many other related experiences? (I should say that for twenty-five years I have also been leading creative writing groups of people connected with the mental health system—patients, psychiatrists, social workers, nurses, rehabilitation workers.) First, I think I have seen the power (and beauty) of people with even severe psychiatric problems to "do the humanities" in an effective way that seems to provide a major positive impact on their sense of competence and self-esteem, the kinds of thing they will need to reenter the everyday world. Second, I have been astonished at the degree to which "severely disabled" people, given the guidance and belief in their competence, can carry out tasks far beyond what one might expect. Third, I have the impression that there is a danger in using the humanities as another kind of intervention for "sick people" with a focus on illness and problems that rather than helping them develop insight just digs the trench deeper into their sense of being disabled and defective. Fourth and last, I have been impressed that when a leader of such groups has reasonable confidence in their abilities and potential, these people can be far more competent and effective than I would have dreamed and that they have been assisted in finding and actualizing that strength.

Loos Geerlings
[*5/4/23*]

With all the awful things that go on in the world, the killing, the destruction, the exploitation, it is amazing—and perhaps strange—that beautiful and great things happen too. I was thinking about seeing Ami, my wonderful physical therapist, this morning and suddenly recalled Loos Geerlings. Loos who!? Loos Geerlings. In 1957 toward the end of the year I spent in Europe, with Piaget and then in Paris, I decided in the spring to take my beloved 250cc BSA motorcycle to Holland just to visit. Riding through Belgium, with its awful roads, I lost my wool sweater, which was on top of my pack on the seat behind me and must have flown off as I bumped along. It was the only sweater I had, and as I was trying to live on $20 dollars a week, I wouldn't be able to replace it. Anyway, I reached the Netherlands, where the roads were lovely and the flat farmland serene. I had discovered that there was a youth hostel in the small town of Axel where I could spend the night. We (my moto and I) arrived there in the afternoon and signed in. No other guests were around so I put down my pack in the dormitory on the second floor and went out to find some place to eat. After dinner, I came back to the hostel and went to sleep in the lower bunk bed I had laid claim to. Still, no one else but me in the hostel. After a great sleep, I awoke the next morning, the sun was shining in through the windows, and what was that I heard—Mozart, someone was playing Mozart on the piano downstairs! Mozart, sunshine, good sleep, BSA motorcycle, I mean what else could someone possibly want? I washed, dressed, and walked downstairs for breakfast. Mozart was still coming from somewhere down there. I went to the dining area and there, near the tables, was a piano. And at the piano, playing away, was a young woman. I had a wonderful youth hostel breakfast. I was still the only guest there so the woman who brought in the food stopped to talk before she went back into the kitchen. Mozart still came from the piano. Finally, the lovely young pianist stopped and came over. We began to talk.

Loos was happy and fun and full of joy. I don't remember exactly how it happened, but soon we were on my motorcycle while she showed me around a bit. I don't know if you have ever driven a motorcycle with a lovely woman behind you on the seat. There are a few possibilities, but the best one is that she puts her arms around you to hold on to something, and you may feel her breasts pressed into your back. There are many lovely experiences in life to be sure, but that is not the least of them. Loos and I spent the day on and off the motorcycle visiting various parts of Zeeland. I think there were windmills, and what I really enjoyed was the flat land. I love flat land (as well as mountains). I had first realized that two years earlier when I was hitchhiking around the United States and discovered that standing out on the road in Kansas, damn, you can see forever! This wonderful open world without borders. Free in the world! So, Holland, at least that part of it, was a little like that. And with Loos on the motorcycle! Well, as we say in French, *Il n'y a pas mieux!* (There is nothing better).

Maybe thirty years later, I noticed an ad for wines in a U.S. magazine. The person selling them had the name of Geerlings. I wrote him asking if he knew Loos. He kindly wrote back that Geerlings is a very common Dutch name, and no, he didn't know anyone named Loos.

Stories, People, Science, and the Mental Health Field
[*4/26/23*]

Reality and the role of stories in the mental health field, that is my subject.

There is a poorly developed struggle in the mental health field between the "true scientists" (mostly biologists) and the storytellers—psychoanalysts and others. I would like to propose that while both these approaches and their modifications are essential to this field, neither by itself is sufficient.

A couple of years ago, I was having lunch with my wonderful friend, Zheala Qayyum, and I was explaining to her that when I am in Paris and speaking in French with French friends that I am a different person than when I am here in New Haven and speaking English with my American friends. I explained further that none of my American friends accept that, they say something like "Well, you just feel different when you are in Paris. I've seen you there, and you're the same person."

I think they just don't understand. But Zheala is like one of those ancient Greek mythical women who are not goddesses but have some superhuman powers—like Cassandra, who could foretell the future but was never believed. Zheala understood immediately. She took the four water glasses that were on the table, placed one in the center and then the others around it. She explained that each of the surrounding glasses related to a different side of the central glass, which was me. Thus, I have many different sides, and each side relates particularly closely to the object nearest to it. "Exactly!" I replied.

Another friend, psychology professor Larry Davidson, occasionally refers to Edwina the dinosaur, who when people tell her that dinosaurs are extinct just leaves and goes to the kitchen to make her prized chocolate-chip cookies. This ministory, totally ridiculous as it may seem, as with the glass and the various containers on the table, conveys an important and unique message.

What is it exactly in what I am calling a story that makes this form such an essential component of understanding psychiatric phenomena? I cannot, of course, begin to approach the erudition and insights of such authors as E. M. Forster and Václav Havel who have written so beautifully about this question. But I would like to suggest that in terms of the mental health field at least two aspects are essential. The first is the degree to which stories provide information about meaning, about how a particular psychiatric state may link to the person's understanding of the world and his or her situation. This aspect of story cannot nearly as adequately be conveyed by a correlation or a significant difference of the stochastic world. And, of course, such understandings may have crucial roles in the etiology of a problem or processes by which the problem can be ameliorated or even resolved. Another crucial and related aspect of story is that it can provide an understanding of the mental and life context to which a particular problem or solution is connected. The examples of the difference in my experiences in New Haven and Paris, or of Edwina's not being understood by the people around her provide introductory illustrations of such processes and effects.

As so often happens, these brief stories can and do convey important messages. With the glasses on the table, Zheala created a story that instantly reflected the concept and its reality. But how, and why, does that work? And what happens to our understanding of "reality" if we insist on only simple explanations ("you are always the same") to complex phenomena?

I propose that what Zheala has done is to create a story—in this case, a relatively simple one—that is a more adequate explanation of reality than the assumption that a person is always the same. Although, of course, both stories may have some truth, her story provides a structure for explaining the phenomenon and its complexity. The story does not prove that it is correct, but it does (in my opinion) represent and explain the phenomenon rather than trying to assume that the phenomenon does not exist.

I would propose furthermore that the "story" provides a structure for further exploration and proof that is more adequate than the simple but incomplete assumption of a continuing uniform identity. If, then, we proceed to one of Freud's accounts or other psychodynamic or complex explanations, does that mean they need to be immediately accepted? Not at all, merely that they are attempts at defining a more complex reality than that proposed, for example, by the dopamine hypothesis or the early childhood hypothesis. Neither the simple nor the complex hypothesis (even with low or modest statistical significance demonstrated) are in themselves sufficient demonstrations of process or truth.

One way of considering that complexity of experience and life was suggested to me by my good friend Camille Paysant. If you consider as one aspect of this problem that the story provides a wider context and perspective on the phenomenon you are trying to understand, then the addition of historical and contextual elements serves to fill out in a crucial way the origins and setting of that phenomenon. And if you don't do that along with other aspects, you cannot adequately understand that phenomenon. Here's an illustration: Several years ago I was asked to do an evaluation of a psychiatric inpatient program. I talked with many from the administration and staff of the hospital and then walked through several of the wards to get a clearer idea of what went on there. On one of the wards there was a nurse writing up notes in the nursing station but only one patient sitting in the day room. I asked the nurse what that was about. She explained that the other patients were out in the yard but this woman was too psychotic to join them. I asked the nurse if it would be all right if I talked with the woman, and she said it would be fine. So I went to the woman, explained that I was reviewing the hospital program. and asked her if I could talk to her a bit. She agreed, and I sat down a few feet from her on the bench and asked her how it was to be in the hospital. We talked for about ten minutes about what she would like to do when she got out of the hospital. Our conversation was entirely "normal" and unremarkable, except, of course, that she was viewed as "too sick" even to be outside in the yard with the other patients. I am not implying that she was not severely troubled, only that in the particular context in which we found ourselves she was totally fine. That kind of situation has happened to me many times, and what it tells me is this: This thing that we call severe psychiatric disorder is very different from our usual concepts of illness. A broken leg or severe cardiac insufficiency are conditions that would make it impossible for someone to run from home plate to first base. There is nothing so clear cut about psychiatric disorder.

Of course, "truth" may require even more understanding, more variables, processes, or sequences than the kinds of examples mentioned above. The assumption that either the story or a correlation is adequate to prove the existence of a process as total explanation is a gross misunderstanding of reality. However, we can assume—and do so here—that in many, probably most, or even all instances, a story must be one of the components of knowledge in our field. In which case, the question arises, what exactly is the nature of a story that is required. A story is a construction to explain a process. In the case of my "dual reality" it may be represented by such simple things as a water glass and a few associated objects. Or a story like Freud's tale of Dora may be needed, or even a fantastic story like that of the Gorgon or Penelope or Pandora's box.

In fact, to borrow again from Greek mythology, one might even say that to require that understanding of human thought and behavior conform to only one approach, the traditional scientific method, is to assume as did Procrustes that all human beings conform to a bed of only one length—and if they did not, they would have to be stretched or have body parts cut off to conform to that one model.

Tempus Fugit
Nobody Says "Ain't" Any More
[5/8/16]

Time flies. It's scary when I notice that I am the only person left alive who remembers certain things. Little things like when the Indian dog Wewim bit me on the wrist up at the Island when I was six. But big things, too, like Dad telling me about going to see a Loudonville doctor who described having been at the Battle of Antietam. That was, of course, the Civil War battle where more American soldiers were killed than at any other. Can you imagine being a doctor in your medical tent, amputating injured arms and legs off kids? Without anesthesia, of course. They would give them a bullet to bite down on and saw off their arm or leg. One kid after another. All day long. Tall piles of human arms and legs outside the tent. Can you imagine?

And Dad and Mom would tell me about the man who lit the streetlamps with a flame on the end of long pole. Those were gas lamps, of course. The lamplighter stopped coming around when electric lights came into being.

That was before my time so I have no memory of it. But there's lots of stuff I do remember. For example, when I was growing up people with little schooling would say "ain't." "They ain't around any more like they was." My grandfather, Sambo, would often say ain't, lots of older people did. And, of course, I am the last person alive to remember lots of personal things, like when Lila Cook saved me from drowning. It was up at the Island, I was four or five. I was running on the dock

("Don't run on the dock!") and slipped off into the water. I didn't know how to swim. I swear I can still see the bubbles coming up past my face. Lila happened to be nearby, saw me, rushed down, and pulled me out. No one else was close. If she had not happened to be there, I wouldn't be here—and if you are one of my kids, you wouldn't be either. Lila and her husband, Bob, came up to the Island many years in a row. Lovely Lila, with beautiful breasts. One day she was swimming and the top of her suit slipped off. She turned her head toward me, smiled coyly, and put it back on. Lila and Bob were friends of my mother's brother, Herb. They knew I liked peanut butter. (I have loved peanut butter pretty much since I was born, still do, make my own now.) One year, when we were celebrating my birthday, August 18, at the Island—birthday cake with candles, about twenty people staying there at the time—out come Lila and Bob with a case of Best on Earth peanut butter, for me. Dave was an owner of the Best on Earth company, I think. They had brought the peanut butter up from Cleveland for me.

Sam and Ralph's was the barbershop in Erie. Dad would take me there every week or ten days to get my hair cut. "The hair on the back of your neck is getting fuzzy." Either Sam or Ralph, who was the thinner one, would fit me in between the guys they were shaving. For that task they used the big shaving mug, full shaving brush, and a straight razor.

At the post office, ordinary stamps were three cents. Penny postcards were, of course, a penny each.

As Edith Piaf sang, *"Mais vous pleurez milord! Ca, je l'aurais jamais cru."* (But you are crying, my lord, that I'd never imagined.)

Behind the Wooden Door
[*3/10/11*]

How is it that after all these years and all this experience with psychiatry—treating patients, doing research interviews, writing scientific papers, giving lectures, and teaching students and residents—I feel I know so much and understand so little? When Bob, my friend since childhood, and I were in junior high and would play cards on his living room floor, his father would pass by and say critically, "If you're so smart, why aren't you rich?" I always resented that since we weren't bothering anyone, but I never forgot the question. I ask it often now of all of us in the mental health field: If we're so smart, why aren't we rich? I don't mean rich in money, but if we know so much, why can't we prevent psychiatric problems? When we see someone who has one, why can't we just say, "Here take one of these every night at bedtime for one week"? Or see the person for a week or two of interviews or prescribe a work solution or a rehabilitation program, and then in a one-month follow-up visit learn that now everything is fine? If we're so smart, why aren't we rich, rich in the sense of being able to prevent and cure within a limited amount of time?

The answer, as Bob's father could have told us, is that we are not yet all that smart. Certainly, things in the mental health field are better than they were twenty or even ten years ago. But just as certainly, we have a distance still to travel to be really smart. We have made progress, much progress, that's for sure. But in some areas, I wonder.

For example, we neglect important things that don't fit into what we have been taught.

In the 1960's I was involved in a research project for the World Health Organization (WHO). About fifteen of us from countries around the world were in Nigeria, where one of our goals was to see some of their psychiatric treatment facilities. To that end, we were taken by our hosts to a small village outside of Ibadan to meet a "native healer." Arriving in our van, we pulled up at a small house on the main dirt street of the village, where there was a lot of foot traffic but almost no vehicles. The building, we were told, served as the healer's office and hospital. Outside it, we were appalled to see a couple of people each with a chain on one ankle, the other end of which was fastened to a metal stake driven into the ground. Of course, we thought, "How horrible, how primitive." We were ushered into "his hospital" by the healer, a small man who seemed to be very impressed with his own knowledge and authority but also to emit a kind of slyness, not the kind of person to whom you would want to trust yourself. Inside the small room he called his office there was a large desk. The walls were lined with shelves on which stood rows of large glass jugs filled with dirty yellow liquid and containing things that looked like skulls of raccoons or other animals of that size. I was happy to leave that oppressive place. Going back once again to the dirt road on which our van waited, I noticed that people who were walking by would stop to talk in what appeared to be a reasonable and caring fashion with the people who were chained outside the building. While we waited to get into the van, I observed what appeared to be ordinary, fairly extended, and caring conversations.

Several years later in the United States, I was doing some

research interviews with patients in a state psychiatric hospital. I had to use a key to enter the door of the massive brick building, where I headed down a long corridor to reach ward C. I knew it was ward C because it had a sign saying so attached to its huge windowless oak door. There were no windows from the ward onto the corridor. I took another key from my set, unlocked the door, and reassuring myself that the key was still in my hand so that I could get out any time I wanted, closed the door behind me. Inside I found another long corridor, off which there were openings into small, sparsely furnished bedrooms. These were empty of human occupants, however, because the patients, about thirty in all, were gathered in a large day room at the end of the hallway. Some were pacing back and forth muttering to themselves. Others sat in chairs facing ahead, not talking to anyone or doing anything. I heard occasional screams punctuating this dreary frightening place and an occasional loud crazy-sounding shout.

I can't help thinking, If I had to be confined for a severe mental illness, would I prefer this or being chained at the side of a road with people stopping to talk with me. There is not even the slightest doubt in my mind, I would prefer the chain.

Comfort
[2/10/15]

Twenty-three years ago, when he was ninety-two, Dad took an airplane trip from Cleveland to visit me in New Haven. I went to the Hartford airport to pick him up and waited at the exit gate for him. He came out, but in a wheelchair pushed by an attendant. I was so surprised to see him like that. At his retirement colony he swam every day, made some of his own meals, and had driven his bottom-of-the-line Mercedes until just a few months earlier. But he was okay, just older. He got out of the wheelchair, and we walked the hundred yards or so to my car.

I had asked Dad on the phone a week earlier if he wanted anything special in the house for meals, and he had come up with only one thing: "You know the Cream of Wheat that comes in those little packets." I had gone to the supermarket and got Cream of Wheat, as he had requested, but in a larger box because it was cheaper that way. The morning after his arrival I brought out the box of Cream of Wheat, and he said, "No, I don't want that. I want it in those little packets." I was quietly furious. "Dammit," I thought, "it's all the same damn stuff, don't be that fucking way!" But I didn't say anything. Dad said, "There's a store around the corner, isn't there? I'll go out and buy the packets." I was still furious when he put on his coat and walked out of the house. He came back several minutes later with a package of Cream of Wheat packets. Most of the rest of his visit went well enough, but I never forgot that damn controlling shit. Mostly he was great, but I sure hated it when he got that way.

This morning, all these years later, I had my small glass of orange juice and was drinking my coffee and eating half of a brown toasted English muffin spread with half peanut butter and half butter, sitting in my warm house with the cold and snow outside, when I thought "How good it is to be here where it's quiet and everything is so comfortable and familiar and known." It felt like being in a warm bed or covered in a fuzzy warm cloak. Then I thought how much I enjoy it when I go to Atticus to have breakfast with Larry every Friday morning and Maricruz comes over and says, only half questioning, "Coffee with milk, orange juice, and a toasted blueberry scone?" And I nod, yes. Or when I go to the Royal Palace restaurant to meet Dave and Michele, and Yan comes over to take our order and, looking at me and says, "Orange Beef, hot and sour soup, and pork fried rice?" And then, when the food arrives, she brings me a knife as well, since I always used to ask for it.

When I'm in Paris, every morning I go to the Kayser bakery. As I approach the counter one of the workers dodges into the back where the pastries are baked and looks to see if croissants have just come out of the oven, knowing that's what I'll ask for, "a warm croissant, if you have one." Then, leaving the bakery, I eat that flakey marvel as I walk to the bus, muttering in French and English, "There just isn't anything better than this." I take the bus to my café, the Danton, which I have known for over sixty-one years. I sit down at my table, the second from the door next to the *baie vitrée,* where I can watch the people and cars pass, and Michel or Dominic, depending on who's working that day, brings me my *café crème* without my needing to ask, and we exchange a few words. Sometimes the Afghan couple is there, sometimes the elderly lady who lives "just around the corner," and we say hello.

And in Paris, at lunchtime I walk up to the café Rostand.

There, if the weather isn't super beautiful, I sit inside next to the window overlooking the *terrasse* and the Luxembourg Gardens, and Elodie comes up and asks, "*Comme d'habitude?*" If I say yes, she brings me my Carlsberg beer and *sandwich mixte* (ham and cheese). I love being known in that way.

So, in the middle of that chain of thoughts this morning, I thought, "Oh that's why Dad wanted his Cream of Wheat in little packets. Now I understand."

But What If It's Not Like That?
[7/21/10]

When I am in Paris, I stay in a small hotel, surrounded by bookstores, where they always give me the same room and treat me like family, and I take my morning coffee at café Danton. On my way to and from the café I pass by a square where three days a week there is a market with fruit that tastes like real fruit. On one particular day, though, a Sunday, I found not the general market but one at which people were selling used books of all types and ages. Now, I don't need more books. All the many bookshelves in my house are full, and I have piles of books on the floor all over my living room and office. Still, it's always fun to look. At this market books were everywhere on tables and in cardboard boxes, and many of the people were selling them by weight, so much per kilo. On the top of one box was a small paperback of stories by Maupassant, whose work I love. Looking through the contents, I realized that these were stories that I had never read, and, well, what harm could it do to have just one more tiny book and to save it from the ignominy of lying there in a cardboard box. So, I bought it, for eighty centimes. It's so strange that you can buy a work toiled over with such care by a wonderful author for eighty centimes. On the way back to the hotel, one block away, I looked through the various parts of the book and discovered a brief history of the life of the author, as one often finds in French books, especially the paperbacks. I learned that Maupassant was infected at a young age with syphilis. He became delusional and severely psychotic and eventually died from the disease.

After thinking how sad it was that someone so gifted should die so young, as had so many artists in the nineteenth century, I reflected on how discovery of the bacterium that causes syphilis and later of the antibiotic penicillin made the disease curable. And I wondered, what if schizophrenia is like that? What if someday someone finds the twisted gene, the abnormal neurological structures, and/or neurotransmitters that cause schizophrenia just as they had found the spirochete of syphilis. All the misery could soon be ended. In that case, my views would be wrong, and the world would be better off. Wonderful!

But what if schizophrenia and many other psychiatric problems are not like that?

He Has a Problem with Communicating
[11/4/14]

Who? Well, that's just the problem, I'm not sure. You've seen those television programs where a relative goes to visit a man who's in prison and they sit on either side of a glass wall through which they can see but not hear each other. To communicate they must use an electric tube or telephone. What I'm talking about it is like that except without the tube. You have two people trying to talk to each other madly gesturing. One mouths the words, "Don't you see, this is really important . . .," but the other doesn't understand.

It all started about two years ago, or at least that's when it all started to become clear. I was upset with the leading psychiatric journal, the *American Journal of Psychiatry*. They publish all these articles about glutamate, ribosomes, and things and others about diagnostic criteria for borderlines, epidemiology of anorexia nervosa, genetic findings in schizophrenia, or comparison of typical and atypical antipsychotics, but nothing about people. So, I wrote an editorial with a title something like "There are no people in the *American Journal of Psychiatry*"—probably not too cool on my part—and sent it in. A few weeks later I got a reply rejecting my submission and saying, in effect, "Yes, there are." The editor was kind but firm. He noted that there was, in fact, an abundance of case histories and biographical accounts of famous psychiatrists and things like that. (I note, as an aside, that case histories are about "cases" not people, but that, of course, is a common medical practice.)

Clearly, he didn't get it, or maybe I hadn't been effective in communicating. I didn't know how to do any better. Over the past year and a half, however, I have been a discussant, an audience, or a reader of "case histories" toward which I have the same outraged feeling: "Yes, I suppose that is a case, but where is the person there, I don't have any idea who the person is!"

It's not that the people doing this work are bad. Many are my friends, very sensitive people. They love literature and things like that. But when they start talking about patients or treatments or treatment systems, it all falls apart. Of course, we have statements such as "This is the first admission of this thirty-four-year-old single white male." In all fairness, this is clear, easily understood, and informative. That is the medical tradition, take a huge amount of often amorphous information ("Well, doc, it sort of hurts here, but it's much worse there, and maybe it began about a month ago, but I think it may be longer than that, maybe three years ago when I noticed this strange feeling in my side") and reduce it to a much more linear clear-cut outline.

But especially in psychiatry that's a problem. Such an outline is perfectly good, but by itself it is grossly inadequate. There is no person there!

Here's what I am trying to communicate. Let's start with Shakespeare. Let's say, King Lear is an eighty-year-old white widower with three daughters. He worked as a king for many years but then gives his kingdom to his daughters—well, at least to two of them. Those two then find him too intrusive and cast him out. He becomes homeless and then psychotic. He improves a while later when the third daughter becomes kind to him, but she is killed, and the old man dies of a "broken heart."

Have I described a person? I suppose a little. But is that

sufficient? Have I just saved you the trouble of reading King Lear?

Well, that's what we do.

Today, at one of our discussions of "case histories" there was an interesting variation on that. The people doing it were again really good and bright people. There were four presenters, and they gave a lot of detail. But it was all in fragments: "She was really likeable." "When I saw her, she was really hyperactive." "She really alarmed me when she threatened to hurt herself." "She was very isolated without any friends." "She can really get along with people and has a way of getting them to open up to her." "It was fun talking with her." "She could be impossible." All really important pieces of information, but there was no apparent attempt to put them together! Who was this person? How did she get that way? What was her problem or were her problems? Did she improve? What about our treatments? Could we have done better? How? What is likely to happen in the future, what problems, what changes?

Now to be fair, this was not a typical "case conference." The focus was on staff experiences with this person, and the participants did a great job talking about that. But at least two things were missing. First, we needed an ethnographic-like statement about the treatment system within which the various participants operate (for example, I would say that it consists of more or less isolated subsystems, so our experience is not communicated and is fragmented). The second need was for some kind of synthesis about the patient: Who is this person, how did he get that way, what are the forces at work, and what is needed to help. Perhaps this could be something like what we used to call a formulation, not necessarily a definitive statement, more a best working hypothesis: "This person had an early life in a very chaotic family and a tendency to need both freedom and esteem in relation to those around her. When she found herself alone and isolated she became psychotic, finally improving when she was in a situation where she had freedom during the day, structure during the night, and people who cared about her. She was also helped by medication. Our various experiences with her were like the blind men with the elephant, each of us saw only one piece of the puzzle, but we were able to begin to put it together at the end. With a person like this who has so many sides to her it is helpful for staff feelings in working with her to make sure for ourselves that we try to put the pieces together by communicating with each other and trying to develop a more coherent story about her."

"I thought King Lear was a nice old man." "King Lear was demanding and difficult." "King Lear didn't have a clue how to deal with people." "He was crazy out of his mind, I couldn't reason with him at all. It was so aggravating." "He was so sad I felt sorry for him."

Or, more "objectively": King Lear was a king. He was old. He was foolhardy. He was demanding. He was later homeless. He became psychotic. He got better.

The pieces, whether described subjectively for the staff or objectively as in traditional medicine, need a story. Without that story I don't think we can understand either the patient or our relations to him and how we might connect more effectively and better understand our own emotional relations the next time. We must have a story.

Is that right? Is the mental health field one where, as in orthopedics, for example, we can often reach a diagnosis through objective means and then objectively prescribe a treatment or is it one where at least part of the task is to get some sense of where the patient is coming from, to be able to some extent put oneself in his or her place. That is the question.

New Mexico Experience 2009

"What brought you to the hospital?" the psychiatric resident asked. "My father," was the reply. "Did he think there was something wrong with you?" "I don't know." The intake interview went downhill from there. No matter what questions the resident asked his respondent provided no information. No way to make a diagnosis, to fill out the questions for admission criteria, even to know why the person had come into the ER.

We were role-playing. A resident was the intake doctor, and I was the psychotic patient. But he couldn't find out what was wrong. After several minutes of this, I suggested that we switch roles. He became the difficult patient with a psychosis and I became the intake doctor. I failed at least as miserably as he had. "World famous psychiatrist falls miserably on his face," I said, and the twenty-five or so residents laughed. Another resident offered to be the intake doctor for his fellow resident, the difficult patient. This new intake doctor was fantastic. He didn't look straight at the "patient" when he was thinking about questions to ask. He talked about concrete things, work, where the patient was living, things like that, and the "patient" began to warm up and to relax.

We were at the University of New Mexico Psychiatry Department. We, the residents, some improvisation actors, friends of the director of education for the department, and I, had started the morning with some warm-up exercises common to teachers of method acting, led by the actors. "Get in a circle, look into the eyes of the person next to you and clap your hands at the same time, then pass it on to the person next to you in the circle." The residents apparently didn't like these exercises too much, but everyone participated, and then we went on to the role playing. I think the exercises had gotten us all going and taken us out of the usual medical training structure, so when the role playing started, everyone was wholeheartedly into it, laughing when the difficult patient stumped the doctor, rooting for the doctor, suggesting questions, and talking freely when the "interview" was interrupted to discuss what was happening and what the doctor might try to do next. We did one interview after another, changing the type of patient and the people involved in the interviewing. On one occasion, one of the actors took the role of patient and started the interview with a loud "Hi doc, how ya doing?" which brought a lot of laughter.

For the last interview, a resident volunteered to coach an actor to take the role of a patient with whom she had difficulty. She took the actor aside and whispered to him. When the actor took the "patient's" seat, the doctor asked the opening question, "What brings you to the hospital?" The patient replied, "I want to be admitted" and proceeded to say whatever was necessary to prove that, but it was never clear whether he was "really" suicidal or just trying to get disability support.

At the end of the morning the training director asked how the session had gone, and the residents said how great it was for all of them to get together, something they had not done before. Was the role playing worthwhile? We didn't want to ask such direct questions at this point.

The next day we had a writing workshop, "Writing creatively about clinical experiences." All the residents that had come the day before were back again. Because of their scheduling demands, the time was shorter than is usual for groups I lead. We had time for only two writing periods of seven minutes each, each followed by residents reading what they had written and comments on the readings by the others. The usual rules applied: "Only comments about what works, what you remember, nothing like 'It was stupid to say that,' 'You shouldn't feel that way,' 'You used the same word twice,' or anything negative." Because of confidentiality concerns, I will only say that the residents were wonderfully open and forthcoming, and of course I learned something new about psychiatry. One resident who apologized that English was her second language and said she couldn't write very well, read beautifully about how she was always so surprised that people who hear voices and feel that someone is after them so often find the courage and trust to tell the doctor, a total stranger, about those experiences. I have seen literally hundreds of patients like that and had never before appreciated that important thing. Like I said, always something new

The third day I gave a lecture to the whole department, including those residents. Of course, I described a lot of those experiences in my talk. The administrative assistant had asked what technical things I needed for the talk, Power Point or whatever, and I had said no, nothing, I just want to talk to the people who come.

For me it was a wonderful three days. I had never had the opportunity to put a series like that together before. For me, and I hope for them, something emerged from that coming together that felt unique and important. Yes, it had something to do with teaching, with being, but also, I think, with understanding the nature of psychiatric disorder and our way of dealing with it.

What did it teach? Something about the degree to which that which we have conceptually separated out as "psychiatric disorder" is embedded in the life and personality of the person who "has" it. And how much the relationship between that person and the people around him or her, including the doctor, is part of that matrix. It is perhaps so much a part that when we separate these things out we risk losing touch with both the nature of the problem and understanding what factors are most crucial in its resolution.

Science and Art, Technique and Feeling
[*1/23/09*]

So she says to me, "Art isn't just a pouring out of emotions, it involves technique, training." "She" was Emily Coates, a fine and experienced dancer who was involved at Yale with the Performance Project. She was interested to see how her work might link to mental health treatment systems and ideas. We had met over coffee once with little meaningful communication, but then, after a large meeting, she said she would like to talk further. Not expecting much, I invited her to another get-together over coffee. This time I tried to explain my experience of how much art had to teach the mental health field, especially about what it meant to be human and about feeling, and how devoid we were as a field, in my opinion, of any kind of ability to grasp in theory or official practice, both those things. I added that, of course, some mental health types were very adept in those areas but that they had to do it on the side more or less, because coming from science, medicine, and academia, we were supposed to be dedicated to cognition rather than feeling in our writing, research, teaching, and much of our practice. However, for me, having technically "retired," I had become free to bathe in the arts and was so impressed by what they could contribute to the mental health field.

This was the point at which Emily looked at me, wide eyed and smiling, and said, "But art isn't just a pouring out of emotions, it involves technique and training." And thus began our discussion. I knew that, of course, having suffered through many years of failed piano lessons, some not so failed art lessons, and most recently a few acting lessons. But I grasped it now more clearly from the way she expressed it, making it more powerful and important.

She described how her training as a ballerina and more recently in modern dance had become absorbed into what I will call her "soul" and given her the means to use those skills and techniques as a way to express and communicate, not just as technical gadgets. I explained to her how, by contrast, one of the bases of medical education is to master one's feelings. You are confronted almost at the start of medical school with the dead body of a human being that you are going to start cutting. When you think about it that way it is a truly shocking experience. Of course, the trick is that you are helped not to think of it that way. The body is all wrapped so you don't really see it, you have partners at your table. and in the anatomy lab you are all doing this together, you talk, sometimes make jokes, struggle to find the femoral nerve or hundreds of other things. In other words, you concentrate on the technical task and know this is just part of the deal. As you go on, you experience doing experiments on live animals; they are anesthetized, but you know they will die after you have finished. Eventually you experience putting needles into live human beings, examining all their body cavities, and then cutting into live human beings. With the actual patients that you start to get later in medical school, you become increasingly responsible for their care and, later, often for their lives and sometimes for their deaths. You must learn to deal with all that. And you do it by learning to distance yourself, sometimes too much, sometimes not enough, but expressing your feelings was not in the past—and, I think still isn't—a central part of learning to be a physician.

What you really need to know, and are taught, is how to

identify hundreds of different diseases and conditions, often in cases not easy to discern; the effects, side effects, and interactions of hundreds of medications, also often complex and subtle; and many other things, things that evolve rapidly with new discoveries and the development of the medical field. I won't bother you with administrative things like setting up a practice, consent forms and legal liabilities, and much more.

If you go into academic medicine and research, there is more, much more still: sampling, statistics, methodology, writing reports, and so forth. Emily and I talked, for example, about the technique for writing an article for a medical journal. For me it is like a sonnet form, rigorous, restricted, beautiful. It allows for so much, so clearly. You know just where to look for each thing, the introduction, goals, methods, results, discussion, conclusion. And you know so easily when someone has not done something properly. Also, but more subtly, like the sonnet form, you can tell when it is just pro forma, done as a vapid thing to get tenure or whatever, and when it is done with "soul" as a meaningful, even important contribution.

As we talked, I started to get more and more confused. So there is soul and feeling in science, and there is technique and training in art. How do you deal with that?

One place for looking at this issue of technique and feeling is in master classes. For several years I have been fascinated, without knowing exactly why, by master classes, in piano, singing, acting, whatever. It now occurs to me that I know a bit more of why. In master classes you get people who are already very skilled. (In the first master class I ever saw, in Paris in 1957, the celebrated pianist Alfred Cortot was teaching some outstanding young pianists.) The student plays a piece or portrays a character and then the "master," the expert, a well-known figure in the field, talks with the student in front of the audience.

Almost always, the teaching is not so much "You should have played C sharp instead of C natural," but more like "Do you like walking in nature? With that passage there try imagining that you're in this beautiful field of wildflowers and the sun is shining down warmly on you." Of course, different teachers at that level have wildly differing approaches to teaching, but from my experience, their main focus is always to try to help the advanced student get in touch with the feeling of the piece or the role, to find that sense.

Of course, there's the personal side. As Emily and I were talking, I realized that this question is not only an issue for my field that I think is major but an issue for me personally, as well. In my life it has been easy to lean into the technical side of things, being careful to make sure everything on my massive evolving list of clinical tasks that need attention regarding patient care will get done. When I was an intern, that meant drawing blood, getting lab tests, checking x-rays, "working up" new patients, checking on "old" ones, talking to informants and previous doctors, scheduling new procedures, writing prescriptions, and on and on. And always, if you screwed something up, something terrible for the patient might be the outcome. And beyond that, keeping the house clean, revising papers, calling my parents, spending time with the kids, and much much more. I did these things successfully and usually with pleasure and some degree of looseness and even imagination, but the creative side, although certainly active, was always held in check. But the last few years, when I have been trying to be much more open to people and ideas, have been wonderful. Papers all over my office floor don't bother me all that much, and I keep on top of the important things. Occasionally things pile up on me and I decide I must be efficient and get a lot of things done. But that threatens to suffocate my new-found freedom and engagement, which is frightening. So I make myself lie down on the couch for a while, settle down, figure out what really has to be done and what doesn't, and get back in touch with myself. The technical (efficient, distanced) frequently threatens to take over the feeling and the creative, and I have become more aware of that and act to avoid that happening.

How Can a Story Have Such Power
[3/4/14]

There I was, with Claude and Linda plus a ton of other people, sitting in a large room in the cellar of one of the college buildings. The cellar is the home of the Yale Cabaret. It has about thirty high round tables, each of which can seat five people, and about sixty additional chairs, arranged around three sides of a stage that rises just a foot or so above floor level. Tonight all the seats were filled. Claude, Linda, and I were at a table having a simple dinner. As we finished, the lights dimmed. After a few light-hearted announcements, the lights dimmed even further and a huge bearded Black man appeared on the stage. He was simply and roughly dressed. With the only light in the large room shining directly on him, he began to recount how he had been in Sharpeville, in apartheid-era South Africa, during the demonstrations of 1984 in which a White official was killed. This man wasn't part of the demonstration but simply watching when police seized him, put him in a police wagon with many others, and took him away. In court a few days later the judge tells him it didn't matter whether he was part of the demonstration or not, he was there, and that was enough to put him on death row and to execute him. The man then described what it was like to be on death row month after month, how the individuals there were summoned at seeming random by their prison number, not even their name, to be executed. This dreadful narrative was interrupted from time to time by one or other of two additional actors, a middle-aged White woman who had the role of friend, sister, or policewoman depending on the moment, and a younger, more slender Black man who represented the protagonist when he was younger and in the prison. The brief appearances by one or the other of these persons moved the story, filled it out, and provided a welcome shift in focus from the grim central narrative. As the huge Black man told his story, he made me feel as though I was there. I had some feeling for what it was like, the whole thing, month after month of waiting and seeing one's fellow prisoners taken to be executed and imagining their minutes of suffocation, of struggle, of pain. Then, his number, too, was called. What was the magic of that performance, that story, told in that way. I have been moved by plays before, but never, never, like that. The reality of being there in that prison, in that situation, was passed on to me—and to the rest of the small audience in that enclosed place as well, judging by the total silence that reigned all around that stage. A couple of days before the protagonist is to be hanged, the post-apartheid regime takes over and he is saved, but his experience left an imprint on us in that audience that will be long in disappearing.

How does that happen that a story can have such power? And what is the role of the way the story is told, whether it is read, recited, or acted out in conveying reality.

Hannah Would Understand
[*5/7/14*]

Hannah Harvey did a CD lecture series on storytelling. I bought it when it first came out more than a year ago and found she was terrific. So, I did what I sometimes do when one of these series (I now have about sixty-five) is particularly great: I found out her e-mail address and wrote to tell her how terrific she was and, also, a little about what I do. One thing led to another, and after a small exchange of e-mails, I invited her to come to New Haven to teach us something about storytelling. She said she'd love to but wasn't sure if she could since they had just bought a farm (she lives in Appalachia, in a corner of Tennessee) and had sheep and chickens to look after as well as a two-year-old child. She added that she had just become a church deacon (or something like that) and for the moment at least she'd have to stay around.

That was that, for then. But, a few days ago, after finishing a long series on the evolution of Asian culture, I took out Hannah's lectures and started listening to them again. She's even more fantastic than I remember. Tonight, I listened to her seventh lecture, "Myth and the Hero's Journey." As usual, she was wonderful, very smart, very well read, very down to earth. She talked about hero stories and Joseph Campbell and Jung and myths and everyday life. She's teaching me what a hero's adventure story would be like and how to think about it and how to relate that structure—hero leaves home for a major reason, hero has a helper, hero faces challenges, hero comes back changed—to your life experiences, however big or small you might want to think of.

This starts me thinking of the time after my second year in college when I hitchhiked for three months and nine thousand miles around the United States, from Erie, Pennsylvania, to San Francisco and from Montana to New Mexico. I worked for the Frontier Days rodeo at Cheyenne, Wyoming, selling hot dogs after I'd smashed my finger working on a Ferris wheel. Late one night, I arrived, a total stranger, in Provo, Utah. The only place lit up was a bus garage and there I found a mechanic, whom I asked where there was a park where I might sleep. He told me and, as I was leaving, slipped a five-dollar bill into my hand. I told him I didn't need it (I had made enough money selling hot dogs), but he insisted, saying, "Take it. When I was doing what you're doing, someone gave me five dollars, I'm just passing it along." On another night, I slept out alone next to a beautiful lake above the tree line at Glacier National Park and woke up at sunrise to see a deer drinking from that lake. Among the people I met, one guy took me to a strip club in Cal City, Indiana, because I'd never seen Cal City. Stuff like that.

But was I changed? I don't remember feeling changed. I didn't feel I'd changed when Dad picked me up in Cleveland at the end of the three months. I just remember sitting and talking with him in the living room of my grandfather's small apartment and feeling relaxed and relieved that all was safe again—even though I had never really felt unsafe when I was out there on the road. But that was it. All I remember was feeling happy, comfortable, relaxed, and safe. I don't at all remember feeling different or changed or anything like that, just relieved. It was entirely different after I returned from a year in Europe five years later, when my feeling was "I don't really belong here (in the States)." Totally different.

Thinking about these stories, it is like they are really the essence of my life. My height, weight, medical history, and so forth, even my name, are important, but these stories are the essence. Hannah would understand.

More Stories
[*5/31/14*]

Last night I was thinking about what I wrote yesterday about the hero's journey and whether or not I had changed as a result of my own journeying, and it was like a piece of music that stopped before it was over—what is it, on the dominant chord, the chord that leaves you just waiting for it to resolve to the tonic chord, the end of the musical thought. So the thoughts continued, and in the middle of the night, or maybe it was early this morning, it came to me: I <u>had</u> changed. But consciousness has never been my strong point. That's why, I suppose, I most often make big decisions and even small ones on the basis of what seems to me to be intuition.

I had changed. But to explain that I need to go back a bit. My father's mother was born of German Jewish parents in the United States. His father, however, was a German Jew who was born in Germany. He came over in the later nineteenth century to avoid the German draft since Jews in the army were treated like dirt. Still a teenager, he'd learned a little banking from his older brother—was that Stephan (my middle name), "the star of the family?" But he ended up in Toledo or central Ohio working for "Aunt Nanny"'s husband, a rag dealer with a cart.

Dad said he hated his father, whom he described as a screamer, a yeller, though never actually violent. Dad could paint one picture in the morning and a very different one in the evening, which makes it hard to know the "truth." But whatever he said was mostly true, I think. I never heard him actually lie, although he was a real storyteller and could stretch things sometimes. Anyway, the negative statement about his father was certainly incomplete. In fact, his father, starting out in small-town Ohio as the assistant to an itinerant rag dealer, soon became co-owner of a dry goods store in the village of Loudonville, Arnholt and Strauss. He later also became the town's banker and was elected mayor, even though his was the only Jewish family in Loudonville.

My father had a horror of becoming a yelling despot, like his father, and he certainly wasn't. However, somehow you didn't screw around with my father. He was kind and gentle, serious and funny, and very smart, but when he looked over the lawn that I had just cut and said, "You missed this place here," I was careful not to make that mistake again. And when I got a C in math in seventh grade and he looked at my report card and said, not at all ominously, "Should I talk with your teacher?" I said "No," and I got all A's in all my subjects clear through to graduation. I never felt menaced, just that he was indicating how one should behave, which I see to this day a beautiful and very important message.

So, as I said, my father was a storyteller, and I was not. I didn't like the way he told all those stories and sometimes stretched the truth to make them better. They were often fun and funny as well, but I didn't want to be like that or to do that. However, as I realized late last night or early this morning, when I came back from my three-month trip across the country, I had many stories of my own to tell, real stories of my hundreds of experiences, true stories, and so I told them, and often people asked to hear them. And that was nice. So, in that way, a big way, I really had changed, although it seemed so normal and natural, not like any big deal or any change at all. I always had tended to tell the truth, only now I had truths that were big deal stories, real stories, of my own.

But there is more. There was that second trip, the year in Europe. At the end of that year I embarked with my motorcycle on the *Île de France* to return to the U.S. I was ready to go but very sad to leave. When we disembarked from that huge black boat, my parents were there on the pier, having come to New York to meet me. I saw them and was glad, but it felt strange, and I wanted to wait until my motorcycle got off too so we could go into New York together with them. They had thoughtfully made reservations for dinner at a fine restaurant, The French Shack, and I was grateful to them for that too. But the portions were too big. (In those days portions in France were small and inexpensive so it worked well to have five or six courses in succession at dinner, a great way to eat.) Of course, I thanked them and didn't say anything.

I returned to medical school at Yale for my third year. The school had kindly made my first rotation to ease me back in, but I wanted to maintain my connection with France. I subscribed to *Le Monde,* which came on fine sheets of onion skin paper. But I soon realized that wasn't working. Then someone backed into my motorcycle and knocked it over, which had never happened in Paris, and I realized that we were just not welcome here in the U.S. in the way we had been in Paris. There is a song—strangely, I just heard it for the first time tonight—"You can hold the candle, but you can't hold the flame." It was no use. Paris was slipping from my grasp. There was nothing I could do to stop it. I didn't renew my subscription to *Le Monde.* Finally, I even sold my motorcycle.

My life was back on track. I liked medical school, loved my internship, very much liked my year of medical residency, and then went into psychiatry, which I also loved. I got married, had two great (really!) kids, lucked into getting my "military" service at the National Institute of Mental Health, and became a drone then one of the leaders of the International Pilot Study of Schizophrenia (IPSS), which took me on trips all over the world. I moved on to Rochester as an associate professor, then to Yale as a professor. I was divorced and, several years after the divorce, bought this house, where I have now lived for thirty years, far longer than anywhere I have lived in my life before. I was very much single, sometimes too single, sometimes beautifully single, and free.

Then, about fifteen years ago, when I was about sixty-five and about forty years after my return from the year in Europe, my great friend and close colleague Larry Davidson and I were invited to be presenters at a conference in Marseille. We went, of course, passing through Paris en route. And I think I realized then, or at least felt, how much I missed that city and being there. After that, whenever I got invited to give a talk in Europe, about three or four times a year, I would stop in Paris for three or four weeks. I went back to my old cafés, found friends, spoke only French, read French novels and philosophy and history, and dug myself into the city. I found a small hotel in the fifth arrondissement, where the people became like family. The owner would take me out to lunch in fine restaurants, I would help them translate their materials into English. They always gave me the same room, a small room on the sixth floor, and at a very reduced rate.In the morning I would go to buy my croissant at the Kayser bakery two blocks away, then take one of the buses on the three routes that travel the rue des Écoles to Odéon, and go to my café, the Danton, where back in 1956 Ann and I would laugh at the "nine o'clock dog" coming by with his master, and in front of which we would kiss (which you certainly couldn't do out in the open in the U.S. at that time). Now, Michel or Dominique would bring me my *grand crème* without my even asking, and Monique, the owner, would come by to talk. One time she said she was having trouble with her neck, and I got up and gave her a brief neck rub, while the waiter looked on in mock surprise.

I would often lunch at the café Rostand across from the Jardin du Luxembourg. Sometimes Alain would meet me there or Sandra the clown, and it was there I met Alma Brami, young woman with big hair who was writing her third novel for Gallimard with a pen on scruffed up sheets of paper. (During this period I myself published about ten papers in French psychiatric journals, including two interviews about my life and career and one interview in a general French magazine called *Books* meant to be like the *New York Review of Books*.) In the evenings I would sometimes have dinner at a Chinese restaurant, the Celeste Empire, perhaps with Pernette, more often alone. It was there I met the Ravanels, Serge and Ida. He had been a leader of the Resistance in the Toulouse area, and the restaurant had a photo on the wall of him with a French general on a balcony reviewing the Free French troops. As the Ravanels became more fragile, I would take food (*potage avec boullettes* [soup with something like matzoballs] for Ida, *crevettes* [shrimp] for Serge) from the Celeste Empire to their apartment, reached by bus 27. As I walked through the Jardin du Luxembourg or was anywhere else in Paris, it was clear to me that I was back where I belonged.

After all those years.

And then about two years ago, after maybe thirteen years of "being back," I started getting fewer invitations to give talks and began having an arrhythmia, which is scary when it happens but under pretty good control. So, I started going back less often. Then several months ago, Alain died in his early sixties of lung cancer. He was so great, really like a brother for me. A couple of months before he died, I sat with him in the hospital for the hour he was having the chemotherapy poison flow into him through his chest tube.

I have not been back for almost a year now. I miss it, of course, but I find that I have transferred some of my life there to here. I meet people for coffee in a café or for a long lunch. I have come to know Marie-Cruz and Veronica, the waitresses at the Atticus Bookstore/Café, and Yan at the Royal Palace, as well as Tom and Tommy at the gas station at the corner (Bill, Tom's father and Tommy's grandfather, died of pancreatic cancer about five years ago).

So, although I certainly miss Paris, I don't need it so much anymore, I've brought a lot of it here for me. I guess I have found my Erie, or my Loudonville, which, with the munificent people, conferences, music, theater, and library that are part of Yale, provide a kind of Erie/Paris mix that is perfect for me. My motorcycle may have gotten knocked over here years ago, but in the end, we (it and I) have won. Bless its soul! Bless its soul!

It's a Long Long While from May to December
[*12/21/08*]

"It's a long long while from May to December, but the days grow short when you reach September." I remember hearing that song one night in a park at the edge of a lake in Skaneateles, New York. It's a lovely place. It was early spring, the night was warm. My Dad and I had just started our trip from Erie in our '47 Ford to visit colleges, Cornell, Yale, Harvard, Swarthmore. Dad was terrific, I didn't really appreciate it fully 'til now. He had reserved rooms at great hotels—not fancy but right for us—all along the way. We even spent a day on Cape Cod, where he arranged for me to go out sailing with a guy on a small sailboat. Afterward, as we lunched in a small simple seafood restaurant overlooking the water, Dad leaned over and said quietly, "Look over there. That's Lillian Gish." And I said, "Who's that?" I had never heard of the formerly very famous movie star. Dad sat back in his chair and smiled, understanding, amazed, a little sad.

"It's a long long while from May to December." The song is about long-lasting love between two people, of course. I had no idea at the time that May-December relationships might also be those between a young woman and an older man, referring to the difference in their ages.

That evening in Skaneateles was the first after leaving Erie. We stayed at a quaint hotel opposite the park and the lake, and after dinner I said I wanted to go out and sit in the park for a little while. Dad was fine with that. I left the hotel, crossed the street, entered the small park, sat down under a tree, and looked out over the water. How many times have I sat in a lovely place looking out over the water? I did it often on our island in Canada, also on my trans-Atlantic crossings by ship, most notably on the *Queen Elizabeth* (the original one) on my first trip to Europe in 1953. I did it that year, too, from a castle in Lerici, Italy, overlooking the Mediterranean. The castle was abandoned except for the youth hostel at the top where I was staying. That night I lay out on the parapet of the six-foot-thick wall with Mary from Wagner College, overlooking the dark sea from way above. The moon was full, music wafted up from the café whose lights you could just make out far below. You think things like that don't really happen? They do.

But this night at Skaneateles, the music was coming from a portable radio a little way from where I was sitting. Two young people, high schooll seniors, maybe, or young college kids, were talking quietly in the dark, kissing, and their radio was playing "The September Song"— "It's a long long while from May to December." It's a beautiful quiet song, and as I sat, thinking of them, looking out over the water, hearing that music, I missed not having someone beside me, someone I was in love with.

I was bathed by the feeling of soon to be leaving Academy High School, where I had gained five letters for swimming and water polo and had my blue-and-gold Academy varsity sweater with five stripes circling the left sleeve; where Bob and I had won a regional debate tournament; where I had kissed my first girl and had been in love with Rose Trimble and then Barbara Love, who was a cheerleader and a year ahead of me; where I had learned to drive; and all those things.

All that was drifting into the past.

And now years and years later, in 2008, I am listening to that song again. In my house. On my CD player. During a beautiful snow. This time, the "September Song" is sung by

Lotte Lenya, the wife of Kurt Weil, who composed it. Lotte Lenya, the Austrian-born former impoverished prostitute who reinvented herself as a dancer and then an actor and married Weil. She became a wonderful singer and actress and he a famous songwriter.

Of course, they're both dead now.

A lot of people are. Malcolm Bowers, George Mahl, Irwin Metzger, Steve Herzog, Sara Lee, Dad, Mom, lots of people.

I am so lucky. I have Paris, and Sandra and Alain and Pernette. I even have Serge Ravanel, ninety-two-year-old, former French Resistance leader, and his wife, Ida. I met them a few years ago at a Chinese restaurant where we had each gone for years. Now I bring them take-out food from the same restaurant when I am in Paris because they are too old and infirm to go out. And wonderful people in my *groupes d'écriture* here in New Haven, and my other wonderful friends here.

God, am I lucky. I have a lovely house, my kids, CDs and DVDs, and new people I meet, new things I'm learning or working on, and Paris, New Haven, Bergen, Rome.

Beautiful snow is falling outside at this very moment, not enough to make tunnels but sufficient to make an angel in it on my front yard, which I did two nights ago.

And yet, "It's a long long while from May to December." Yes, it is, and in September, "the days dwindle down to a precious few," as the song says. But it's not that. For me, it's more that it would be wonderful to hold that May person, a young woman— admit it— where we could look out at the snow together, or make matching angels, or cocoa, or sit in a park looking out over the water and hear that song together, or make love, wake up together in the morning, and smile into each other's eyes.

Well, I guess you can't have everything, can you? But I've got almost everything.

Writing Assignment One
[*8/10/15*]

Dear Dad,

    Wow, today I had lunch with Vivian. She feels just like I do about at last being in New York. She's at Columbia, which is more uptight than NYU, but maybe that fits her better. Anyway, it took me only one day to get over my feeling weird and a little scared about being in this huge city and away from home, but something happened during lunch today so all that apprehension just peeled away and I felt wow I'm here! I had my first class this morning on songwriting. Of course, I know some of this from Wagon Wheels, but the idea of actually having a class on songwriting, and that the college is good with that and that the teacher actually teaches it—well. I just have to say it again, wow! The kids seem good, dressed in all kinds of ways. I think some know more about music than I do and a couple have even made CDs of stuff they've written. Well, I'm not there yet, but hey Toto, I don't think we're at the lesbian butcher shop anymore.

    Grampa John is coming down next Tuesday. I think he wants to go to a museum, maybe the Frick, which he says is good and not so huge. He wants me to choose a place to eat, I'll find a place near the Frick that isn't too expensive because I know he doesn't have as much money as we do and also doesn't like spending it as much, but that's fine, it's good to be with him and I know he likes being with me.

    Anyway, poor Vivian. I know she likes being at Columbia, but they have all these traditional classes, no music writing for her. But since she's a pre-med I suppose that's what she wants, maybe she'll change her mind. Can you imagine, spending four years, and then a lifetime on organic chemistry physiology and whatever! Poor Vivian.

Anyway, I've started writing a new song. I'll accompany it with my ukulele and Nemo has agreed to back up with guitar. Of course, he's so great he's not really back up, more front up. It's great having him do this stuff with me. He says he even knows a little bar/restaurant where they have a big room where if you're good enough they let you have it for an hour as part of an evening of new songwriters. Wow (again)! New York, songwriting course, performance space, Nemo. John's trying to get me to stay in the East. Who knows, but I think I'd miss LA and you guys too much.

Loveya,
Petula

Writing Assignment Two
[*8/12/15*]

Hello again, Ronald. We're making progress, crossed the Zambezi today. Not without problems. Using rafts of logs bound together with hide, some rapids but not huge. Suddenly a huge croc we hadn't seen tried to climb up on one and turned it over. One of the porters fell off and was lost, poor soul. Otherwise, all fine. One of the porters we call Tommy, young, handsome, smart, has been particularly good helping out in many ways. Also amazingly good sense of humor. We've made him chief porter for our group and he helps with the fire at night, even exchanging jokes. Never saw anything like it. So now he's carrying my gun and my most important personal things. Almost not an African, he's that handsome. I don't know how long it will take us to reach you know who, or whether he's even still alive. Meantime I'm sending my reports back to the paper and we're slogging ahead with all the usual annoyances. Bee got in my ear two days ago. They like to lay their eggs there. Devil of a time to get her out, but finally Tommy, bless him, succeeded. He's really a gift.

    I have to tell you about a particular kind of tree we see in this part of the country. It's tall and grows all by itself on a mound of earth. The lions love them, use them for shade at midday, scratch their claws on the bark. These trees the locals call baobabs don't seem to have any fruit or anything the animals eat and don't seem to need much water, but they're all over the place. When we see a dead one, we use it for firewood and it burns beautifully, emitting an odor a little like sandalwood. Amazing place out here, such a mix of desolation and disease on the one hand and beauty and marvels on the other. And so far from the dirt and crowds of New York and London! Sometimes I hate the veldt, but other times it's the most beautiful, solitary, quiet, miraculous place in the world. And the stars at night, you would love that!

Monty's grumbling as usual, pretty much about everything, weather, food, bugs, even the lions, he thinks they look scrawny—wait 'til one jumps on him. Some of the porters are down with malaria, but that's pretty much expected. The hartebeests around here are so abundant that you have to practically scare them off. No wonder there are so many lions just waiting to get hungry again, lying with their prides under the trees, watching.

I write to Maude every week. I haven't gotten a letter from her—or anyone else—for over a fortnight. No women here, of course. I told Tommy about her. It appears he had a wife too, but something happened to her, he wouldn't say what. I guess he's had a complicated life. His mother was killed by some disease, doesn't seem to know much about his father. He was raised by missionaries, which is why he's so comfortable with us, I suppose, but they were so holy he finally slipped off to the village he came from. Didn't know exactly where he fit in so set off to find an expedition to work with, perfect mix for him of black and white. He seems really good with that. Oh, oh, here comes Monty again.

Well, we have a long trek across the plain tomorrow, no more rivers for a while. We're getting there! I hope the paper's happy with our reports. They certainly were eager to have me do this, but now I don't hear from them.

Hope you are well, take care,
Henry

A Formulation
[*12/9/18*]

In psychiatry it has been the tradition at the end of the discussion or "write up" of a "case" to provide a formulation. It is a way of describing one's thinking about how the person developed his or her disorder and the nature of that disorder. A diagnosis is also provided. Thus, we have adapted a traditional medical approach for the field of psychiatry. The "case history," with its description of the problem, the evolution of that problem, other problems, family and social history, is then summarized into a diagnosis and formulation. This is a useful and powerful way of collecting and synthesizing information about the patient for the purposes of identifying the disorder and its causes and for determining treatment and predicting outcome.

As a psychiatrist, I have done personally hundreds of these patient "workups" and judged and commented on hundreds of others that colleagues or trainees have carried out. So now that I am working on an autobiography it seems reasonable that I might produce a formulation of myself.

But I find I can't. Partly, it is because I am in the middle of it all, which makes it incredibly difficult to get a fix on my life, to get far enough outside it to see it clearly and more or less objectively. But partly, I think, it may be more serious than that. Perhaps the "formulation" of a life is not possible. Perhaps a life is too complex, too entangled, to many-threaded, to have a "formulation."

Well, of course, a life is not a disorder, but in psychiatry are they really that separate? If we take seriously the "biopsychosocial" foundations of understanding psychiatric problems, doesn't that overlap considerably with having a life? Isn't the formulation, the story, pretty much the same for both?

A Story
[*11/28/16*]

So today the psychology prof tells me to take the story of Vronsky in *Anna Karenina* and write about his psychology. I love that book, but I hate Vronsky. He looks as though he's trying to do the right thing but *au fond* is a rigid cold sonofabitch. If you met him, you wouldn't know that right off (unless you were my daughter Sarah, who doesn't miss much). I would have thought that, yes, he is a bit cold and formal, but really they all are, unless they are emotional highly strung people whom you can't count on for anything—well, perhaps for making a scene and a fuss, but not good for anything else.

But you'd think you could count on Vronsky, Count Vronsky. He will do what he is supposed to. I suppose you could even say he is more or less supposed to make it with Anna. I mean, she has married an even colder, more disgusting man, and she is crying out for love and warmth, why not. Well, she finds Vronsky. They are called lovers, but shouldn't that word be reserved for people who are really in love, not just—well, you know. So they hook up and then live together, and she loses her home and her son since she isn't supposed to wander off like that. But it doesn't work out. I mean, how could it—between a basically uptight guy who can go on living like nothing ever had happened and a girl who has lost her connections, especially her son, and for what—this piece of cheese?

So what happens? Well, she throws herself under a train, this wide-eyed Goldilocks, Cinderella maybe, or Rapunzel. I mean all these women have pretty much the same problem.

They are expecting a prince, a real prince, a prince of a man, loving, fun, responsible, and, of course, it won't hurt too much if he is rich, really rich.

But the prof says I'm supposed to be talking about Vronsky. To which I say, I am. At first Vronsky looks like that prince, but when he takes off his clothes, think of Donald Trump. Sure, he's still rich, but he's mostly just a fat blubbery guy, no more toupee, just a fat ugly man. Well, Vronsky isn't fat but otherwise, not much to him—*nul,* as they say in French, nothing.

So, the prof wants me to write about Vronsky. Well, I am. He's a nothing. I think I am supposed to be more insightful, dig down deep, reveal his soul. I don't think he has a soul, or much else, except a lot of money and a fancy uniform. He looks to Anna as though he has a soul, but she is a bleary-eyed, desperate woman. To me he looks more like a naked Donald Trump, except outwardly reliable and responsible and not so horrible.

Poor Anna, she needs something that is very rare—if only she had found Pierre from *War and Peace*. But she is desperate, Vronsky is handsome, noble looking, solicitous, if you didn't mind that he never laughs. Poor thing, terrible mistake she makes. Naive but that shouldn't be a ticket to suicide, although you see that it sure can be. Poor Anna, she thought Count Vronsky was something special. Maybe my prof did too, "Well, basically everyone is deep and complex." Nope, not Vronsky. He's just a shallow asshole, if that image isn't too impossible.

Congratulations
[*10/15/19*]

I returned late last night from my granddaughter Sophie's wedding. At some point in the process, guests lined up to greet the newly married couple, and I heard many people congratulating them, or was it just the new husband? I learned long ago that one only congratulates the husband, but I am not sure that every one of the two hundred people at the ceremony observed that bit of decorum. When I got to Sophie what came out of my mouth was "Good luck." Unfortunately, I hadn't thought ahead about that moment and would never have said that if I had. But at the moment and even now, two days later, I think it the most apt wish one could possibly have, and the most informative, although seemingly unkind, for the just married.

I have just finished writing my autobiography. Two years and four hundred pages after I started, what has most surprised me is how much I learned in the process. When I began, following the request of a wonderful doctoral student to interview me about "my life and work," I thought what would be involved was merely writing down a chronology of events and experiences, "First this happened, then that, then that, and so forth." I did do some of that, but then I would wander off here and there in the process of writing and get lost in describing what it was like to canoe alone through the islands late at night after visiting a friend on an island near ours and sitting out on a massive rock as the moon rose talking with her about Peter Ibbetson or what her life was like at St Catherine's, Ontario. Or I would find myself writing about a stranger in Provo, Utah, when I was hitchhiking in the summer of 1952, who gave me a five-dollar bill and, when I tried to refuse it, said, "When I was doing what you're doing, someone gave it to me, and I'm just passing it on." The chain of being among kind people reaches across the millennia.

But mostly I found I was too chronological or too non-chronological in my writing until an editor came along who added chapter headings and managed to mix things up without losing the thread, rather as when you add the cornstarch dissolved in kirsch to the almost ready fondue and see the cheese and wine mix into a beautiful silky collage. So, she blended the chronologies with the moments, the predictable and the unpredictable, in a way that I liked.

Anyway, the problems of writing an autobiography can mirror those of trying to understand the life it aims to reflect and the problems of understanding that life.

So, in the process of writing and rewriting the autobiography, naturally I thought more and more about what a life is and, of course, how you think about and describe it. Now whatever you may think about getting married, for me, based on my own experience and what I see around me, marriage is what Victor Hugo describes as a *"tournant de la route,"* a shift in direction, one in which what will follow is pretty much hidden in the shadows. So, "congratulations"? They seem appropriate when you graduate from college or win a swimming meet or even when you have a baby. They are for an accomplishment. Is marriage an accomplishment? I remember one friend saying, "All you need to do is ask someone and if they say yes..."

Getting married is a huge deal. And you really don't have a clue as to what will happen next. I remember when I got married, and it was a happy event, we headed from Boston toward

French Canada. We stopped for the night at a hotel that was at the farthest point east of the United States. I got up early the next morning all excited to see the sun rise before anyone else in the country. I shook my bride to see if she would join me in the adventure. No, she replied, she wanted to get more sleep. I didn't know it at the time, but that was pretty much the tone of our subsequent marriage. I'm reliable, but love occasional adventure, even perfectly safe things like seeing the sun rise. She was solid and really avoided extremes of feeling, at least as far as you could tell. In a way, that was very good for me. But at a twenty-year point it began to feel that there was something empty about this. How could you tell that early on? I certainly couldn't. I don't think even a much wiser person could have.

Congratulations? Sometimes yes, sometimes no. Marriage is, indeed, a *tournant de la route,* but where that new route will lead you, how can you know? Sometimes, I think it's wonderful, even super wonderful. Sometimes, it's awful, soul killing even. And often it's somewhere in the middle, isn't it? I guess that's why, out of impulse, I said to the new couple, "Good luck." I wasn't being ironic or mean, I was reflecting what I believe. But I really should have said something more socially acceptable, I know that.

Doing Autobiography
[*12/5/18*]

I've told you that I've been working for over a year on an autobiography. What has been shocking to me about this attempt is how much I've been learning—about me, about describing a person's life, maybe even about being human, but I'm not so sure about that last thing yet.

Just having everything out there is in itself an amazing experience. There are pieces of your life that you had forgotten or that you hadn't connected with other pieces. And having some sense of, having written about, the whole thing, well, it's hard to describe the impact of that. Maybe, it's like having seen almost all of a movie like *Casablanca* rather than just a little part.

But there's something further that relates directly to time. If you think of your life, probably you think of one thing following another, sequences, even if there are long gaps between each part. It's a little bit like listening to music, a concerto, a song, one part of it. But when you have the autobiography out there, it's also like looking at a painting. You may notice one thing or another, maybe by chance or because something stands out. You can also see the whole thing in one glimpse, get the effect of the totality. I'm getting closer to being able to do that now, at least I have realized the concept, something that had not really occurred to me before.

And if you tell someone about the autobiography or if someone reads a draft, they may say shocking things, things that are obvious but somehow have never occurred to you. It may be something really "simple," in the sense of obvious (to them), such as "You don't write much about your mother" or "I get almost no idea about your sister." And, of course, even if you have noticed that yourself, it is shocking that it is noticeable to a friend or a stranger. Oh, my gosh!

There are more subtle things too, not that much more subtle, but still apparently only noticeable to someone who is particularly attuned. A person who I think is becoming my editor and who I think is probably really terrific, said to me over lunch when we were discussing the manuscript, "Of course, you are your mother's child." That almost drove me through the roof. "You mean I am as much a failure as she was. You mean I'm as troubled as she was, as incompetent, as discouraged, even as proud, as snooty, feeling as special?" Of course, I didn't say any of that out loud. In fact, although my reaction was strong, it was also inchoate. I didn't trust enough to say anything.

One thing my possible editor added to preliminary suggestions about my draft shocked me. In writing about my grandfather, I had said something to the effect that "we" called him Sambo, which she changed to "Only people in the family called him Sambo." Sambo was the family patriarch. His real name was Samuel or just Sam. But we never called him anything but Sambo. "We," who's we? Why, us, of course. Us, the members of my family.

I knew it all along, like I know that grass is green or the sky is blue. No one ever told me, I just knew it. That's how the world was, "we" called him Sambo. But when my editor identified "we" as "the family," I was shocked because I had never thought about it, had never put it into words.

So, what's the big whoop? I have spoken before of one of my patients who was born and raised on Nantucket and who referred to people who were not from Nantucket as "offislanders." She was the member of a small group of people, a couple of thousand perhaps, which for her seemed to constitute the world. The rest of the people in the real world, numbering billions, had a shadowy existence at best. notable only as being not of the island. The name "Sambo" for my grandfather shows the same thing. "We" belonged, everyone else in the world did not. There was this tight little boundary around "us" that gave us an identity, connections to each other, a meaning, and all you other people out there, you're okay but you're not "us." Oh my god, yes, it's true, that's how I felt and I never noticed it. Now what does having that feeling mean?!

In the past, I have felt something like that when I was overseas (offisland?) about being an American. I just now happened to tune into George Bush's funeral and the huge army chorus and orchestra were singing and playing something loud and pompous. I suppose that same feeling about being so special and protected was true also of British subjects around the time of the Empire.

That's what writing an autobiography is like.

Feelings
[11/5/19]

I started attending a six-day "course" on romanticism yesterday. The professor is from Yale, one of our group of emeritus professors, I think. He is very good and very knowledgeable. I learned, for example, about the distinction between the beautiful, the sublime, and the picturesque. As I was listening to him, my mind wandered a bit. I began thinking about my grandfather who was born in 1876, the same year that Henry Morton Stanley trekked across Africa, the dark continent, and found Dr. Livingston, the missionary whom Europe had thought was lost, perhaps dead. Then I thought of my seventh-grade civics class. In one section we were asked to describe the career we hoped to have, and I wrote about becoming a big game hunter in Africa. The teacher seemed angry at me at first, figuring I was making fun of her and that I wasn't taking the assignment seriously. But I was taking it seriously, and as she questioned me, she realized that and so accepted what I had written.

I mean what else would you want to do besides being a big game hunter? I didn't have any desire to kill animals or to help other White people do that. Somehow, I would just be there and know how to handle all the situations that might come up. Trekking across Africa, the endless sky, the veldt, the amazing animals—lions and elephants, leopards and cheetahs, elands, hartebeests, wildebeests, and water buffaloes, flamingos, vultures, eagles—and, of course, the night sky with a million stars and the magnificent, many-colored sunsets. There were, to be sure, dangers to deal with. The wild animals could be dangerous. A fer de lance (iron of the lance) snake could kill you with a single bite. Bees might settle in your ears, as one did with Stanley. And then there were the diseases, malaria, dengue, and so many others. But, oh, those skies, those animals, all that nature and those spaces. I had read about Osa and Martin Johnson, who made wonderful documentary films of their safaris, and many others, explorers, white hunters. I had not yet read *Out of Africa* by Isaak Dinesen nor seen the movie with Robert Redford and Meryl Streep, which came out many years later and confirmed all my romantic beliefs about the continent, helped along by a musical score that featured Mozart's clarinet concerto.

Our professor was now talking about William Cowper, whom he pronounced Cooper, and about John Constable, some of whose paintings were projected on the screen. But I was still off on my own travels. I was crossing the Isthmus of Panama with Balboa and seeing the Pacific Ocean for the first time, the monster body of water that makes the Atlantic seem like a puddle. Then I was on to Brahms and his magnificent piano concertos, which make my heart pound, and his violin concerto, the second movement of which makes my soul weep and which I began to hear in my mind. Then to Keats and Shelley and to my special buddy, Victor Hugo. I am still reading in French *Les Misérables*, but I can only manage two or three pages at a time because they are so rich.

I had a sudden thought: Knowing the distinction between the beautiful, the sublime, and the picturesque is kind of interesting, of course, but thinking in those terms has a sort of Medusa-like effect. When people looked at her with her hair all snakes, they turned to stone. Perseus knew about that problem and so looked at her only in the reflection on his mirrored shield and thus was able to kill her. Now Brahms was incredibly knowledgeable about the rules of harmony and melody and somehow didn't let them rule him and so could write those magnificent concertos. Similarly, Victor Hugo knew the French language inside out but rose above the particulars to write the magnificent *Les Misérables*. The part about Jean Valjean coming to a village at nightfall and not being allowed to eat or stay at the inn because they realize he has been a galley prisoner, so sleeping on a park bench, resonates with me. Hugo was the first person I had met or read who could mirror my experience of arriving in a residential area of Provo, Utah, in the middle of the night and not knowing what to do. Jean Valjean had it worse than I did, of course, but at least I now had met someone who realized what it felt like to arrive in a strange place, know not a person, and be totally alien.

So, knowing and analyzing stuff is important, but you can easily be turned to stone, losing the feelings. You can talk all you want about hormones animating adolescent love, but can you remember that feeling!? Robert Browning's poem "Andrea del Sarto" describes a painter who was technically perfect but painted without soul as a convenient way to earn a living. When I took an acting class, the wonderful Doug Taylor was trying to help two students do a scene from *The Philadelphia Story* where the two leads are supposed to be falling in love. "Try it again with the card table between you," Doug said, and it didn't work. He tried other things. Nothing worked, the scene lacked feeling. "Okay," Doug said, "Now try it again and fix his collar as you are saying your lines." She did, and voila! the feeling was there!

Kindness
[*3/8/19*]

It started about ten years ago. I was in Paris on bus 57 going from Maubert, a couple of blocks from my hotel, to place d'Italie about a half block from where Pernette lives in her apartment off the courtyard. (Her apartment is lined with books except for the large space in which she paints and has a tiny kitchen, dishes usually in the sink.) It was about 7:00 in the evening, and Pernette and I were going to go out for dinner.

When I got on the bus at Maubert, it was full, so there I was standing in the aisle holding onto the bar among a crowd of other people. I looked down and there was this young girl, about seventeen, looking up at me. She got up from her seat and asked me, please to sit down there. I didn't know what to think, do I really look that old? How kind of her! I smiled and thanked her *mille fois* (a thousand times) and sat down.

From then on, and increasingly as I got older, when there was only standing room on the bus, someone would get up and offer me a seat. Do you know how that makes you feel? Like royalty, like being offered a nice warm blanket in a world that otherwise can be pretty cold. You are the recipient of totally unselfish kindness.

And it began happening to me in the United States as well. One day I was going into the Westville Post Office, and an old lady, maybe sixty-five or even seventy (I must have been eighty-five) who was also going in opened the door for me and held it open as I went in. My goodness! What is going on?

A few years ago Larry started opening the door for me if we

happened to arrive at Atticus at the same time for our breakfast on Friday mornings. Then he began offering to to pick me up in his car if we were going somewhere, and he or Maryanne would drive me home after I had dinner at their house. Claude, too, would offer to pick me up when I was bringing the fondue dinner stuff to prepare at their house, and he would bring me home after we had finished dessert. I don't think I have ever done that for someone.

My kids, Jeff and Sarah, also began to look after me more—well, it tends to be mutual as it should be, but that is a shift, and I love it. Other people too, as in my writing groups, seem kindly accepting of my increasing incompetencies. Yes, I began to feel like an old person. Yes, in some ways that was sad, but it was also a fact. And yes, I began to feel special, being taken care of like that.

Of course, I have had people who helped me all my life. My parents paid for my college and med school and really provided more than adequately for me. I think, too, of all those people who picked me up when I was hitchhiking around the country, or went out of their way to show me something special, like the guy who took me to Cal City and the striptease joint. But this is something new and special.

Yesterday I had asked Larry if it was all right for me to attend Lexy Davidson's high school play in which she had the role of Helen of Troy. Larry came and picked me up. We drove to the school theater. Maryanne arrived at the same time. They matched my retarded pace without even mentioning it as we went into the school and to the auditorium. After the play we went for a drink. Again, they did not go on faster ahead of me, and Larry held the door open. They insisted on paying. The same thing happened at the restaurant where we went next, although kindly they did agree that next time we would dine at a restaurant they would pick and I could pay for that. Then Larry drove me home and opened the car door for me to get out.

It feels so good, even overwhelming, not getting old and infirm, but the wonderful kindness not even asked for. It's just there.

I came in on the final minutes of the *Wonder Woman* movie on the Turner Movie Channel three nights ago. There's a lot of gratuitous violence and bullshit, of course, but other stuff too. At the very end, Wonder Woman, is fighting this guy who says to her, "You see, people just go on killing each other and are driven by greed and hate and won't stop," and she replies, "Yes, I know that, and yet they are also so much more, so much more." And dammit, she's right!

Magic Moments
[*7/30/19*]

I think listening to Poulenc's "L'hommage à Édith Piaf" must have brought this on. One early evening when I was in Paris I was walking near the edge of the Luxembourg Gardens. I was just walking. It was September, the air was warm, just perfect, and as I got nearer and nearer to La Closerie des Lilas, I began to worry. You see, in those days the Closerie, a mostly outdoor restaurant where much of the terrace was enclosed by walls and a cover of leafy vines, made some of the finest *duck a l'orange* (duck with orange sauce) in Paris, hence the world. The skin was crisp, the meat tender and juicy, and the orange sauce a mix of piquant and sweet—it was perfect. And c*anard a l'orange* was also one of my favorite things in the world.

But there was a problem. The restaurant's serving of *duck a l'orange* was for two people, and on this particular evening I was alone. As I walked closer, I so wanted to sit down to such a wonderful meal. But that was impossible, it was for two people after all. I really couldn't do a thing like that. Or could I?. True, I came to Paris three or four times a year in those days, each time staying for three or four weeks. There would be other times. Probably. But, of course, one never knows. And if I had invited someone to go with me, we could have shared the dish. But again, who knows when I might get this chance again? Oh, all right then.

So I entered the restaurant and addressed myself to the maître d'hôtel. With that wonderful French capacity that you sometimes encounter, especially at fine restaurants, he was polite, nothing special here, and showed me to a table. The waiter responded in the same fashion when I, one person, ordered the duck for two people as well as a half bottle of Sancerre rouge.

It was wonderful! And I took a very long time, several hours. The evening became night as I finished the last morsels of tender meat and crisp skin and the rest of the wine. I was sorry I had no room for dessert. I paid and walked out into the garden, singing softly to myself.

Another peak moment occurred five thousand miles away from La Closerie des Lilas and thirty years earlier. It was during that summer after my second year in college when I was hitchhiking around the United States. I had been on the road for almost two months. I had met so many people, seen so many things, was sometimes lonely, often enthralled. Now, you know how I love music. In those days everyone had a radio in their car, they often listened to music even when we were talking, and west of Cleveland it seemed that the only music they listened to was country and western. Now, I like country music, and as I got farther west, into Wyoming, Colorado, Utah, it seemed a perfect fit for the world there.

Now I was in Utah heading for Salt Lake City. I knew, of course, that it was a big city and also had the Mormon Tabernacle, which I wanted to see. My ride let me out in the middle of town in the early afternoon, and I soon found my way to the Tabernacle. It was huge. When I entered through the large doors, what did I hear? Music. Not country and western music, but music music. I headed toward it. In a large auditorium I found a choir rehearsing. I think it was Bach. Real music. I took a deep breath. I relaxed my shoulders. I sat down in one of the seats in the back of the hall and savored it all. Here was music, real music, all over, all round. I was home.

Stories and Psychiatry
[*3/7/17*]

In the beginning was the word—and very shortly thereafter came stories. Stories that described the basic beliefs of cultural groups, stories that made it possible to avoid the total sense of being adrift in a mysterious, unpredictable, and dangerous world. Stories gave structure and sense to what otherwise was an amorphous mass of uncertainty. And that basic need for a story, for stories, has not changed much from that time long ago to this very day.

Stories are crucial even to help decide basic next moves. For example, when I was in high school trying to decide which college to attend, it was a story that made it possible to choose, just a little story made all the difference. My father was the first one in his family, German immigrants living in a village of central Ohio, to attend college. He went to Oberlin for one year, was drafted (it was the time of World War I), and after he was discharged went to Harvard. During his first year there, both his parents died, and he left college to work in the Cleveland steel mills. When I became a senior in high school, I applied to Harvard and Swarthmore (as well as some other schools) and was accepted by both. (Neither had that many applicants from Erie, Pennsylvania, in those days.) When I visited Swarthmore, I loved that it was next to a forest, that the male students didn't wear ties, and that people were so friendly and informal. Harvard, all male at the time, in contrast, seemed rigid and unpleasantly satisfied with itself. But I didn't know which to choose. My dad didn't put any pressure on me, but aware of his sadness at not having finished at Harvard and the cachet in Erie of having a son at Harvard, I knew that he wanted me to go there. At the time I was on the high school swimming team. During Christmas or spring vacation, the high school pool was closed so I worked out at the YMCA. One day I ran into one of the administrators there who asked where I was going to college. I told him I was torn between Harvard and Swarthmore. He said to me, "I had a friend who went to Swarthmore. He really liked it there." That did it. Somehow that was all I needed. It was okay to go to Swarthmore. I decided.

So, there you have it. A story within a story. A piece within the life of a person. Just one person, just one piece, but an important piece for that one person.

So, that's a story. We all have them. They shape our understanding of ourselves and the world, in huge things and small, as they have for millennia. But what relevance does that have for understanding mental illness?

Let's try this. People are always primarily in the process of constructing their lives. Like spiders with their webs or bees with their hives, we are always building and patching, surveying and fixing. From this point of view, the work of Piaget and of developmental psychology in general can be seen to be learning about this process of constructing our sense of self and the world. This construction involves not only cognition but feelings and somatic aspects as well. Even at the far end of life, the old man rethinking his younger days is often engaged not just in idle recollection but in rethinking, reconstructing his experiences, his background, his actions—in short, the same process as the spider uses with his web, building, fixing, in a sense, the coherence of his life or, you might say, its meaning.

Furthermore, I would suggest that all during one's life the same process is essential to one's life itself. It is the basis for decisions, for actions, for situating oneself in the world, for identity, and for understanding one's context. And all these things are basically stories, stories that we construct that illustrate who we are and the nature of the world in which we live. A child psychiatrist friend has suggested an interesting way of viewing this construction, as if children's blocks were used to form a structure with bridges, isolated compartments, tunnels, connecting and distant units, barriers and walls, and so forth.

This process of construction apparently requires some combination of activity on the part of the person with certain contributions from the people and the general environment around him. Thus, in considering psychiatric problems and improvement, the old light bulb joke often applies: How many psychiatrists does it take to change a lightbulb? One, but the bulb has to want to change.

So again, what has this to do with mental illness? Now this process of construction can be interfered with in many ways, bio, psycho and social, by brain injury or development, by experiences such as "sleep deprivation." A man who worked as a torturer in a CIA "black site" has described the process of "sleep deprivation" that he used on prisoners. He quit government service because he couldn't stand it any longer. Sleep deprivation, he said, is not just sleep deprivation. The prisoner is put in a windowless room and hung by his hands from ropes attached to the ceiling so he can stand up but not sit or lie. Or other devices may be used. He has no access to the outside world. If he tries to sleep, he is awakened at irregular intervals by one of the guards and before long has lost all sense of how long he has been in that room, how many hours have passed, how many days have passed—or haven't passed—where he is, and then finally, who he is. The torturer recounted that before long the person, totally disoriented, begins to lose his personality. And as far as the torturer knew, once broken, the person never fully regained the sense of who he was.

Or the process of deconstructing might involve something as subtle as being in a family or group setting. For example, in early Tavistock group seminars conducted in the United States, in which some normal members would develop psychotic symptoms, the group process itself seemed to undermine the capacity for meaningful construction of the idea of self and context. The undeservedly discredited "politically incorrect" work of Lyman Wynne and Margaret Singer studying "communication deviance" in parents of a schizophrenic offspring is another potential source of thinking about such a process.

I'll tell you about a psychiatric patient with delusions that I saw in a follow-up study. This well-educated young woman described how when she was walking from the bus stop to her apartment one winter evening she noted how the lights in some apartment buildings had a pattern. Ah, now I understand, she thought, that is a sign that the FBI is spying on me. She had turned what was certainly a random pattern into a story to give meaning to her previous situation. That situation had involved a sense of severe disorientation following several difficult life events.

Sarah Kames has described the experience of "Ur homelessness" in people with psychotic disorder. Is one importance of stories that they allow us to keep a sense of who and where we are and the nature of our context?

It would be helpful in this inquiry to be able to define stories reliably. I suggest, however, that the world of stories defy such an effort. Starting with the idea of putting words together in a particular form or taking data or details and putting them together in some form is not very helpful. Dictionaries and various literary sources contribute no idea of stories that seem particularly useful. The problem is how to think of "Little Red Riding Hood," *Anna Karenina,* and James Joyce's *Ulysses* together in a way that is meaningful. The idea of a linear story isn't adequate, nor is the question of truth or fantasy about a person, an event, or anything. Why bother? Because there appears to be something in what may be called "open narrative" that is crucial to thinking about psychiatric disorders and the people who have them. Without a story broadly defined, those people, not merely their defining characteristics, cannot be portrayed in a useful way.

I am suggesting, therefore, that for our understanding of mental illness we need two kinds of information, the traditional kind of data subject to testing reliability and measurement, and this other kind, related more to the arts and involving more global, less easily definable phenomena. So, what can stories do to help us improve our field that reliable measurements, careful sampling, controlled experiments, and statistical analysis cannot provide?

1. Communicating feelings.
I was letting thoughts run through my mind several minutes ago and for some reason recalled a little story that I had heard a long time ago. I grew up in the United States during "the war." "The war" was the Second World War. I was thirteen when it ended in 1945 so much of my childhood was spent listening to war stories on the radio, seeing reports of the war in the newspapers, mapping the progress of the troops with colored pins I put on maps hanging on the wall of my room, and, when I started going to movies, seeing movies about the war. The story I just recalled was about a marine, probably on Okinawa. He was part of an infantry engagement in the jungle, and suddenly a Japanese soldier appeared in front of him with his hands in the air signaling

he wanted to surrender. There had been a lot of trick attacks so the marine kept his rifle pointed at the soldier as he approached. Suddenly the soldier put his hand inside his shirt, and without hesitating the marine fired and killed him, thinking the soldier was reaching for a pistol. Examining the dead soldier, the marine saw that he was holding something in his hand, and it was not a pistol. The marine found that it was a photograph of the man standing beside a woman and holding a baby, probably his wife and his infant child. The soldier had apparently reached for the photograph to reassure the marine that he was just an ordinary family man with a wife and child.

That story doesn't have anything to do with mental illness or treatment, but it may be best to start our inquiry at a distance from that topic. How would you get that story into measurements? Does it have something special just as a story that you can't reproduce by the usual scientific methods? Is that "something special" necessary for our field? If so, what is it?

The most obvious thing is feelings, of course. Our problem is that to have a mental health science we wanted to be scientific, and feelings aren't scientific. "Affect," maybe, even "emotions," but not "feelings." However else that story about Okinawa works, it has the capacity to elicit feelings. It leaves me with a sense of waste, useless killing, unnecessary destruction, sadness, remorse. And what about the Japanese soldier, surely he was motivated by naive hope. But none of these more scientific descriptors leaves me with the feeling the story itself does, that mix of feelings, the sense of what the experience might have felt like.

That reminds me of the story, which I have told before, about a waiter who brought me a doggy bag of lamb chops, proudly proclaiming that he had washed them. What he meant was that he had carefully scraped all the meat off the bone and apparently had washed the bones, which were now totally cleaned off and pure white. Since one of my favorite things was chewing on the meat stuck to the bone, I was devastated.

One more story, just to drive the point home. A man capsized his small rowboat and found himself struggling in the water. Fortunately, a man in another boat saw the accident and rowed over to help. However, as the drowning man came up for air, his supposed rescuer took an oar and pushed him down in the water again. This sequence was repeated two more times. Finally, coming up for air out of reach of the man's oar, the person in the water shouted out, "What are you doing?" The man in the rowboat shouted back, "I'm waiting 'til you came up the right way."

I think we have done something with our field akin to what the waiter and the man in the rowboat did. To make it what we have (falsely) assumed was scientific, we have entirely cleaned the bones of anything that wasn't totally neat, namely feelings, and we are now left with "clean" variables that are no longer messy, measurable variables, reliable variables, variables that can be managed statistically with precision. But this piece is not a screed against such variables. In our work studying diagnosis, outcome, and its predictors, it would be hard not to be impressed by the beauty, power, and necessity of measurement. No, my point is definitely not that measurement is bad, only that it is not sufficient. We can't clean off our understanding of human experience to rid it of all that might be messy and not readily measurable. We need to use every means we have to attend to all the parts we know that make up our experience.

Actually, let's talk a bit more about feelings. In psychiatry the tendency is to list them: fear, anger, sadness, terror, maybe happiness and love. And perhaps several others. There is reason, of course, to have such a list, to do experiments, look at brain responses, and so on. But let's go to the real world.

In fact, there are many more feelings than the basic few used for experimental purposes. For one thing, there are many foreign words describing emotions for which there is no English equivalent. Take, for example, *gigil* (a Tagalog word expressing the joy felt in the presence of overwhelming cuteness), *wabi-sabi* (a Japanese term conveying recognition of the transient nature of things combined with aesthetic appreciation of that impermanence), and *tarab* (the Arabic word for an ecstatic response to music). Learning to identify and cultivate these experiences could give one a richer and more successful life.

Have you ever felt a little *mbuki-mvuki*, the irresistible urge to "shuck off your clothes as you dance"? Perhaps a little *kilig*, the jittery, fluttering feeling as you talk to someone you fancy? How about *uitwaaien*, which encapsulates the revitalizing effects of taking a walk in the wind? These words, from Swahili, Tagalog, and Dutch, respectively, represent very precise emotional experiences that are neglected in our language. And if Tim Lomas of the University of East London has his way, they might soon become much more familiar. Lomas' Positive Lexicographic Project aims to capture the many flavors of good feelings, some of which are distinctly bittersweet, found across the world, in the hope that we might start to incorporate them all into our daily lives. After all, we have already borrowed many emotion words from other languages—think *frisson*, from French, or *schadenfreude*, from German—but there are many more that have not yet wormed their way into our vocabulary. Lomas has found hundreds of these "untranslatable" experiences so far—and he's only just begun. Learning these words, he hopes, will offer us all a richer and more nuanced understanding of ourselves. "They offer a very different way of seeing the world."

And feelings are even much richer, diverse, and nuanced than that. My brief experience with acting classes and attending master classes in music and drama opened doors for me to lands of which I had only the vaguest notions. The master class teacher told the already very expert student, "You said you liked nature. Now try playing that again and think about taking a walk in the woods as you play." What resulted were the same notes and rhythms but with a massive shift to new and powerful feeling. And then there's my oft-repeated story of the acting class in which two students rehearsed a scene from *The Philadelphia Story* in which the characters are falling in love. The teacher suggested successive ways to make the scene work—to no avail. Finally, "Okay, try it again. But this time fix his collar as you say your lines." Like magic, the scene came alive.

In most of our studies of feelings, even in our language choices, we have tried to make our observations "scientific" by reducing them. But in these instances this reduction comes at a huge price, major distortions of the things we are trying to understand. In trying to become scientific we have become less scientific. It's a little like the old story of the moose and the bears. To do a controlled study comparing moose and bears the scientist got a large number of each species. Then, to be able to compare them more accurately, he cut the antlers off all the moose.

Given the complexity of the real human mental world, an understanding of it can only be reached by giving some structure to our inquiry. We require not only nouns to describe qualities as "things" but some means, too, to identify the relationships among themselves and with the environment and the sources of change. Thus, we see the many attempts in the various theories including those that be considered as structuralist e.g. psychoanalytic theory, Piagetian theory, and Gestalt theory, our various ways at attempting to make sense of our mental processes and their relationship to context.

What else can stories do that traditional scientific methods cannot? Beyond being an effective communicator of feelings stories entail several other things: sharing experiences with others, taking you somewhere you have never actually been, making sense of complex sequences, re-understanding the past, trying things on, and representing human truths. .

2. Sharing experiences with another human being
Stories enable you to be there. To explain this, I must refer again to *Les Misérables* and the arrival of Jean Valjean, newly released from galley imprisonment, in a small village. Hungry and tired, he goes to an inn to get food and lodging, but they turn him away as soon as they realize he is a released prisoner. He goes to the jail to see if he can spend the night there, but the jailer tells him that only if he commits a crime may he stay there. This episode reminds me of an experience of mine, no way so desperate to be sure, while I was hitchhiking around the United States as a student. One day I was fortunate enough to get a long ride that brought me that night to Provo, Utah. Arriving after dark in a strange place, I searched for signs of life. The only light I saw proved to be in a garage where I found a man working on a bus. When I explained that I was on a big hitchhiking trip and looking for a place where I could lay out my sleeping bag to sleep, he told me of a nearby park. I thanked him and was turning when he said, "Wait a minute."

He reached into his pocket and handed me a five-dollar bill, a lot of money at the time. A few weeks earlier I had worked at the Frontier Days rodeo in Cheyenne, Wyoming, selling hot dogs, and had made $50. I didn't need money and tried to give it back. He insisted, however, saying, "When I was doing what you're doing, someone gave it to me, so I'm just passing it on." Obviously, I have never, even now sixty-five years later, forgotten that experience. (In fact, as you know, I tell the story a lot.) When you are in the middle of nowhere, a total stranger, alone, knowing no one, and someone reaches out to you like that, it is an incredible experience. Clearly, I did not have an experience as isolating as Jean Valjean and was much more fortunate, but I have at least some sense of what it might have been like for him, and it is a powerful link. So, stories have the capacity to reflect major connections between human beings, even a story written over a hundred years earlier, to reassure you that you are not alone.

3. Taking you somewhere you have never been

In *The Heart of Darkness,* Conrad the author has the storyteller in the novella describe his experience traveling up the Congo River in Africa. On his way down the African coast to reach the mouth of the river, his ship passes a warship that is lobbing shells into the jungle. The picture of that event sticks in my mind to this very day. I can see the large grey ship with its guns trained on the jungle that reaches even to the shore and the shells from the guns landing one by one in that vast green expanse. A little puff of smoke rises where each lands and then vanishes, leaving no evidence from a distance of any disturbance. I can see it, really see it. If I could paint, I would paint a picture of it. And yet in the book or elsewhere there were no pictures. The story painted the picture in my mind. I don't think you can do that with numbers and rating scales, unless of course you put them in some kind of story context.

4. Making sense of complex sequences
For actions, especially those that unravel in complex sequences, stories provide a way of communicating possible causal sequences. Several years ago we carried out a four-year follow-along study of people with psychotic disorders admitted to psychiatric services who were not involved with substance abuse. By combining our data from this research with data from several follow-up studies we had hoped to use time series methods to describe pathways of change or non-change during the follow-up period. Consulting with an outstanding biostatistician, I learned of the myriad data points and huge sample size we would need to develop a statistically valid set of profiles. It was clear we would need to set our sights much lower and to generate a series of impressions regarding patterns of change over the follow-up period. We did so using brief stories to illustrate our impressions. Thus, one pattern we suggested was what we called "woodshedding."

5. Re-understanding the past
In his discussion of Sophocles' *Oedipus* in his Great Courses lecture series *Understanding Literature and Life: Drama, Poetry and Narrative,* Arnold Weinstein notes that most of the action of the story has taken place in the past. However, what happens in the narrative is an understanding of the past, what the oracle had predicted, that the man Oedipus killed at the crossroads was actually his father, and that the woman he then married was actually his mother. As Weinstein notes, we

can't change the past, but we can understand in new ways its meaning and its implications. Yet another aspect of stories.

6. Trying things on
In an opinion piece published in the *New York Times* on Feb. 23, 2016, "Don't Turn Away from the Art of Life," Weinstein also notes the importance of literature as a way of trying things on, getting a feel for what this or that way of life might be.

7. Representing human truth
"*L'exactitude n'est pas la vérité*" (Precision is not the reality), Henri Matisse

The specificity and diversity of the processes discussed above cannot be overemphasized. Now, however, I must return to my complaint that the mental health field, especially in its theory and practice, has so grossly underestimated the area of feeling, its power, communication, and nuances? And how can we do better?

To quote Larry Davidson (quoting the song Tina Turner made famous): "What's love got to do with it?" What does this area of feeling have to do with the mental health field? Well, for one thing it is present in the importance to the patient of someone who cared, someone "who took me seriously."

Some argue that the area of feelings has been sufficiently treated in professional writings about mental health and illness. However, it seems to me that this area has most often been treated by converting it into cognition. (A famous example is Freud's essay "Delusion and Dream in Jensen's Gradiva," said to be the first psychoanalytic study of a work of literature.) Although such translation serves some purpose, it does not go far enough. Puccini's *La Bohème* is more than notes on a page, as is a Mozart piano concerto. *Hamlet* and *King Lear* are not just words on a page either. If you are fortunate enough to be a musician or an actor, you will know how much more work must go into a performance. If you have been fortunate to see some of the master classes as I have, you will have seen the master musician telling even the most advanced piano student such things as, "You said you like nature. Now try playing that again and think about taking a walk in the woods at the same time."

Feenition. Is there such a word? Rather than assume that cognition and feeling are separate, we need to explore whether they do not form a whole. Taking a class given by Doug Taylor using methods of the Actor's Workshop, I was mesmerized. In the initial exercise I realized how much the content of words is only a limited part of human interaction and meaning. The tone of voice, body attitude, and look on the face were all essential to conveying meaning. Are you telling me that as an experienced mental health professional and psychotherapist you didn't know that?! Yep. Somewhere I did but never consciously. I never really understood the importance of those so-called nonverbal aspects of an interchange.

Dear Eliza,

Perhaps you will understand what I don't think anyone else might. I was at a house concert at Barbara's last night. The performer was Jim Trick. He was wonderful in many ways, but especially in his songs and singing and playing he reminded me of the opera *Madama Butterfly*, which I had seen a few months ago.

But first let me tell you about an experience I had when I was hitchhiking across the country many years ago and my last ride of the day landed me in a small town late at night. I found a field to put out my sleeping bag and soon fell asleep. Awaking early the next morning as the sun was coming up, I looked around, and away in the west, for the first time in my life, saw the Rocky Mountains! Those mountains with the sun glinting on them rose from the prairies and reached all the way from one end of the horizon to the other. Never in my life had I seen such a thing.

Human experience, I think, is something like that. And it seems strange to me now that at various times the conditioned reflex, the stimulus-response learning model, behaviorism, even the studies of emotions and psychoanalytic theory could have been offered as explaining the whole of human experience. It is as though someone had taken one piece of one mountain to that vast mountain chain (in fact I have a small piece of one of those mountains) and said, "Here it is, this is all you need to know. This is the whole thing."

Now think of Maria Callas singing "One fine day" from *Madama Butterfly*. You know that this young woman, Cho Cho San, with her beautiful optimism, will one day see her "husband," Pinkerton, with his "real" wife and realize that she had only been his temporary wife, and you will think of what she sings then. Her singing, the music, the words, the whole story—with Pinkerton, his wife, the marriage broker—all of that together tear at your heart. How much the blending of all those things does something, reflects something, that none alone can match. The human experience can be that big, that powerful. It is like the Rocky Mountains, reaching all the way from one end of the horizon to the other.

Your "simple" study of mothers singing to their babies captures in some way that immensity. Not that you have to or can explain it all at once. But there is in front of us is that immense chain of mountains, a "simple" phenomenon filled with complexity and power. And it's as if you have been the first one really to notice.

Yours,
John

Subjectivity
[*9/29/14*]

Strange, here I am about twenty years into writing and thinking about subjectivity and I am only just beginning to realize how hard it is to describe a feeling. I mean much of my career has been based on asking people with severe mental illness questions such as "Do you hear voices?", "Have you felt depressed?", and things like that, with my point in research mostly being that we don't pay enough attention to the real quality of experiences in psychiatric patients.

But I got my first comeuppance when I started to have episodes of my heart beating too fast and my doctor asked me what it felt like. What it felt like? How do you think it felt? No, I didn't say that. I answered politely, "It's really hard to explain, like an emptiness in my chest?" "Emptiness?" he queried, politely but a little incredulously. It seemed to me that he was saying "What does that mean? Can you do any better than that?" Well, I couldn't. I still can't. But now I can add to it. I've just been through two days of vertigo. I'm not used to being sick, so this was a doozy. Yes, you have the sense that the room is turning, but it's much more than that: It's totally disorienting, you can't do anything, and during one episode I was so incapacitated I couldn't even find the phone, which was right next to my bed, let alone pick it up to ask someone for help. I didn't need help, but if I had . . ..

So when you start to think about experience, about subjectivity, it gets worse and worse. It is harder and harder to describe anything adequately, even the good stuff too—a

Grand Marnier soufflé, a fine rum, a sky with clouds ranging from fleecy white, to purple, to very dark grey. How about the hundreds of greens you see when you look at the woods while driving, the Appalachian Mountains, or the quiet series of single notes, beautiful notes you hear in the second movement of Ravel's piano concerto in G, or the laughter of a little girl as she throws a ball? Man, how do you describe ANY experience adequately?

You know what baseball umpires say about calling strikes, "I know one when I see one" and "It isn't a strike until I call it." Maybe subjective experience is more like that. But then what do you say when the doctor asks, "What does it feel like?" Or when you're trying to describe to a friend the most beautiful sky you've ever seen or what it's like to lie on your back beside the woman you love on the huge rock that makes up the island in the middle of the night watching the northern lights covering the sky like an undulating blanket of soft light? And I'm too shy to even get into trying to talk about making love.

The Delivery
[*7/24/19*]

I was sitting in the living room this morning watching the Tour de France on television when I saw a huge Federal Express van pull up in front of the house. Two men got out, opened the back of the truck, and with the help of a cranelike device extracted a huge box, a carton, a cube, twice as high as either of the men. They wheeled it up to my front porch, one rang the bell. and then, obviously sweating from their efforts, both walked back to the truck, got in, and drove off.

I went to the door and opened it slowly. There on the porch was this immense cardboard box. It was much too big to bring in through the door so I went to the cellar, got out my twelve-foot stepladder and carried it up and out to the porch. Fortunately, my box cutter was easy to find in the kitchen drawer, so I angled the ladder up one side of the huge carton, took the box cutter, and succeeded in cutting, one by one, the various cords and tapes that held the box closed.

Finally, I was able to throw back the flaps and peer down into the interior. It was dark inside and so almost impossible to see what the box contained. I knew from my earlier contacts with the sender what was probably in there, but for now all I could see was some glinting from a shiny surface. Finally, by squeezing of the corners, I wrestled the box into the house and there, again with the use of my box cutters, was able to peel away the sides of the carton to reveal . . . !

This happened, more or less, only four days ago. However, what I received was only figuratively a big box. The delivery was of a far more subtle kind. It came as an attachment to an e-mail. It was the advanced version of my autobiography, on which, with the help of some wonderful people, I had been working for more than two years. It all started when a young psychologist friend asked if she could interview me about my life and work. She recorded the six hours of our interviews and arranged to have them transcribed. I had been very impressed by my clever and knowledgeable responses to her questions but found them distressingly inadequate when I read them in their written form.

I then decided to write my autobiography and do it effectively. The first draft, a chronology, was deadly dull and a disaster. The second was a chaotic mess. I had thought this would be so easy, after all you're just recounting your life experiences. Distraught, I gave up for several months, then following some advice, decided to see if I could find an editor to help me get the thing together. I couldn't find any such person.

Finally, at lunch with my friend Stan Possick one day, I asked him if he knew an editor. I didn't really expect him to, so I was surprised when he replied, "The stepsister of my wife is an editor with a great deal of experience." Having failed so far at my search, I figured she would probably not be a good fit, but what the hell, I didn't have any better idea. The stepsister and I made some initial contacts and arrangements, and she went to work on my mishmash. She worked, we corresponded, she made suggestions of things I needed to write or to amplify or to clarify. Her suggestions were often ridiculous, "Write more about your career." "My career, I don't have a career. I've never had a career!" "Why did you spend so much time in Paris? Was it for your work?" "You must be out of your mind. I went to Paris because I loved it!" Things like that. Of course, I tended to be more diplomatic. But she got me to say something about the things that she or any normal person would expect to hear about and then to explain how I saw such things, the vastly divergent perspectives from "outside" and from "inside" that Claude and I have talked about. So I wrote, and she edited and organized. And she sent me little notes such as "Did you know that the hotel you mentioned when you first stayed in Paris in 1953 is now called the Rostand?" She wasn't doing it to be put in the autobiography, only because she thought I might be interested. Or she wrote, "I know your favorite words are "terrific" and "wonderful," but is it all right if we just say here, "I was very pleased"?

We worked for well over a year. As the work went on and she would send me edited versions of what I had written, I began to see the unfolding of my life in front of my eyes. When I had tried to do my own editing, I couldn't really pay attention to the words. It was as though reading them started this movie in my head and I could see, and hear, and feel, the events that the words had recalled to my mind. But somehow, by working together with my wonderful (see?) editor, I could just absorb the text that disclosed my life with a breadth of perspective I had never had before. Sometimes it was wonderful (!), sometime scary, confusing, or disconcerting.

We continued on. Then a few days ago, this "box" came by e-mail, a revised version of the whole damn thing, all together. I haven't read it yet, just the table of contents: (She created the chapter titles although checking with me: "An All-American Childhood," "A Change in Our Lives," "Retirement" (I put the quotation marks around Retirement). You have no idea what even a simple thing like organizing the parts and giving them names can do to "focus the mind" (as the man said about why he hit the donkey with a board from time to time). But so far, I have only looked at the table of contents.

So that's where I am. I've opened the huge box that was delivered but haven't yet been ready to look in detail at what is inside. Writing a dumb thing like an autobiography isn't obvious. I have such a different perspective on my own life now. I have a much clearer view of what is involved in trying to write about or understand what is involved in the life of any human being. But when I tell people, they don't seem to get it.

I don't understand that anymore.

The Island
[*3/3/18*]

Dear Bob,

Thank you for mentioning the Scram, which I guess you were too young ever to know. I knew it well.

The Scram was a mahogany boat that lived throughout my childhood. It was our big boat and wonderful. In addition to its beautiful mahogany, it had red leather cushions and one or two Chrysler Marine engines. There were three rows of seats, two in front of the engine compartment and one at the very back. Susan and I used to love to sit in the back. When the boat started to move forward, the back sank down and the bow went way up (it had a V-shaped hull), but then as it began to plane the boat flattened out and you went like the wind. The spray formed a beautiful curtain on both sides of you in the back seat, and the wake left by the boat was high, full, and magnificent. When I got to be about ten, Joe would let me sit next to him and manage the two levers that were on the steering wheel hub, one was for the spark and the other one I don't remember. Joe was incredible at driving it. He could take it at speed around Gull Rock, where the channel of deep water was very narrow. Joe and Herb were the only people who drove the Scram, although I think people said Sambo could too. Herb was always working on the engines. I'm not sure if they really needed it, but maybe they did. I can still see him, wearing baggy shorts and no top, with the doors to the engine compartment thrown wide open. The doors were set on invisible hinges on each side of the boat and met at a longitudinal midway point.

When he worked, only the bottom half of Herb was visible, his head and shoulders being down between those two open doors as he messed around with the engines themselves. Sambo had bought the Scram from rumrunners. It was the fastest boat in the area. Such a beautiful boat, I can still hear the booming purr of its engines.

One day when I was about seven, I got bitten by the brown Indian dog Wewim. A year or so earlier I had been bitten by Hitchy Mitchell's white dog, Sailor. That time it was my fault. I had kept trying to put a paper cup on his nose, and he finally bit me. But with Wewim, it was not my fault—he was just being nasty. Anyway, Dad and Herb took me in to Parry Sound to see old Doc Appleby. And naturally we took the Scram, Herb drove. We got into Parry Sound and tied up at Scott's Boat Livery as always. They got the car from the big lot people who kept their boat at Scott's used, and we drove up to Doc Appleby's house/office at the opposite end of town. The drive took about five minutes. At that time, Parry Sound was even smaller than it is today. It had no traffic lights. Doc Appleby washed the bite, put a bandage on it, and gave me a tetanus shot. We drove back to Scott's, parked, and got into the Scram.

It was twilight by then and getting darker quickly since it was the end of August. As we left the bay opposite Scott's and went through Two Mile Narrows it was noticeably darker, and by the time we reached Five Mile Narrows it was black. I may have told you that when it got dark up there, the islands, which we all knew by heart, disappeared into an indistinguishable black mass, and if you didn't know exactly where you were, it was impossible to find your way. Herb was pretty good, though, and he drove the Scram where we needed to go. That is, until we hit one passage where there are many rock formations just under the surface of the water. The navigable channel is marked by long nine-inch-diameter red and green stakes driven into the bottom. Years later Jeff taught me the saying "red left out, red right return," meaning that you kept the red stakes on your left as you were leaving Parry Sound and on your right when you were going in—and, of course, the opposite for the green ones. In reality, it's a little more complicated than that since it's not always clear when you are heading in or out because some channels are perpendicular to that direction. However, that was not relevant on this occasion because in the dark it was no longer possible to tell the colors of the channel markers. The red ones had pointed tops and the green ones flat, but even that was hard to tell in the dark. We were going at moderate speed in the Scram, and as we were approaching one channel marking, suddenly we heard a horrible scraping sound on the bottom of the boat. We were on the wrong side! I will never forget that sound. Suddenly, you wonder if the water is going to come flooding up from the bottom of the boat. Was that wonderful protective being that had carried you like the wind just a thin shell that was now a coffin? Would it now sink quickly from under you and leave you fully dressed floundering in the cold water, now in the dark not knowing where the islands were, which way to swim?

Fortunately, this time the bottom of the Scram held. It looked like we were safe. Dad and Herb took off their shoes, rolled up their pant legs, got into the water over the front and pushed the Scram back off the rocks. We were okay! Twenty minutes later we passed Bear's Head, turned right and turning right again at our channel. We were home.

I remember when the Scram burnt up. The mechanics at Scott's Boat Livery were working on it in the middle of the bay. The poor Scram caught fire and sank. The workers dived off it to save themselves before it went down. At least that is what we were told. A wonderful but troubled boat!

So you have the green and white pennant from the Scram, how great!

Yours,
John

The Past Isn't Even the Past
[*6/17/20*]

Damn, what is that quote? It's from Faulkner, I think. Yesterday, I participated in the third biweekly zoom sessions with my cousins. How weird that is! I have known them, of course, since they were born, because, at age eighty-seven, I am the oldest of the brood besides my sister. There are eight of us altogether. The first one to die was actually the youngest. He died just last year.

These cousins all grew up in Cleveland, grandchildren of my mother's parents, Sambo and Nanny, who were also born in Cleveland. Sambo died at the age of eighty-three in 1959 after Nanny. I went to his funeral in Cleveland and sat with my father. Dad leaned over to me, indicating some people at the back of the room. "Do you see those people back there? They are old musicians of Sambo's dance orchestras, from the 20's." Sambo was born in 1876, the year when Henry Morton Stanley was exploring the Congo River after having found Dr. Livingston in Ujiji, in what is now Tanzania.

Sambo was the patriarch of "Our Family." He grew up in Cleveland, his mother having been deserted by his father. "Gramma Rosenthal" owned a small grocery store, and Sambo had to leave school in the "eighth reader" to drive the horse-drawn cart for delivering the groceries. Somehow, he later became a violinist in the Cleveland Symphony and then a millionaire real-estate dealer. He and Nanny had four kids, each of whom married and had two kids, my sister and I and our cousins.

While the cousins grew up in Cleveland, my parents, sister (Susan), and I had moved to Erie when I was six months old. It was the depth of Depression, and Dad couldn't find a job in Cleveland. With Sambo as a senior partner, he bought some apartments in Erie, and he became the manager of this complex. Thus, I grew up in Erie.

But we remained closely tied to Cleveland as if by an umbilical cord. Every Sunday morning my mother would call her sister Ruthie and other members of the family and in an exaggerated voice would say "Hello! How ARE you?" (We teased her about that.) Every three weekends we drove up to Cleveland through Painesville, Ashtabula, Conneaut, and the other towns. Susan and I, sitting in the back seat, would play "Horses and Cows," getting one point for each cow, two points for each horse, and five points for any white horse. And, of course, we would argue briefly about whether a horse was really white or maybe just grey.

On those weekends, in the early days we would stay at "Nanny's house." (Don't ask me why the house was "hers," because Sambo was certainly "king" of the family. I don't know, that's just how things were). When I got older, I would stay with Eddie and Ruthie, sharing the room of their son, Eddie, Jr. He and I did things like put pennies on the "rapid track" (used by the fast streetcar), though we stopped after we learned that Uncle Art had been run over by a streetcar. That was how he lost his leg and why he now had a wooden one.

The family gathered for holidays, Sambo's birthday, and Christmas. Yes, we were Jews, but we celebrated a nonreligious Christmas with a big tree and antique ornaments and presents, which Sambo would hand out after Christmas dinner at Ruthie's house. Pretty much all the women were good cooks. My mother would have made the family recipes of Christmas cookies in Erie before coming up. The cookies had names like *Pfeffernüsse*. My aunt Rose made *Schnecken*, the best in the world. You might call them "sticky buns" or something dumb like that, but yours would be nowhere near as incredible as hers, which were doubly raised, with pecans—oh, my god! We children didn't know, of course, that these names were German, we just knew the names.

Every summer, we went up to "the Island," or "Canada" as we called it. The Island was actually three islands, located one hundred and sixty miles north of Toronto, that Sambo had settled in 1918. We had a small cottage there as did the Markuses (Ruthie and Eddie). Everyone else except Sambo and Nanny stayed in the "Clubhouse." This large plain building had an immense living room where the eating area was marked by two long tables that could seat twenty people, a kitchen, and a bunch of primitive rooms on the second floor. The living room also had a Buck stove for heat and a floor-standing windup Victrola. In the kitchen were an ice box, kept cold with real ice, a large woodburning stove, and a hand pump to bring up water from the "drink." There was no electricity until I was fourteen or so. Sambo and Nanny had a small cottage on the smaller island "across the way." It had no running water or anything else, but, of course, water was all around—you just took a pail to get it. And we had outhouses, two on the big island and one "across the way."

So, every summer the Strauss family (the four of us) would stay there for two, three weeks, or whatever and bring up guests. There were often as many as twenty people on the Island at a time. Sambo would always supervise and sometimes do the cooking and make repairs. He also liked to shop in town after taking the forty-five minute boat trip on the Scram to Parry Sound.

Several winters some of us went with Sambo and Nanny to Miami Beach for a month or so. Someone who owed Sambo money had a bunch of cottages where we could stay. One year Susan and I even went to school there for a while at Normandy Isles School, Mr. Huberman's school.

So, why am I telling you all this? Well, over the years, the core of the family stayed in Cleveland, but my generation, the cousins, started to move away—at least some of us. I went to college near Philadelphia but stayed with Mom's brother, Herb, for the summer at the end of my final year to take a course in English composition for med school. I also took courses in solfège and piano at the Cleveland Conservatory. Susan spent a summer in Cleveland to meet people before going to Antioch and then to live in New York, Eddie, Jr., moved to Wisconsin, where he became a bigshot lawyer for Monsanto, Stuart moved to Florida, Herbie to Washington, D.C. Progressively, the cousins spread all over the country, but those raised in Cleavland kept in pretty close touch with each other.

Over the years, Nanny and then Sambo died. Ethel, the youngest of my mother's sisters—and maybe the loveliest and most musical—died of breast cancer very young, then Herb, then Ruthie, then Mom. The cousins organized a family reunion for Dad's ninety-fifth birthday (he and Mom had finally moved "back" to Cleveland about thirty years earlier). Dad wrote and read a story about Elmer the Whale at the reunion dinner. Elmer was a personage we had all grown up with. Dad was never handy with practical things, but he was a terrific piano player and a wonderful storyteller.

Then Dad died. After that the whole of the remaining family got together for each of the funerals of the uncles and aunts, but otherwise, especially the Erie- raised ones, Susan and I, became more and more distant from the rest. But suddenly, so it seemed, about fifteen years ago, or about ten years after Dad died, someone decided to organize a family reunion. Everyone came. It was wonderful. Then about two years ago, at around the time Stuart died, another reunion. Again, almost everyone came, except Susan, pretty much immobilized in a Bronx retirement center after her husband Mike died. There were about fifty people there! All the cousins who were left, their spouses, and their kids. Terrific. I took a plane from Hartford. David, Ethel's son, picked me up at the airport. I got in around 8 a.m., so the poor guy had to get up very early to meet me. We went to breakfast together. He told me how helpful Mom had been when Ethel had died while David and his sister, Louise, were still little. I had had no idea.

After that second reunion two years ago, nothing. Until the coronavirus came along, and everything was shut down. Someone suggested—was it I?—that we have a regular Zoom meeting for the cousins and their spouses. Herbie organized it. We started six weeks ago and have done it every two weeks.

I am having more contact with my cousins now than I have had in more than sixty years! It is so weird! We know each other from way back. They call me Johnny. Bob is Bobby, Herb is Herby. We have these old links that I guess have been there all this time, just lying there, waiting to be called up. It's like, oh, the family is there again. We talk about plain stuff, mostly not anything deep—getting food safely, operations, when can Bobby play golf again, how is Susan, how can you be with people with all the virus restraints. Just stuff. Just like we've been together forever. Which in a way, I guess, we have. And, of course, at the same time, we have not.

And it continues. Lovely Kathy of the next generation has just sent me an e-mail. (A short digression on technological development: I am relatively comfortable with computers.

Susan, my sister, on the other hand, four years older than I, has never used one, and Dad and Mom used to talk about what it was like when the first electric street lights were installed, of the days of the earliest autos that still had buggy-whip holders so people wouldn't feel too alienated, the first airplanes, the early telephones.) Back to Kathy's e-mail. She told me that the Rhodes, who had bought our main island when my parents' generation sold it (how furious I was about that!), are now too old to manage the island and have just sold it. I do understand that. At the age of seventy-eight I fell off the deck of my small Sunfish sailboat for the first time in my life. I knew then that I had lost the ability to do many of the things that I so loved up there and have never gone back. After sixty plus years of going up every year!

As Faulkner said, "The past isn't even past." It is, and it isn't.

The Plague
[*6/4/19*]

In his novel *The Plague* Albert Camus describes a city in North Africa that is suddenly stricken by a plague. One by one the citizens are affected and then die, an author, a grocery seller, the mother of three little children, two of whom have already died of the plague, the city doctor. The gates of the city are closed, and no one is allowed to leave or to enter in order to prevent the plague from spreading.

A year and a half ago I bought my first iPhone. I learned to use it as a telephone to send and receive calls but after a short while stopped. It was partly because I was so sick of people on the street who are so stuck to their phones they cross without noticing cars coming, all but bump into you, or ignore the person they're with. I see lovely young couples in the coffee shop or restaurant both so involved with their iPhones or computers that they might as well be alone. In addition, I just wasn't in the habit of using my phone and slowly forgot how to manage it. My daughter gave up calling me on it because I took so long to figure out how to turn it on and respond to an incoming call.

Three weeks ago I watched the movie *Passage to India* on Turner Classic Movies. Since high school I have been very attracted to certain Indian philosophy and the sense of peace and order that it can bring. I loved the movie *The Razor's Edge* and read a great deal about Buddhism. Then during my second year in college I decided to take a year out to spend the time on a sort of pilgrimage to India. I had all the information I needed from the Peninsular and Oriental shipping company to book passage from London. But then my parents, and some administrators from college advised me not to go at least until I finished college, so uniquely in my life I followed the advice of others that ran counter to my strong impulse. Years later when working on a WHO research project, I finally did go to New Delhi and to Agra and had many beautiful experiences with people there and, of course, was mesmerized by the wondrous Taj Mahal.

During that second year at college, I had a wonderful roommate, Ralph Brown. Kind, very knowledgeable, ironic, he came from an old Yankee family and had spent a year at school in England. While a senior at college, he married a woman that his other friends and I found extremely difficult to be with and so Ralph and I saw little of each other after that. I've seen him three times since. He became a lawyer and made tons of money as a big deal at Gulf and Western in New York, where he had a huge corner office overlooking Central Park and 57th Street. They also had a monster apartment, the kind where you get off the elevator directly into the apartment, I think it was on Park Avenue. They invited me to celebrate their anniversary one year. They hosted about sixty people at a sit-down dinner in the Metropolitan Museum. Ralph even introduced me during the presentations as his oldest friend there.

Several years later I saw him in New Haven. He and his wife came up for the funeral of the secretary of Yale, who was related to her, and we arranged to meet at the Atticus Bookstore/Café. Ralph, wearing a grey three-piece suit, had become very fat and was terribly pompous. I was horrified. I brought him a paper I had published that I thought might interest him, and he had stuffed it in his pocket without so much as looking at it. His pomposity vanished during a ten-minutes period when his wife went to the bathroom. He turned to me and, out of the blue, explained why it had been so important to him to earn a lot of money. His family, he said, although patricians, had been so poor that money was always a problem for them. When Ralph's wife returned, he became pompous again. I was desolated.

We had no further contact for several years. But a couple of weeks ago, after seeing *Passage to India*, I had this serious urge to call him again. Somehow the Anglo and aristocratic characters in that movie and Ralph seemed connected for me. (I do love that movie.) The next day I called him. He was delighted to hear from me and invited me to come to his weekend house in Cornwall, Connecticut. (He actually had three homes: the main one in New York City, their country place in Cornwall, and another large apartment on boulevard Saint-Germain opposite the church of Saint Germain-des-Prés in Paris.)

He sounded like the old Ralph, like the person who had been such a wonderful friend so many years earlier. So I began to make arrangements to visit him in Cornwall. And what, you may ask, does all this have to do with my iPhone?

Well, I needed to figure out how I was going to get to Ralph's house in Cornwall. I tried to use Google Maps and MapQuest on my computer, but I find computers too damn nosey. The computer screen on my car tells me as I turn on the engine to be careful when I drive. I constantly get advertisements on my computer screen at home when I am trying to work on a paper or send e-mails. And once I tried to find out what a university professor was writing and ever since have received daily messages from some finding company about how I can get private information on him. And, of course, I get many calls daily from people I don't know or non-people, trying to sell me crap I never asked for. All thanks to computers!

But I figured now was the time to learn to use my smart

phone so I could use its GPS to get directions to Ralph's place. I consulted my iPhone for dummies and my "for old people" book and made a little progress, but then I ran into problems with the direction piece. I went out that night for dinner with Barbara to a restaurant I've gone to for about twenty years and where over that time the waitress and I have gotten to know each other a little. At the restaurant, after Barbara and I had finished our dinners, she tried to show me ways in which I can access an "app" to get directions. The waitress I know had been serving us, and she and I had been exchanging memories, but when she came to say goodbye, I was in the middle of trying to figure something out and by the time I looked up she was gone. As Barbara and I left the restaurant, I tried to find the waitress, but she had vanished, and I had to leave without saying goodbye. I guess stuff like that is normal these days. But not for me. Computers, smart phones, they are intrusive, they distract, they interfere with normal human interactions. They are a plague.

The Project
[*2/10/16*]

The four of us were in the room together. The chairman, Dave Sells, Larry Davidson, and I. The chairman had just announced that he had received a considerable gift of money and wanted to fund a project on schizophrenia that one of us might propose. I went first, trying to think as best I could about how to make use of this new possibility: "I would carry out a qualitative study of maybe about twenty subjects, people between the ages of twenty and thirty with schizophrenia. I would take a biopsychosocial perspective in my inquiry." The chairman interrupted: "You know, of course, that the evidence for brain disease is significant. Would you include people like Leonard Grimaldi?" I didn't know anything about Leonard Grimaldi and tried to fudge it. "Well, inquiry into brain function would, of course, be part of the study. I would try to clarify the processes involved in the onset and course of disorders by carrying out a series of interviews and various tests to trace the longitudinal factors involved." I was beginning to worry since this sounded like much of the research I had done in the past, which had been useful but certainly did not need repeating. "By taking a non-theoretical orientation, not assuming total psychoanalytic, biological, or other mechanisms, . . ." I began, trying to suggest that that an atheoretical orientation would be different enough to warrant the project. But the chairman interrupted again, this time not with words but a look that suggested "So what's new about this?"

I decided to take a new approach. I said, "Here's an example. At the APA three years ago, I saw a film entitled *A Sister's Call*. It was made by Rebecca Schaper about her younger brother, Call, about his developing schizophrenia and then improving. The film starts with a picture of him at a time when he had just developed schizophrenia. He looks bizarre and disheveled. A few days after this picture was taken, we are told, Call disappeared into the woods that surrounded the family home. He was away for several days and came back speaking strangely, unintelligibly. At this point he appeared to have a disease that had seemingly come out of the blue, perhaps genetic, perhaps something like Huntington's chorea—a relatively straightforward kind of problem, even if it was difficult to discover its specific origin. The family tried to get treatment for him, but he disappeared again. This time he was gone for twenty years, during which time they had no word of him whatsoever.

One day there he was again, looking terrible, in rags, long beard, mumbling, and apparently disoriented. The sister then took him under her wing, and over the subsequent months she was able to find him an apartment, get him connected to a social worker who also spent much effort on him. Gradually, he began to improve, to dress better, speak more coherently, take his medication, and to do better generally.

The film now fills in some family history. Rebecca and Call were the two children of a couple who at the time of their marriage were considered the ideal pair. The father was a newly returned veteran of the Second World War. He had made sergeant, and when he came back from Europe his picture appeared in the Atlanta area paper as a kind of conquering hero. The mother had graduated from her high school as one of the most popular girls, and a picture of her in a beautiful white gown at the time of graduation was in the society section of the paper. When they were married, pictures of the wedding were in the paper as well.

The film returns to how Call was improving but then gives more background. It turns out that Call had come home one day to find his mother sprawled dead on the floor. Over the next few days they learned she had committed suicide by drinking a large quantity of alcohol and then taking some pills as well. She had been Call's main ally in the family, which was especially important since the father had been quite abusive of Call since shortly after the boy's birth. It was shortly after the death of the mother that Call became psychotic and disappeared into the woods.

The film continues to intersperse scenes of Call's improvement with the help of the sister and the social worker with more family history. We see Rebecca and her husband and their two teenage daughters at the dinner table. They are having a heated discussion because the children feel that she is spending too much time with Call and not enough with them. She apologizes and says, well, she needs to be both with him and with them and will try to do better. Then we learn that a month or so after Call's return home, Rebecca and her husband had been told by one of their daughters that their grandfather had sexually abused them. The parents were furious and within a few days confronted the grandfather with this information. Two days later he was found dead. He had shot himself while taking a shower.

The film shows more of the evolution of Call. He is beginning to develop a sense of humor, has started seeing some of his old friends, and is looking so much better. This is where the film ends.

When the film was presented at the APA, a question-and-answer period followed with Rebecca at the podium.

One audience member asked how it was Call had gotten better. Rebecca responded that his meds had been changed to Respirdol, and she thought it was from that. She did not mention at all the huge effort that she and the social worker had made.

I didn't think the chairman was impressed by my project or by the message I thought was conveyed by this film, the message that we make assumptions about the cause of schizophrenia and discount or even fail to collect data that might give us a more complete biopsychosocial picture, instead trying to maintain mistakenly the dominant ideology. In this era that is the ideology of biological causes and treatments. Dave Sells, who had been quiet all this time, commented, "John, you really have to clear up some of the clutter on the floor of your house." I realized that was a good idea and also realized I had been listening to myself tell this story out loud as though I was both the speaker and a listener. That seemed strange. Then I realized I was lying down. Then I realized I was in bed. Looking at the clock on the table, I saw that it read 5:33 am.

Twenty-two
[*2/23/14*]

At Mary's retirement party I was pleased to be invited to sit at the head table. There I was next to Mary's daughter Jean, whom I had known since she was about three, and Jean's daughter Lindsey, whom I had known since she was born. Of course, the guest of honor was Mary herself. She looked great, bright and cheerful, and was busily talking to all her friends and making sure everything at the party was going perfectly. Mary was retiring now, but she had been the head of small but successful non-profit community organization for over thirty years. I had first met her a long time ago because of my own involvement with studying psychiatric patients who had been discharged from hospitals. She was kind, caring, and so impressive, and we became friends. We would meet every month or so for lunch and got to know each other and our particular ways quite well. It came as no surprise to me, for example, that when several years ago I was thinking of retiring and then about to change my mind not to, she said to me, "You better do it before it's too late." That was the best advice that anyone has ever given me. At her work Mary had this miraculous ability to keep any fifteen projects going without a hitch, reapplying for grants, making sure that all the paperwork was in order, getting funding, and keeping track of the people who worked for her and of the organizations with which they were involved.

The retirement party was a pleasure. For one thing, I really enjoyed the opportunity to talk with Lindsey, who was now fourteen, and with Jean. We had, after all, seen each other at least annually over many years when I went to Mary's apartment to help them make Christmas cookies. The three of them would already have started the work when I arrived because Mary's yearly effort to make Christmas cookies for what seemed like almost everyone in New Haven was not an effort to be taken lightly. We had a whole routine. Jean would mix the dough, Lindsey and I would stamp it out into the various shapes (Christmas trees, Santa Claus, and so on), paint on the icing, and pour on the sprinkles, while Mary organized the actual baking and cleaning up. The result was hundreds and hundreds of cookies, of which we ate our fair share (of the crispest ones). In the process we naturally talked and joked, and I had the chance to ask Lindsey, bright like her mother and her grandmother, about what she liked at school, her progress with her music, and what she had been doing more generally.

But now Mary was retiring. She was sixty-five, and as she told me out of the blue, matter of factly but with the tiniest hint of wistfulness, at our lunch a month after the party, she had "halfheimers disease." But I could tell she was really as sharp as ever. The sparkle in her eyes, the memory that recalled everything and everyone from at least twenty years ago, her terrific sardonic sense of humor, they were all there. I said, "You don't even have noheimers disease." She just looked at me, as always not accepting any amendment to what she had told me, not arguing with me. There was no way I could have an impact on what she believed, just as always, unless she had actually come to me specifically for an opinion.

At the retirement party person after person from the nonprofit and from the organizations they dealt with got up and extolled Mary's almost unbelievable capacity for work but also her terrific sense of humor and caring for the many projects with which they were involved. But at our lunch that month later that word "halfheimer," characteristically both joking and serious, interjected itself into our otherwise happy world.

Two months later, at another lunch, Mary and I recalled the various jokes and tributes from the retirement party. I said it was really too bad that Henry, Mary's husband who had died a few years earlier, couldn't have seen how respected and beloved she was. "How long has it been since he died?" I asked her. "I don't know," she answered. "My god," I thought, "she wasn't kidding."

I looked forward less and less to our lunches after that. It was always good to see her, but the "halfheimers" was getting grave, scary, and sad. "Lindsey came back from a trip to Spain where she and the chorus she's in were singing," she told me. We also talked about how Mary's former non-profit was doing and about my kids and my granddaughter, who had just become a student at NYU. "Lindsey came back from a trip to Spain where she and the chorus had gone to give singing concerts," Mary said, apparently unaware that she had just told me that a few minutes earlier. I asked if Lindsey had liked Spain as though the information were new to me. I paid for lunch, and after I drove her back to her apartment, she said, "Thank you, but next time I'm paying." "Then we need to go to a really fancy place, not our usual diner," I said. We hugged goodbye.

A couple of months later I went to pick up Mary for a lunch we had arranged, but she wasn't at home. I rang and rang at her door, and her sister finally answered. "Mary went to a movie with her friend," she told me. I thanked her and left. I called Jean to say I was beginning to worry. We both agreed, but we both knew how stubborn Mary was. She advised me, "Before you go to get her, call first, that's what I do."

Later Mary called to apologize. Apologizing had never been her strong point and she kept it short. She added that she had gotten a present for me and wanted to bring it over. I said I'd be at home when she came. She had been to the house many times before since she had kept an eye on it for me when I was on trips to Paris. But she called a few hours later and said, a little sadly, that she had set out for my place but then couldn't remember how to get there so just returned home. I said, "No problem, I'll come and pick it up." I did.

We continued to have our lunches every month or two as before. Pretty much every time she told me about Lindsey who had just come back from her singing trip to Spain. Pretty much every time I would tell her about my granddaughter at NYU and her various activities there including being a songwriter. "How old is she?" Mary would ask. Twenty-two, I would answer. Mary talked about her problems with the Social Security office. Jean had told me that Mary had forgotten to file important information, but Mary just said the office was confused.

Yesterday Mary and I had lunch again. I picked her up as usual, but this time when she came to the door she looked old and worn. I had never seen her before like that. Her face was so, what was it, tired? She wore no make-up. I hadn't been aware before that she used make-up, but I realized she had since her skin was now kind of washed out. Her eyes looked tired, and her hair was scraggly. She said, "This time I'm paying for you," to which I said, "Great". We went to the diner a few blocks away and sat down at a booth. Mary looked out the window, but she didn't really seem to be seeing anything. Her gaze was empty. I asked her how things were going, and she told me that Lindsey had just got back from Spain where she'd been with her school's singing group. I asked what had happened to the possibility that Mary could move to a place where people could help her with things. "I don't want to do it now, maybe in the spring. Jean wants me to be where I'll live closer to her." I told Mary that my granddaughter had been up for the weekend and had two friends, one a Yale student and the other from Wesleyan, drop by the house; we had all sat together in the kitchen, and it was really fun talking with them. Mary started looking through her pockets. "I wanted to pay, but I must have forgotten my purse," she said. Last time she had forgotten her house keys to get back into her apartment. Mary looked at me a little sadly, then asked, "How old is your granddaughter?" "Twenty-two," I said.

Understanding a Life
[3/1/19]

During lunch yesterday my editor noted the shifts there had been in my work between the "scientific" and the "humanist." Those are my labels, not hers, but she was right. It has been almost like a sine wave for me, at first the humanist (psychodynamic), then the scientific (IPSS), then the humanist again (still paying attention to the subjectivity of the "patient," but not so much to the subjectivity of the observer). Just like that old problem of not being able to put two things together, just like that jigsaw puzzle when I was six, I haven't been able to solve this either. Proposing multiaxial diagnosis for DSM-III was an attempt, but it was really a failure or at least grossly inadequate. People are not axes; we are more a unity than that.

There are actually two related problems. The first is how to think of and describe a person. Listening to a CD series of lectures on the diplomatic history of Europe from 1500 to the present, I noticed that for the nineteenth century the professor first talked about the wars and treaties and border changes on the continent and then went back to the beginning of the century again to talk about the imperialist moves of that period. Thus, one thing, the history of the century, is described by breaking it into two pieces, although, in fact, it was one massive history. So how do you do that? Why does it seem to work so well? And how would you do that for a person, how, for example, describe my mother's "illness" and her competence?

Another possibility is that in separating the scientific from the humanist approaches we have broken down a unity into two separate pieces that prevent you from bringing them together. It's like the old story about the traveler who asks the Maine native how to get to Millinocket. The answer is, "You can't get there from here."

So, as I said before, here we are again with my jigsaw puzzle at age six. One possible answer may be in cheese fondue. In making that, you start with melting cheese in a pot. As you do, you add white wine. The two don't mix and actually make a kind of mess. Then, when the cheese has completely melted you add cornstarch and gently stir. The two separate substances become a silky smooth unity. For us as people, we live without problem with the scientific and the humanist pieces. Have we found without noticing it the emulsifying agent that puts the colloid together? Or was it a mistake to have ever pulled them apart in our minds? Do we need to start over, reconceptualize the whole thing? I'm still working on that jigsaw puzzle from age six.

Is John Still Alive?
[5/25/21]

"Is John still alive?" Luc, a colleague I have known for years, asked in a recent e-mail to Courtenay, another colleague, both of whom I consider as friends. Courtenay let me know of his inquiry. I am thinking about answering him: "Yes, I think so," "As far as I can tell," in the fashion of Descartes' *cogito ergo sum*. Perhaps, "Hier j'ai tendu les pelouses, donc je pense que oui" (yesterday I cut the grass so I think yes).

It is a strange, striking, wonderfully direct question, "Is John still alive?" And I know why he asked it. He is ninety or more, I am eighty-eight. We both know many people, some close friends, for whom the answer to his query would be "no."

It's strange to ponder the weight and immediacy of that question. After all, living or dead is really a big deal. As is the certainty that death's not all that far off and definitive.

Irving Yalom, the famous, now elderly, psychotherapist, gave a talk at Yale last Friday. He is alive. But he talked and was asked about his health, about death, about his life. In all these years I have never heard anyone talk so normally about living and dying and even about his failing memory (which was not apparent during the talk). It was creepy. But important. And in some ways beautiful. It seemed so natural and reasonable. Someone somewhere said how strange it is that current experience keeps us so far from many of the natural aspects of life, such as death. During that talk my thoughts kept going back and forth between "this is so weird" and "this is so normal."

To Build a Fire
[*1/14/25*]

I was a fan of Jack London's when I was a teen, but what I remember about him most now was the story "To Build a Fire." I have not read it since my teen years, but essentially (and some of the details of my memory are vague) it was about a young man who was traveling by dogsled in deep winter in the Alaska wilderness. The snow conditions got so impossible that he stopped while still in the woods. It was terribly cold, and he wanted to start a fire. He collected branches and took out his one remaining match to light a beautiful fire to warm himself up. A few minutes later, but too late, he realized that the fire was melting the snow overhead in the trees. A mass of snow fell. It extinguished the fire. He proceeded to freeze to death. That was the story.

For some reason I have been thinking of that story now at age ninety-two, seventy-eight years after having read it. Sometimes now memories from decades ago just pop up like that. So I went to my friendly YouTube to see what they had on that story. There were many entries, many readings of the story, a short film of it. Each started with a one- or two-sentence summary of the story. Some of my memories were mistaken (it was set in the Yukon, not Alaska), but they were roughly accurate. Each of the entries made comments on the story, usually things like "it was an example of such and such kind of literature." None said "wow" or "W0W."

What is wrong with these people? They talk about existentialism or whatever, but no "WOW." For me that story is truly powerful and so underspoken. Can't you see yourself out there in the terrible, freezing cold, in the darkness, having taken out your match and succeeded in starting the warming fire on which your very life depended, then to have bunch of snow fall and put out the fire. In that moment you are realizing you are going to die. I mean, my god!

The commentators miss the point, miss the whole damn thing. Sure, existentialism, naturalism, whatever, but this guy about to freeze to death! What is wrong with you people?! Noticing this little thing or that? This guy is going to freeze to death!

So that's my point. What's wrong with these people or maybe with me? They don't even mention that horrible realization, "Shit, I'm going to die," and then he does. And they're talking about existentialism or whatever. I mean it's like being in a trench being attacked by Germans with poison gas and shell fire, and what are you thinking about, existentialism? What is wrong with you anyway?!

Being Human and the Mental Health Field
[11/16/24]

As I was walking, limping with my cane, across an open lane of the CVS parking lot, a poorly dressed, grizzled man walked past me and then, noticing an approaching car, stopped, faced the car and held up his hand to stop it until I had safely crossed. I am profoundly grateful and thank him profusely. He has done a kind and wonderful thing.

And what he has done, is it biological, psychological, or social? Clearly, it is all of those things. So how do you understand it?

Why is it so hard for us in the mental health field to deal with all three of these domains at once? Why do the biologists deal almost exclusively with biology? Why do psychoanalysts deal almost exclusively with psychology? And who deals with social issues? I would suggest that sociologists occasionally have useful ideas, but really in each of the three domains it is rare that anyone deals helpfully with all three as they exist in reality, interacting deeply with each other. Certainly, any one of these perspectives is simpler than looking at all sides of the phenomenon at hand. It's as though there are large concrete walls in the middle of a river that divide the flow of water. But in the end the water in the river will come together again. When will these currents in psychiatry come together?

To be fair, in treating some problems, such as PTSD, they do. But for most areas of inquiry, including anxiety, bipolar disorder, and schizophrenia, they are largely kept apart. The assumption is, I suppose, is that these areas fall only in one or other of the domains. I suspect, however, that our failure to look at the whole picture derives simply from our particular trainings, disciplines, and preferences. We separate the flow (to return to the analogy above) more because of our perhaps unconscious specific preferences than because of the nature of the things we are trying to understand and influence. But how can we do better? Practitioners do— the better ones, as I see it.

Puccini's opera La Rondine begins with a scene in a Paris salon at which a young man, a poet, sits down at the piano and begins to play a beautiful piece that he has composed. But he stops, and when urged to continue, says he can't, he doesn't know what comes next. Me too. I have tried to write something and what comes out is just more of what I've said before, and I don't know how to finish it. But just now, I thought of the story of Pandora. You know it. This young Greek girl who is curious and into everything finds a mysterious box at her front door. A sign on it says, "Don't open me." She can only resist for a short time before she opens it. All the evils in the world fly out, greed, cruelty, selfishness. She hurries to close the cover, but these terrible things have already escaped. Then she hears a little voice from inside the box, "Let me out." Still curious, she does. And out flies hope.

So maybe the issue for us lies also in our failure to come up with an adequate theory. I would say that our problem is in not trying to use the illness metaphor for our field to see it more in a double way. Yes, something has gone wrong, of course, but another part of the picture is the effort to understand things optimally and act effectively, to manage the resulting difficulty, to survive. And, in fact, many practitioners faced with the real world do that as well. Was my guy in the parking lot making a bio-psycho-social intervention? And is there a theoretical structure to support the recognition that we are dealing with a double reality of illness/competence. I believe strongly that the assumption that "mental illness is an illness like any other" is misleading, even harmful. We need a conception that recognizes both the problem and the person's effort to survive it and make it better,

Isn't that how we already think and act? In practice many clinicians do, but we don't have a developed conceptualization that really helps them, or do we? Perhaps behavior theory? Rehabilitation theory? What would such a conceptualization look like? Here, like the piano player in La Rondine, I have to realize that I'm not sure. Would it be like behavior therapy, confrontation therapy, some combination of approaches, or what?

Points of View
[*10/21/20*]

Points of view: first, second, first, and third person

It's late afternoon. I am lying on the couch as I often do at this time of day. It's a good time of day just to let go, to stop being or even trying to be productive. I can see out the window to my left the sky of deepening blue at this time of day, a few white clouds, edged with just the slightest pink from the descending sun out there in the west. A large eagle is sliding across the sky, way up there. See it? A pair of bald eagles lives in Edgewood Park. The park is only about a mile away so I see them often a couple of times a week, way up there, wings motionless. Oh, maybe there's some movement, a feather here or there, but not that I can see from down here. Maybe this one's going to the Hamden Mall about four miles away. I think that would take him about three minutes. He's already disappearing from view. I would be cold if I were up there, though perhaps not if I had feathers.

Can you imagine? No traffic, no tunnel under the ridge of hills, no traffic lights. The freedom to go wherever with just a little tilt of my wing. The ability to look down and see all these people scurrying around, to see forever, go wherever. But I think that after a little while all that power, that beauty, that freedom would get boring. Then what could I do? Go back to my cold nest? Land on that squirrel way down on the ground, minding his business looking for acorns. Land on and kill the innocent, unsuspecting little thing. Start eating him. Raw! I saw an eagle do just that in my backyard three years ago. He looked very noble, but there he was, pecking at the guts of the squirrel at his feet. Maybe it's better just to watch the eagle ease by, way up there in the air. Just leave it at that. Realism screws things up.

You can lie here for twenty minutes, but then you need to get up and take something for dinner out of the fridge. Ham? Ribs? You don't have to decide right away. See that eagle up there. I'll bet he's cold and lonely. You think you'd like being an eagle, but you'd get damn bored after a few minutes. Well, maybe you could learn some flying tricks, but that wouldn't hold you for long. You're better down here, on your couch, in your nice warm house.

You're always saying things like that. Be afraid of this! Don't do that! You want me to be glued to this couch? You drive me crazy with your worries and your warnings. I hate it when you do that. If I listened to you, I'd be like Immanuel Kant who never ventured out of Königsberg. But I would never have written all the great stuff he did, just rattled around Königsberg like an idiot.

There he is, see him over there? Lying on his couch like an idiot. He does that pretty much every day. You wouldn't think to see him now that he used to do all kinds of things. Did all the house cleaning, even mowing the lawn and trimming the shrubs. Even cleaning that intricate chandelier when it needed it. He bought all the groceries, fixed the meals, washed up. And all that was on the side. Mostly he did research, worked as head of a research team that published five, maybe ten articles a year, all in first-rate journals. And he gave talks and stuff and led writing groups on top of that. Yes, I know, he's older now. That's what happens. It's weird though. He seems happier, more at peace, at least most of the time. And, of course, he's waiting for the autobiography he just finished, three hundred and seventy pages, to come from the publisher. Still, there he is now, just like a worn-out ragdoll, lying there on that stupid couch, watching that stupid eagle again.

Poisoned Sauce
[*2/24/22*]

Like poisoned sauce poured over our only meal seeping into every morsel, today the Russians have invaded Ukraine. Like Nazi Germany invading Czechoslovakia "to help their mistreated people," Russia, the country that some suggest deliberately used its ethnic minorities to lead their charges against the Germans in the Second World War, resulting in their decimation, has now decided why not grab some territory, something to chew on, and distract the masses. The country that starved millions not so many years ago in the same location now says, well, what does it matter if there are a few thousand more dead and wounded, a few more thousand lives mutilated one way or another. The country that has done much the same in Chechnya, Syria, and the country of Georgia. The country that has moved its own people around like disposable bundles of paper dolls into the gulags and other places of exile. Starve a few hundred thousand here, destroy the lives of a few hundred thousand there, what's the difference? The country that has given us Dostoyevsky, Pushkin, Tolstoy, Gogol. The country that has given us Tchaikovsky, Prokofiev, Scriabin, Stravinsky. The country that has given us David Oistrakh, Baryshnikov, and that lovely fifteen-year-old ice skater to whom they gave drugs, resulting in her disqualification from the 2022 Olympics. The country of ballet, music, literature. The country that has given us brutality beyond measure and beauty also beyond measure, is now showing once again how you can destroy tens of thousands of lives without much worry, just like that. Amazing sauce, poisoned sauce.

The Dance
[*10/27/21*]

I was just twenty years old when I saw Margot Fonteyn dance at Covent Garden. I was spending the summer in Europe, freeing myself in Paris and traveling in ways I could only barely grasp, and now I had arrived in London to hitchhike around Britain. Posters proclaimed that Margot Fonteyn was dancing at Covent Garden, and though I had almost no money I was able to patch together a few dollars to buy a ticket. She was magnificent. Of course. And last night, sixty-nine years later, totally by chance, I saw a notice on YouTube that there was a film of her life story. So, there I went. Over two hours later, at 2 a.m., I finished it, totally disassembled.

Margot Fonteyn was not only one of the finest English ballet dancers ever to have lived, she was one of the finest dancers in the world. She had a grace, an élan, a beauty, unmatched. I could see it again in the various parts of her performances that I watched last night. You would not imagine that a human being could do such wondrous things. And if you are dismayed by all our inadequacies and evils, seeing Fonteyn will allow you to realize once again that humans have wonderful abilities as well.

It had been so long since I had seen her and watching her was a joy! There she was dancing over the years with her many partners, and especially with Nureyev! You would not think people could move like that, could be like that.

But her life was complicated and far from easy. This lovely child danced just by nature, even when she was three or four, but her mother, did she exploit her? She traveled with her mother between the father in China and a kind of homeland and dancing instruction in England. She became more and more successful, but was she used by her mother or helped by her? Always more graceful, more musical, more beautiful, and dancing, dancing. She married a Panamanian diplomat, politician, and arms dealer. He was shot and rendered quadriplegic but never gave up his attempts at power grabs and, as much as he could manage, affairs. She danced on and on and found the perfect partner in Nureyev, with whom she had a serious affair. Her husband took the money she made as though by right. To rescue her ill-managed finances, she gave a final stage performance in Miami at the age of sixty-six. She died from cancer five years later.

The United States, our country, is struggling now, perhaps in the death throes of our democracy. We are filled with both love and with hate and fear. Can we survive, revive? It is a country of so many beautiful and wondrous things. The incredible beauty of Glacier Park and of Oregon's coastline, where the Pacific Ocean pounds against the rock formations. The generosity of a garage worker who told me during my hitchhiking days across the country, "Here, take this five dollars. When I was doing what you're doing someone gave it to me. I'm just passing it on." Will we survive? Will we crash and burn?

We cannot tell whether things will get better or worse. In some massive way, either beauty or misery is possible, perhaps even both.

Too Much
[8/13/20]

It was impossible to do everything needed to provide the essentials of adequate care. It was already late. And I still had eight more patients to evaluate and decide on a likely diagnosis, to plan further evaluation, and, as far as possible, to start treatment. Clearly, I would not finish before 2, maybe 3, in the morning. I was known for my efficiency, but this was clearly pushing my limits.

And you want me also to be kind? To spend time with each person talking with them about what their worries might be, were there other problems we needed to discuss? You know, sometimes you are just stupid, ridiculous, disgusting even. Get off my back! I am nice, kind, that's already pretty damn good, given the stuff I need to do to get through this day responsibly.

I have been watching the Great Courses lecture series on the French Revolution. I saw it once before, several years ago, and even wrote the lecturer, Suzanne Desan, to congratulate her on it. This time, however, it seemed completely new, and I was totally captivated, not by the dates or even the events or historical meanings, but by the feeling I was living in that time. It was something about how Suzanne presented it, as though it were a driven narrative, a complex narrative, looking at the situation both in Paris, where the people were running out of bread, and in the countryside, where in several places counterrevolutionary groups were rising up and attacking the people who were trying to forward the revolution, developing economic and educational programs and new administrative structures. At the borders the Prussians were moving to attack, and the Austrians, British, and Spanish as well. And of course, there were the diverse factions and interests within the National Convention, the Girondins, the Jacobins, the Plain, the Mountain, the Hébertists. Somehow Suzanne interwove all these threads and brought me among the people who were involved with this whole thing. What would it feel like to be Danton or Robespierre, or General Dumouriez? And what would I have done, how would I have felt, in their place? There you are, Robespierre, in Paris, a kind of skinny guy, a bit on the rigid side, trying to hold this whole damn thing together. Someone rushes in as you are trying to decide what to do about your old friend Danton, who seems to be threatening the success of the revolution. Do you have him arrested and his head cut off by the guillotine? Then someone rushes in and says, "General Dumouriez [who had been leading the French troops against the Prussian invasion] has gone over to the side of the Austrians." You hear the noises outside. The wives of Paris are rioting because they have no food for their families. Hébert, who has been sitting quietly as you try to respond to these events, has come up with a tax plan that may provide enough funds to be able to pay the troops for a few months. But Hébert has to wait.

"How did I get into all this?" you think, but there is no time to answer. The success or failure of the revolution depends on your decisions, your skills in understanding what is going on, and your ability to find solutions.

I wake up. The French Revolution, evaluating and deciding about the lives of five more patients on the ward, your own life—each involves the interaction of so many elements, your own decisions, the happenstance of your body, the problems of the patients on the ward and of the general who is trying to defect. Everything is unpredictable, totally beyond your control, yet you must try to address them, decide about them, handle them. And, of course, as soon as you decide about one and begin to take action, three more totally different, crucial things intrude, for some of which there is just nothing you can do to manage. How is it possible to handle all this?

Knowledge
[7/10/23]

So, Lexi, Larry Davidson's college student daughter, has started giving me some serious help with my second (and last) attempt at a definitive book. She is terrific—bright, quick, effective—and, as I learned today, surpasses me in computer smarts by about five-hundred-fold. But there's more. She was trying to help me figure out how to structure this thing I am trying to write. She suggested that when I put together a group of writings under one of the headings we are trying out, headings like "People," "My Travels," things like that, that I summarize for each group what I want people to concentrate on, learn, or become.aware of. But while realizing that might be all right from some traditional academic points of view, I knew that wasn't really what I was trying for. And I was having trouble figuring out how to explain that to her.

But what am I trying for? As usual with me, I don't have a clue. But I told Lexi a story about my hitchhiking experiences around the country when I was young. I said when you get in a car of someone who stops for you, the driver asks where you are going, and you say, if you're in Indiana, perhaps, "The west coast." Then you laugh and he (the drivers who stopped were always men) does too, and your conversation has begun. And they tell you some of their experiences when they were doing what you're doing. Or they say, "It's good you're in college. When I was your age, I wanted to go to college, but it was the Depression so my family couldn't afford it. So here I am driving this hearse for a living." A little wistfully, he says again, "It's good you're going to school."

What's happening, I explain to Lexi, is that I am learning about this person's life, about life, about what it can be like. And how exciting that learning can be. And, of course, I'm telling him about my life and how I see things from my perspective (limited as it then was). And I'm learning still more by trying to put into words how things are for me.

So, Lexi says to me, "This morning I was with a group in a poor part of town, and I was telling this homeless woman how she might get certain kinds of help from the city. That's what our group does. But this lady—we were sitting together on the curb—was telling me about her life." As Lexi described this, her tone changed and became warmer, indicating greater interest and involvement. She told me more about the encounter, and it was really lovely.

So, here we have two kinds of knowledge. One is information about the resources that the city of New Haven has available for this lady, and that is clearly important. The other, derived from the human contact between these two people, is what Lexi learned about this human being's life, thus enriching her own comprehension of the world and of what it means to be human.

Thinking more about this second kind of knowledge, maybe we humans are somewhat like horses, "herd animals," animals that need others of their kind to survive. Maybe not as much as horses, but almost. Perhaps that's why solitary confinement without any physical torture is such a powerful punishment. Most of us need other people, really "need." When Lexi was sitting on the curb with that homeless woman or when I was in a car with someone who had picked me up while I was hitchhiking, there was that necessity of connection. The reciprocal impact of "being with" another person, of connecting, of sharing, is somehow just as powerful as a meal ticket. As they say, a person "does not live by bread alone." So, when we limit medical visits to fifteen minutes (many of them spent with the "caretaker's" computer) or limit "case histories" to just the facts, we are acting as though this other side of knowledge, of reality, does not exist.

And Now for Something Completely Different
[*12/5/20*]

The phrase "And now for something completely different" comes from the wonderful British comedy troupe Monty Python, who in the middle of a skit would suddenly stop it and start a new skit that was supposedly, well, "completely different." What I will discuss here is "completely different" from most of what appears in this volume but also intimately linked with all of it. My subject is something "we do and know already" but in fact often grossly underestimate, especially in research and publications, that is the relationship between the treating person (the therapist or case worker) and the "patient" (the consumer). By considering the arts we can see the magnitude of what we don't know or appreciate and learn possible approaches to the necessary goal of doing much better.

First, we must dispel the assumption that "we know it (do it) already." What I am talking about is usually encompassed by the rubric "non-specific factors," which means that it is pretty much ignored. Nineteenth-century German philosophers promoted a concept called "historicism," one aspect of which is to assume that human thought is now proceeding intelligently in contrast to earlier times when people didn't know enough or perhaps were misguided or even not too bright. This meant that earlier interpretations tended to be discarded totally and also, ironically, that current thinking was likely to suffer the same fate at the hands of the next generation. I submit that our mental health field has fallen into the same trap.

Recently, a colleague in reviewing an article of mine complimented me on it while at the same time noting that it reflected a focus on questions and methods that were true in the past. He suggested most politely that the world has moved on and that the methods I and my colleagues used were now outdated and the focus no longer relevant.

While such a critique might be valid, it may also reflect the goldfish bowl phenomenon, in which the goldfish assumes that what is right around it (the water) is the only thing there is because that's all it sees. Of course, this problem is ubiquitous, and I have sought help from a professor of the history of ideas to see how one's own work might stand up within that broader context. I did respond to my colleague to thank him for helping me think about the context of my work and also to suggest politely that he might try to do the same evaluation of his own efforts, which are in a different but currently much more popular area than my own. The problem for all of us then is how to understand that we are all in a sense, goldfish in a bowl, and that it is difficult indeed to understand what is outside that bowl and its implications for our own work.

In this essay I wish to stress the point that in the mental health field an area that is currently neglected, an aspect that is rarely noted, requires much more attention than we give it and should not be dismissed as something we know/do already, that is, the understanding of the relationship between the treater and the patient.

An example: A psychologist friend of mine was discussing his work on behavioral treatments with me. I asked if I might observe him in a session to get a better idea of what he did, and I was able to do that. In our discussion afterwards, I said that I was impressed by his behavioral methods but also by how before and after the "behavioral" part, he spent a lot of time greeting the patient and generally engaging in friendly talk and comments. He replied, "Of course, you have to do that. You just can't go in there and start with the behavioral stuff."

So he assumed that this other part, the part besides the "behavioral stuff" just doesn't count. Hmmm. It has struck me that in our encounters in the mental health field we tend to assume that we are experts in the kinds of skills these encounters involve. Yet, in contrast to us, actors and musicians spend years, often lifetimes, sharpening the kinds of awareness and behaviors that somehow we tend to assume we completely know already. I have described elsewhere some of what I have learned in taking acting classes as well as observing master classes in musical performance. One of the areas is listening. In the first session of my acting class, we did an exercise in which we paired up and one person made a comment to the other about an obvious part of their appearance. One might say, "You have blond hair," and the other reply, "I have blond hair." You continued repeating those exact phrases back and forth. The acting teacher stopped us and said, "But John, you're not listening to her." (What me, John Strauss the wonderful psychiatrist, not listening?!) But gradually, I realized he was right. Of course, I heard the words and responded "appropriately," but I wasn't really listening. I hadn't paid much attention to her tone of voice, to the look on her face, to the movements of her body. And as I began to notice these things, even at a basic beginner level, I began to realize how much was going on between us that I hadn't even recognized.

But it got worse (or better). Several sessions later I began to learn that it wasn't just what was going on in the other person, or between us, that had eluded me, I began through Doug's teaching to learn that I didn't even know the things that were affecting my own behavior and way of being. It happened like this. Much to my own surprise, after several sessions I was even able to try improv, improvising a real scene with another student. Doug had taught us the general approach to doing improv, and the other student and I had decided I would be an older lawyer and he would be my ne'er-do-well son. The situation was that I was planning my first vacation in years when he came to me for help with yet another scrape he had gotten himself into. We had started and I thought we were doing well when Doug stopped us. "John (referring not to me but to the character I was playing), where did you go to law school?" "Doug, that's not relevant, this is many years later." "Where did you go to law school?" "Okay, (I invented) Harvard." "How many children do you have?" "Doug . . .," well, I just gave in. "Okay, Doug, (again I invented) three." "Okay, you can continue." Damn him anyway! But if where I went to law school and how many children I had seemed irrelevant to this scene, I'm damned if knowing those details didn't make me feel more like a real three-dimensional person. The scene was now better. It didn't make any sense. Yet, of course it did. Doug summed it up repeating as he had so often in so many situations. "The life is in the details. There is nothing general about life."

Let's get back to the mental health field. In my life as a professor of psychiatry I became increasingly interested in subjectivity, but I found there was limited official interest in that area. (One interviewer said to me, "But you've been working on that a long time," suggesting that the two years I had spent with it was all anyone should need to solve all the major issues. I didn't dare mention that Shakespeare and others more talented than I had spent a great deal longer.) I was no longer able to get grants. I was told by my department that I had to do something to earn my salary, being a tenured professor notwithstanding. It was suggested that I could become "medical backup" for a group of psychotic patients, two hundred and fifty of them! I was assured that it was a half-time job, leaving half my time free for research. It seemed impossible to me, but colleagues who were "medical back-up" psychiatrists on other treatment teams reassured me it was totally doable.

I tried. The system was that I would see most of the patients for ten to fifteen minutes every six months to update or renew their prescriptions. I tried, I really did. "How have things been going?" "I still hear the voices, but I can manage, and I take my medications." "That's good, but I'm also interested more generally, how things are going." "I still hear the voices, but I can manage, and I take my medications." I would repeat my question and usually by the third time the patient would realize that I was really interested in how things were going, and we would have a real conversation. Of course, the problem was you can't really do that in ten or fifteen minutes per patient. So, I was working full time, not half time, and still not keeping up. And I was messing up the whole system. Many of us had thought that all patients could tell us was about their symptoms and whether they took medications. In fact, we had taught them that was all we cared about and they had learned well. It seemed to me that's how the system had come to focus on bureaucratic fictions like "bringing the patient to baseline" and even to creating positions like "medical backup." As Doug said, "The life is in the details." But in our treatment system patients had been taught that we were not really interested in their lives or in their details. They had adapted. The psychiatrists had adapted too. And everyone was happy. Except me. I couldn't stand it, and after trying to deal with what seemed to me the non-human process for six months, I decided to retire.

But does attention to the "life," to the "details," as part of the treatment, really matter? After all, if "treatment" is really "meds," their selection and dosage, what else is actually important? In another medical situation when the orthopedist made the diagnosis that I had a torn hamstring and prescribed reduced stress on that leg, the "details," the "life," were not really particularly relevant.

How would we even know whether attention to the "life," to the "details," is important? We haven't really begun to inquire how to do that, to consider the vicissitudes of human engagement. In the course of a research project in which our interviews focused on the study of the course of disorder and improvement, we asked patients, people with schizophrenia and other severe disorders, including people who had "improved," questions such as "What has been the most important thing in your improvement, what do you think has been most important in your getting better?" Often, they responded with statements like "Someone who took me seriously" or "Someone who cared." We have also learned, partly from the work of Susan Gottschalx to ask questions like "How has your illness affected your life?" And people have responded saying things like "You are the first person who has realized I have a life."

To attend to the details of human engagement we need a tool that could provide detail analogous to that of the electron microscope or genetic analysis in biological research. Otherwise, our efforts would be comparable to trying to understand cellular microstructures with a magnifying glass. For more adequate attention, we need to turn once again to the arts. And such consideration may require getting outside of our goldfish bowl to notice how people in other areas learn about and deal with the realities of human engagement. For example, in a master class for students of piano who are already very proficient, the teacher will not be spending time with basic fingering arrangements or timing but focus rather on feelings and attitudes. I have mentioned elsewhere the instance where the famous pianist Cortot said to a student, "You said you liked going out in nature. Now try playing that (a Chopin étude) again while you think of walking in the woods." We should be considering analogous sophisticated approaches in our teaching about working with patients as well as in considering approaches to data collection and analysis for research and theory.

On YouTube you can watch master classes in operatic singing conducted by Joyce DiDonato. In one DiDonato helps a soprano, an advanced student, reach a certain feeling in the Puccini aria "Donde lieta uscì" from *La Bohème*. After several progressions the student succeeded. DiDonato then told her, "Wonderful! Now, you can't just try to do the same things to repeat what you accomplished. You have to start from an idea of what you're trying to accomplish and figure out how to do that all over again." The idea for us, of course, is that developing "a technique" for dealing with patients is not enough. We need to learn how to be flexible enough, how really to listen, in order to know how to proceed. (Remember, "But John, you're not really listening!")

The organic nature and complexity of connecting with another person, of communication and expression, constitute a subtle phenomenon. How to connect is not a mechanical or simple thing. The idea of "being there" for another person is not a mechanical process. There is no recipe for "taking someone seriously" or being "someone who cares." For example, it is rarely possible to accomplish that in an interview of ten to fifteen minutes in length every six months. It is almost certain not even to come automatically in learning to do psychotherapy or psychoanalysis. In my essay "The Story: Its Role in Medicine and Other Human Science" (see above) I described how I assisted in a class for third-year medical students on how to "bring bad news") to patients. It seemed to me that the women students were often more effective than the men, perhaps finding it more natural to deal with feelings and communication.

The physicist Werner von Heisenberg noted that our research methods will generally not teach us about things we do not know to ask. "What we observe is not nature itself," he said, "but nature exposed to our method of questioning." I am not saying that connecting with another person in a meaningful way is necessarily the only treatment required, but rather that very often it is an essential part of a treatment program and that our current theory and practice indicates that we grossly underestimate its importance and complexity. We need to give it major attention in our practice, teaching, research, and theory and to learn from the arts how to go about it.

The Ghost of Christmas Past
[*8/14/23*]

It wasn't that strange recurring dream of being a corporal in the French Army and dying during Napoleon's retreat from Moscow. Not this time. And it wasn't the wonder of arriving on the *Queen Elizabeth* at Le Havre during the May after my junior year at Swarthmore. As that monster ship docked, I could smell the Gauloises being smoked by the blue-smocked workers way below us on the pier. A while later as we headed to Paris it wasn't the new sight of the four-wheeled railway carriages with the corridor on one side or the orange tile roofed houses and the small automobiles. It wasn't even the huge glass-roofed station, just like in the movies, that our train entered in Paris, or finding a hotel on the corner of boulevard Saint-Michel and the rue Racine, L'Hôtel des Étrangers, where I stayed a couple of days with my shipmate until he left for Israel. Somewhere something happened—and it was a barely, almost not noticeable thing—so that rather than going to Perugia to study Italian as I had planned, I decided to stay in Paris. I knew no French but found a pension on the rue Madame, enrolled in the Alliance Française, and got my blue-covered learning French book, and started learning French. I mean I had to. The people at the pension only spoke French, and besides the language was like a beautiful song.

No, it was none of these things. Rather, it was a question that occurred to me for the first time, now seventy years later: How was it that the last times I spent in Paris, these last years, how was it that the owners of the small hotels where I stayed on the Left Bank invited me to lunch with them at fine restaurants, even La Tour d'Argent. It wasn't that I stayed in fancy rooms—in fact, at Le Hôtel Saint-Jacques, I always requested and got room 28, a small room on the top floor, which they would save for me—or that the owner, M. Rousseau, asked me to call him "tu," as did Brigitte at the reception.

The relationships were so naturally warm. For example, Madame Mouton confided in me that she wished she had not given up her maiden name of de Monjean ("a real name') for her husband's name of Mouton ("sheep"). Afterward they took me for lunch at a wonderful restaurant up the street. Madame Angele, the chamber maid at a hotel in the same area of the fifth arrondissement where I stayed several times, would bring me flowers left by people in their rooms when they left the hotel.

Recently I have felt a little as though I've been visited by the ghost of Christmas past from Dickens' *A Christmas Carol*. In my case, though, instead of showing me bad things from the past (as he did with Scrooge), the ghost has taken pleasure in showing me wonderful things from my life. He has often showed me times I had with people who have died in the past several years. One was the time I visited the psychiatrist Johan Culberg in Stockholm and he took me to meet his brother, a well-known artist who sells his paintings to museums as well as wealthy collectors. Oh, yes, and the brother also has schizophrenia. Johan and I spent several hours in his brother's studio. He worked on a large painting while we were there and we talked about art, about what it is like to be an artist, and about the things of ordinary life. I don't think we mentioned mental illness or psychiatry; they never came up. Afterwards, Johan took me to meet his wife at their apartment, and we had a wonderful dinner of fish and white wine. The wife played a CD of Schubert piano music, which she then gave me as a gift, I have it still, love it still, and beyond the music, it holds wonderful memories for me. About a year ago I learned that Johan had died.

Thank you, ghost, for helping me revisit that wonderful time in the past.

On another night, you took me back to the café Rostand in Paris. I was sitting at the *terrasse*, of course, since the weather was beautiful, and along came Alain, Alain Bottero, a very close friend, like a much-loved brother. He had walked over from his office on boulevard Montparnasse. He walked through the Luxembourg Gardens to reach the Rostand just as I walked in the other direction when I went to his office to meet him. It was wonderful seeing him again. As usual we talked about everything, his little house in Greece that he is fixing up with his own hands, how some day it would be so nice for him to come to our island in Canada, about music, Klimt, Rilke, his daughter Milena, and even psychiatry, since we are both psychiatrists. And we planned when I would come over to his apartment for dinner with him, his wife and kids, and his sister Françoise. Alain was a wonderful cook, and, my, did he know brandy. When we once went to the Grand Vefour, one of the best restaurants in Paris, for lunch, we decided to have cognac after our coffee. The waiter brought the cognac table on wheels around, and Alain picked out a very special one. When I tasted mine, I had never had an experience like that in my life.

Alain died about four years ago. Of lung cancer. He was younger than I. When I sat with him in the hospital while he was getting a perfusion into his chest, I asked if he wanted to talk about death. I had never done that before, but I had heard Sandra the clown asking the question when she visited elderly dying people in hospital. Alain, however, said, "Thank you anyway, death is boring." I must say, I was relieved.

He died a few weeks later. A week before his death he called me in New Haven from Paris, but he could only talk for about twenty seconds because he was so short of breath. Thank you, ghost, for letting me revisit Alain.

Oh, and I must mention one more person in Paris, my wonderful friend Pernette. For a long time Pernette was the only person I knew who was older than I am—just by one year, but still. I have told you something about her elsewhere. She was the daughter of an archaeologist who invited her to join him on a dig in Egypt, where she took up the job of drawing illustrations of his findings. When I met Pernette, there must have been something we liked about each other because we rapidly became good friends. Whenever I was in Paris we would set a time to meet, and I would take bus 57 to her apartment on the boulevard des Italiens. Pernette lived in a building that you entered by pressing in a code at the door outside. Then you passed through an august high-arched entry way and emerge into a courtyard. On the left was the plain wooden door to Pernette's apartment, a doorway encircled by vines and flowers, and the ghost placed me outside this door again. I rang the bell, and she appeared smiling, slender, and with a face that sparkled. Behind her I could see bookcases full of books up to the ceiling. Inside I entered a kind of large anteroom, beyond which lay a room filled with large easels bearing paintings in progress. To the right of the anteroom was a large dining table, and beyond that, a small kitchen. We would have dinner either there or at a nearby restaurant. (There was a wonderful Chinese restaurant in the neighborhood and a terrific French restaurant run by a Chinese family, where they served the finest foie gras I have ever eaten.) Or we would meet during the day and go to an art exhibit and have lunch. Pernette was wonderful. I don't think I ever knew someone who knew so much about so many things. And it wasn't just book knowledge. It was as though she had really thought about each topic and somehow integrated it with what else she knew. She understood it and had important ideas about its relevance. She was really terrific.

When I was back in the States, Pernette would send me envelopes containing small paintings she had done. Of course, I bought frames for the paintings, which are hung all over my dining room. You could talk with Pernette about anything, anything personal or academic, feelings, history, art, whatever. But now she, too, is dead. She died about a year and a half ago. Her daughter, Manon, wrote to tell me that she had died in her sleep. Pernette was wonderful. Like Aeneas' Trojan sailors, these people have sunk "beneath the waves never again to hear someone call their names."

I have other clear memories, of course. When I was twelve, my friend Douggie Young would come to the back door of our house and yell, "Hey Johnny!" He never rang the bell or even knocked, he just yelled at the top of his voice. But the ghost of Christmas Past has played no role in reminding me of that. In fact, he seems to have moved on after taking me to visit Pernette again. Who knows, maybe we will meet further.

Scrap Trailer in Driveway
[*4/22/25*]

"Scrap Trailer in Driveway," so said the note left in my screen door. My beloved trailer that I have owned for at least fifty years, the trailer that carried my small sailboat lovingly from Rochester to Parry Sound, Ontario, and back, then from New Haven to Parry Sound and back. Now someone's telling me it's a piece of scrap. He must be kidding! Does it really look that bad? Is it really that bad?

It is old, I suppose. And it does look bad. But it works fine—or does it, still? I mean I haven't used it for what, maybe twenty years. Perhaps it's just like me, old looking but still robust. Or is it really just a "scrap trailer" now. Me too, maybe I'm scrap or getting there. I mean we've both been around a long time, me much longer than my wonderful trailer. And I wonder about that "scrap thing," too. Too old to be of much use. Just hanging around. I wonder increasingly about that, you know. Even just a year ago or so I was taking walks of at least nine blocks. I was using a cane, of course, but now I couldn't do it without a walker, maybe even with a walker. Then it was the ankles. sometimes the hip. Now the knees are starting to go, to say nothing of the eyes, the teeth, the ears, and on and on.

Yet it still feels dumb, even unnecessary to feel sorry for myself. At age ninety-two, almost ninety-three, I'm still alive, which is a hell of a lot more than I can say for most of my contemporaries. Most of them are dead. I can think of one who's a year older than I, doing much worse than I am. I can walk (with a cane), write, read, and watch television. I can listen to incredibly beautiful music; in fact, I can enjoy watching and listening to the full version of *La Bohème* (with Freni and Pavarotti) on YouTube. I can even write on this computer! And joy of joys, I can spend time with wonderful friends and have many contacts with my kids, even read to my great grandson snuggled next to me on the couch. It feels a bit spoiled and is too much to complain.

Both my trailer and I are pretty battered. But we are still somewhat usable and, in our own weird way, kind of beautiful.

Scrap trailer in driveway indeed! Hard to feel sorry for myself for too long.

Taps

"Don't believe it," my father said,
"When they talk about the golden years."
He lived to ninety-five.
Drove a car 'til he was ninety-three.
I didn't pay much attention.

"Don't believe it when they talk about the golden years,"
My father said
He gave piano concerts for the "old folks"
when he was ninety-two,
"It's easy" he said,
"They fall asleep, they don't notice when you make mistakes."

He wasn't a depressive person,
Told jokes to the lifeguards at the pool in his nineties.
But he lost the use of one of his eyes
So was grateful when I visited and cleaned the refrigerator.

He never stopped thinking or telling jokes
Until that day when he was ninety-five
And I came to Cleveland to see him
And he was in the hospital bed
In a coma
Never to awaken.

Taps: music at the end

played by bugles.
I could never hear it
before.

But My Favorite is . . .
[9/24/23]

I was lying in bed this Sunday morning thinking of the sad two-day conference on the paintings of Turner I recently attended. The participants were academics at their worst, discussing (often in tiny voices) topics they had selected like Turner and the Insurance Companies. This was petty, trivial stuff, the sort of thing they fuss over in the backs of huge libraries, never coming out to see the sun.

But one thing leads to another, and I began thinking about the paintings they showed during this conference, the *Burning of the Houses of Parliament*, *The Fighting Temeraire,* things like that. And that, of course, led me to Turner himself and other painters who I think are incredible.

I love Turner's paintings. He is absolutely my favorite painter. I admire especially his later paintings in which he blends the realistic and impressionistic. Then, still lying in my bed this Sunday morning, I ask myself, who else do I think is really superb. Well, Rembrandt of course, I have his self-portraits in mind, the three ages so different, so deep. Then there is Vermeer, the quiet pensiveness, depth, and beauty of his scenes , of his people. Oh, yes, and Delacroix. I love Delacroix's house, hidden away in the place de Furstembourg in Paris' sixth arrondissement. The house is a museum, where you see none of his big flashy pictures but wonderful small studies of people and of places. You can visit the garden in back as well. And have you read his memoir? What a blend of wonderful art, wonderful living, right there in the heart of Paris. And while we're at it, there's also Matisse, particularly his line drawings of people and faces.

Okay, and how about writing. Victor Hugo, of course. *Les Misérables,* the people, the places, the feelings. "What do I do now about this poor man who is going to be put in prison forever for my crime?" And Shakespeare and Heine, Joseph Conrad, Dostoyevsky, and Isak Dinesen. How about the Dave Dawson series by R. Sidney Bowen and the Lucky Terrell flying stories by Canfield Cook? Well, no, but all right, we'll give them an honorable mention. And P. C. Wren, author of the *Beau Geste* trilogy about the French Foreign Legion? Okay, him too. Is that all? Well, we have to let in Saint-Exupéry. Of course.

What about music? Well, Brahms, of course, who wonderfully mixed the romantic and the classical. Ravel, Chopin, and—I'm almost embarrassed to include him, he's such a romantic, but I will anyway—Rachmaninoff. We must include Mozart and Bach and Rachmaninoff. I'd say, Prokofiev. Hey, and don't forget Puccini! And I want to sneak in the song *Le Temps des Cerises* and Barbara singing *Septembre,*

What an incredible gift of beauty these people have bestowed on us! have given us, It is a wonderful thing to recall when we think of the horror and misery we humans have also brought on ourselves and our planet.

One more thing: Can we add in Johann Strauss and his waltzes? Oh, all right. But that's all!

www.ingramcontent.com/pod-product-compliance
Lightning Source LLC
Chambersburg PA
CBHW020235170426
43202CB00008B/90